How to
Raise a Family
on Less Than
Two Incomes

How to Raise a Family on Less Than Two Incomes

**THE COMPLETE GUIDE TO MANAGING
YOUR MONEY BETTER SO YOU CAN SPEND
MORE TIME WITH YOUR KIDS**

Denise Topolnicki

BROADWAY BOOKS

NEW YORK

BROADWAY

This book is designed to provide accurate and authoritative information on the subject of personal finances. While all of the stories and anecdotes described in the book are based on true experiences, most of the names are pseudonyms, and some situations have been changed slightly to protect each individual's privacy. It is sold with the understanding that neither the Author nor the Publisher are engaged in rendering legal, accounting or other professional services by publishing this book. As each individual situation is unique, questions relevant to personal finances and specific to the individual should be addressed to an appropriate professional to ensure that the situation has been evaluated carefully and appropriately. The Author and Publisher specifically disclaim any liability, loss or risk which is incurred as a consequence, directly or indirectly, of the use and application of any of the contents of this work.

HOW TO RAISE A FAMILY ON LESS THAN TWO INCOMES. Copyright © 2001 by Denise Topolnicki. All rights reserved. Printed in the United States of America. No part of this book may be reproduced or transmitted in any form or by any means, electronic or mechanical, including photocopying, recording, or by any information storage and retrieval system, without written permission from the publisher. For information, address Broadway Books, a division of Random House, Inc., 1540 Broadway, New York, NY 10036.

Broadway Books titles may be purchased for business or promotional use or for special sales. For information, please write to: Special Markets Department, Random House, Inc., 1540 Broadway, New York, NY 10036.

BROADWAY BOOKS and its logo, a letter B bisected on the diagonal, are trademarks of Broadway Books, a division of Random House, Inc.

Visit our website at www.broadwaybooks.com

Library of Congress Cataloging-in-Publication Data
Topolnicki, Denise
How to raise a family on less than two incomes: the complete guide
to managing your money better so you can spend more time with
your kids / Denise Topolnicki.—1st ed.
p.   cm.
1. Finance, Personal.   2. Households.   3. Family—Economic aspects.
I. Title.
HG179.T59 2001
332.024—dc21   00-027265

First Edition

Designed by Chris Welch

ISBN 0-7679-0565-2

01 02 03 04 05 10 9 8 7 6 5 4 3 2 1

With love to Tim,
our daughters Emily and Robin,
and my parents

Acknowledgments

I am very grateful to all of the mothers and fathers who generously shared their anecdotes and advice with me. Like me, they had quit or cut back on work to spend more time with their children. That means they are busier than ever, of course, so I am especially thankful that they found the time to converse with me.

Thanks also to the many experts who answered my questions, updated information for me, or read my manuscript for factual accuracy. Howard V. Hayghe, a supervisory economist at the Bureau of Labor Statistics, gave me the latest data on mothers, fathers, and work. Keith T. Gumbinger, vice president of the financial publishing firm HSH Associates, commented on my chapter about housing costs. David S. Rhine, director of family wealth planning for the accounting and consulting firm BDO Seidman, commented on my chapters about taxes. James Hunt, a former insurance commissioner of Vermont who is now with the nonprofit Consumer Federation of America Insurance Group, carefully read my chapter on insurance and gave me lots of excellent advice. Karen Ferguson, director of the Pension Rights Center, a consumer advocacy organization, answered my questions about pension plans. Carolyn Cheezum, a spokesperson for the Social Security Administration, answered my questions about disability and survivor's benefits. Jennifer Frighetto, a spokesperson for Hewitt Associates, an employee benefits consulting firm, updated some of her company's reports for me. She also put me in touch with two of her colleagues at Hewitt who commented on sections of my manuscript—Mike McCarthy, who specializes in defined contribution retirement savings plans, and Michele Schwanke Halle, who is a legal consultant. Deidre Zapata, media relations manager for FEMALE (Formerly Employed Mothers at the Leading Edge), was also very helpful. If any errors remain, I take full responsibility for them.

Thanks, too, to my brother, Walter Topolnicki, who helped refine the proposal I wrote for this book. My friend Barbara Owen also gave me some useful suggestions, as did my agent, Daniel Greenberg of James Levine Communications. I am indebted to Laurie Calkhoven, an editor at Book-of-the-Month-Club, for introducing me to Daniel. It was a pleasure to work with Jennifer Griffin and Suzanne Oaks, my editors, and all of their colleagues at Broadway Books.

My deepest thanks go to my husband, Tim Smith, who read every word of my manuscript, some more than once. His corrections and insights were invaluable. Most important, he encouraged me to follow my heart and quit my job so I could spend more time with our children. He is an optimist and an achiever, and I draw much inspiration from him.

Contents

You *Can* Make Your Dreams Come True

re you sick of rushing to pick up your child at day care on time when your boss calls a late afternoon meeting? Do you wish you were home finger-painting with your four-year-old instead of sitting in traffic on your morning commute?

Do you fantasize about quitting your job or cutting back on your work hours so you can spend more time with your kids? Do your wonderful daydreams always end abruptly when you start worrying about how you'd pay your mortgage or send your kids to college if you stopped working?

If you answered yes to all of those questions, we have a lot in common.

Three years ago, I was an editor at *Money* magazine in New York City, pregnant with my second child. I'd hired a terrific live-in nanny to care for my four-year-old daughter, but I was still sick to death of playing supermom. I hated commuting between my home in a New Jersey suburb and Manhattan, a twenty-four-mile round-trip that took three hours on a good day. I longed to eat dinner with my daughter on week nights, but our schedules didn't allow it. Instead, our nanny fed our daughter before my husband and I got home from work. My husband and I then ate together at nine o'clock or later after putting our daughter to bed. I wondered daily why I was working so hard to pay another woman to take my child shopping, swimming, and out to lunch.

Every day, I thought about giving up an interesting, well-paying job that most journalists would die for. But I didn't have the nerve to do it. Like most two-income couples, we had plenty of good reasons for feeling that we had to keep both our noses to the grindstone full time.

I worried that my husband and I wouldn't be able to make it financially on less than two full incomes because we spent freely. Our daughter went to a top-notch and very expensive preschool. My husband and I went to the opera and ate at pricey Manhattan restaurants. We also paid plenty for necessities like housing and auto insurance just because we live in an area where costs are high. I also fretted about what we'd do if I quit my job and my husband ever lost his job, with its group health insurance. How could we ever afford to buy individual health insurance, since my husband has had diabetes since the age of seven? I also worried about destroying the career I'd been working hard at since my high school days. Could I keep up my skills and contacts if I quit a staff job to write occasional magazine articles?

My frustrations festered until I told myself that I had to stop worrying and *do something*. So I sat down at a desk piled high with our family's financial documents and went to work. I toted up our savings, figured out how much money we spent and what we spent it on, then agonized about how to spend less. I used all of the knowledge I'd gained in fifteen years of financial journalism, and you know what? I figured out that we'd barely notice any difference in our lives if I earned just *one fifth* of my old salary. Sure, we wouldn't be able to save quite as much money for our retirement or our daughter's college costs. Yes, we'd have to trade some of those expensive nights out in New York for cheaper fun closer to home. But we wouldn't have to drain our savings, give up vacations, or start shopping at secondhand stores.

After my second daughter was born, I took a year-long maternity leave and had plenty of time to think. When my leave was up, I resigned my job and haven't had any regrets ever since. In fact, things worked out so well for my family that I decided to write this book to help other families with young children get off the two-income treadmill.

This book isn't just about me, however. I reached out to other parents for help because I know that every mom or dad who quits or cuts back on work to care for their kids has very personal reasons for doing so. I also figured that other parents would have plenty to say about how they manage to live on less than two incomes. So I surveyed more than 100 mothers (and a few fathers) who've ditched the two-income life. I first questioned relatives, friends, and neighbors. They then graciously introduced me to their relatives, friends, and neighbors. Soon our chain letter stretched from New England to Alaska, and included families who live in big cities and on farms as well as suburban cul-de-sacs. I met mothers who had once worked as accountants, speech therapists, and teachers. Their husbands work as bankers, ministers, and truck drivers. I've told their stories in this book just as they told them to me. However, I've changed the names of the parents who generously shared their experiences with me to protect their privacy.

Contrary to popular belief, mothers who trade time at work for more time with their children aren't an endangered species. Indeed, the stereotypical supermom is the exception, not the rule. Even today, most mothers quit or cut back on work outside the home when their children are young. Slightly less than a third of married mothers with kids under age six work for pay full time, year round. What about the rest of mothers with young kids? Surprisingly, slightly less than one-third are full-time, stay-at-home moms. The remainder work part time or part of the year, which can mean for as little as one week out of fifty-two.

What about dads? Although stay-at-home fathers get a lot of press, dads are still a rarity on the playgrounds of America during weekdays. Only 1% of fathers in married-couple families care for kids under age six while their wives work full time, year round. That's why I've addressed this book to mothers, though I hope interested fathers will read it too.

The parents I spoke to came from all walks of life and had many different reasons for deciding to raise their families on less than two incomes. Unlike my husband and me, some parents I surveyed never tried to juggle two full-time jobs and children. Some women knew they wanted to be stay-at-home mothers long before they had children. Once Amy Jones gave birth to her first child, she never had any second thoughts about quitting her secretarial job. "When I first looked at and held the precious miracle of God that had been growing inside of me," she recalls, "I instantly loved her and was willing to do my best to protect, teach, and care for her." Amy's firstborn is now twelve. Amy and her husband George, an electrical engineer, also have two sons, ages ten and eight.

Other women concluded that the two-income life wouldn't work for their families while they were pregnant with their first children. Nora McElrath was an advertising executive who routinely worked ninety-hour weeks. When she went into preterm labor, she knew that she and her husband, who also worked in advertising and had a similarly grueling schedule, couldn't both continue to work and expect to spend much time with their child. So Nora quit her job and is now at home with three children, who range in age from seven to two.

Some mothers returned to work only to quickly discover that they'd rather be at home. Elana Skinner had a dream job; she was a child life specialist who helped children prepare to undergo surgery at a major hospital. After the birth of her first child five years ago, she took a twelve-week maternity leave, then returned to work part time for about seven months. She had intended to ease back into full-time work, but couldn't bring herself to do so and resigned. "I had the perfect child care situation," Elana recalls. "But I *truly* missed my baby. Although he was in a very loving family day care home with my sister's son, I just needed to be at home with him." Elana and her husband Lloyd, an attorney and engineer, now have three kids who range in age from five to one.

Sometimes child care problems pushed women who were wavering to quit their jobs. Sandy Provost, who worked in human resources for a corporation, went to a three-day workweek after the birth of her first child. Then the terrific baby-sitter she'd worked so hard to find quit after just two months. "I didn't want to go through the hassle of finding *quality* care for my son again because it took me such a long time to find my first sitter," says Sandy. "I really wanted to be home, so this became my excuse to be home." Now Sandy and her husband Doug, a manager for a security company, have three children, ages five, two and seven months. Sandy's still "very glad" to be home.

There are also plenty of mothers like me who'd played supermom until they'd finally had enough. Take Louise Rubenstein. She worked full time as a screenwriter and producer; her husband is a financial manager. They maintained a hectic lifestyle until Louise one day forgot to pick up their third child from day care because she was racing home to meet their eldest child's school bus. "I knew then it was time for a change!" she says wryly. Louise, whose kids are ten, seven, and three, now controls her own schedule as a part-time freelance writer and producer.

Parents also have different reasons for trading time at work for time with their children. Irene Ryerson, a former dental hygienist who stopped working during her pregnancy, has been home ever since with her daughter, who's now five. "I'd tried for a long time to get pregnant and then had a miscarriage," Irene recalls. "When our daughter was born, my husband and I both felt that we couldn't leave her with anyone. I wanted to spend as much time as I possibly could with her and felt no one would care for her like I would."

Some parents feel that baby-sitters and day care providers won't impart their beliefs to their children. Says Yvonne Lowry, an elementary school teacher who taught part time before giving up paid work after the birth of her third child: "I felt very strongly that I wanted to raise our children with our values, which I believe could only happen if we spent lots of time with them. Opportunities to teach and discuss come up all day long." Yvonne and her husband Tom, a graphic designer, now have four children who are six years to one month old.

Finally, I want to thank Merle Traylor, a former engineer and mother of four children who range in age from nine to one, for having the courage to mention a reason for giving up the two-career life that's politically incorrect yet oh-so-true. "When I stopped working, my husband could concentrate more on his job," Merle says. Mind you, this comment comes from a woman who always thought she'd continue to work after she had children. Moreover, she's married to a man who was willing to share child care equally. Here's what happened. When the Traylors' first son was born nine years ago, Merle took a two-month maternity leave. When she returned to work full time, her husband Drew, who's also an engineer, took an unpaid six-month leave. After Drew went back to work, they hired a baby-sitter to care for their son. Then Merle began to feel that she wasn't spending enough time with her son to really know his moods and habits. "At least when Drew was home with Bernard, he could tell me when Bernard was getting tired or hungry," she recalls. So Merle, who worked for a company that tried hard to retain working mothers, started working part time. She worked seven hours a day, three days a week, but still wasn't satisfied. "People told me that I had the best of both worlds, but I felt like I had the worst," she explains. "I didn't have enough time to finish all of my work and when I was home I was too busy doing the grocery shopping and other chores to really have much fun with my son." By then, she was pregnant again. After she had her daughter Kelly, she took a year-long leave from her job, then quit. Back when Merle worked part time, Drew had to leave his office before five o'clock to pick up Bernard on days when Merle worked.

"Now Drew sometimes doesn't come home until eight, nine, or ten o'clock at night and his career has really taken off," Merle says. "I'm sure it's partly because he can put in long hours."

Merle makes a good point. It takes hard work and often long hours to excel. Plus, it often takes even longer hours to prove to bosses and coworkers that you're the type of person who excels. I'm sure that neither my husband nor I won many Brownie points at work when we were both desperate to rush home at 5 P.M. One of my unmarried colleagues, who actually ranked below me in the hierarchy, used to bid me farewell by asking "Half day?"

You've got your own reasons for picking up this book. Maybe you're expecting your first child and wondering whether you and your husband can survive on less than two incomes. Perhaps you already work part time or stay home with your kids full time and find it tough to pay your bills. Or maybe you manage to get the bills paid but worry because you're saving little or no money. Perhaps you're just fine financially, but you'd like to spend less on necessities like insurance and more on things you really value, like music lessons for your kids. This book is also for you.

My aim is to help you work less, spend more time with your kids, *and* still live your personal vision of the American Dream. I'm not going to tell you to sell your minivan and take a bus to the grocery store. And I'm not going to tell you to cut up all of your credit cards or start buying day-old bread at thrift stores. I *will* tell you how to cut your mortgage payment, get a great deal on a new or used car, pay off credit card debt, and spend less on groceries without stinting on quality. Yes, living on less than two incomes requires some sacrifice. If you manage your money well, however, you'll never feel deprived of the things that matter most to you and your loved ones. Here's a peek at the advice you'll find in this book:

Part One, which includes three chapters, will help you analyze your financial situation and make plans for the future. You'll figure out how much money you spend—and what you spend it on. You'll also find out how much money you and your husband would take home after taxes if you stopped working or worked part time. I'll also explain how to subtract your debts from your assets to determine your family's financial health.

Part Two, which includes nine chapters, features hundreds of tips to help you slash your spending. I cover taxes, housing, preschool, cars, credit cards, insurance, health care, food, plus fun stuff like vacations and nights out.

Part Three, which includes three chapters, shows you how to save more even though you're earning less. I discuss saving for emergencies as well as long-term goals like your retirement and your kids' college costs.

Part Four, which includes three chapters, tells you what you need to know about work (the kind you get paid for). I'll tell you how to quit your job gracefully without passing up any benefits you deserve, like disability pay after you give birth. There's a chapter on part-time work for mothers who need extra income or just don't want to give up their careers completely. My final chapter is about how to reenter the full-time workforce when you're ready, and on your own terms. You may not use the advice in that chapter for five or even fifteen years. You may never use it. But knowing it's possible to find a fulfilling (and well-paying) full-time job after you've been home with your kids for years should help you get up the nerve to quit working now.

A final thought before you delve into Chapter 1 and start

plotting your family's new financial life: It takes two to *joyfully* raise a family on less than two incomes. Both you and your husband must want to make it work, and you've got to appreciate each other's efforts. You shouldn't nag your husband about getting a promotion that'll solve your money problems; he should *never, ever* even *hint* that staying home with children is a vacation.

If both you and your husband believe that you're doing what's best for your family, you'll feel pleased and proud to be playing a new role in your partnership, whether you choose to do it forever or just until your youngest child is old enough for kindergarten. Listen to April Orseck, a stay-at-home mother with a two-year-old daughter and eleven-month-old son: "When I was an area manager for a chain of photography studios, I worked sixteen-hour days, six days a week, and traveled a lot. My husband was a high school English teacher, and I made more money than he did and helped put him through graduate school. I based my worth on how much money I brought home. Now that he works in human resources for a big corporation and I no longer work for pay, I base my worth on how much money I save our family and how much time I save my husband. The less work he has to do around the house, the more time he has to spend with the kids and me."

I feel the same way April does, pleased that I've been able to manage my financial life to suit my family's needs. I hope you'll feel the same satisfaction after you read my book.

Part
One

Get a Grip on Your Spending

I f you don't know how much money you spend or what you spend it on, you're not ready to hop off the two-income treadmill. You've got to know where your money goes if you want to start living on less without drowning in debt.

Sure, tracking expenditures is tedious, but I guarantee it'll pay off big. When I got a handle on my spending, I realized that my husband and I were together blowing about $45 a day in cash! That's more than it would cost us to eat out every night. What were we spending that money on? The list was long, so I'll name just three little indulgences that'll be familiar to many two-income couples. My lunches, because I was too busy every evening to even think about brown bagging it the next day. Taxi fares, so my husband and I could work past 5 P.M. and still rush home before we had to start paying our nanny overtime. Saturday lunches out, because we often spent the entire day doing errands that we didn't have time for during the work week.

The parents I surveyed spent lots of money on other types

of goods and services when they tried to live the two-income lifestyle. Do any of their stories ring a bell for you?

Nancy Krzywicki, an ex-magazine editor who now freelances part time so she can spend more time with her five-year-old daughter, recalls dropping about $40 a month on dry cleaning when she worked in Manhattan. She used to spend $150 getting her hair cut and colored every five weeks. Now she waits at least eight weeks between salon visits, and saves about $500 a year. "I've also given up manicures," she says. "I never liked them but felt I *had* to have my nails done when I worked in a full-time office job."

Before they had their first child two years ago, April and Ben Orseck were so busy working that they ate out four times a week. Now that April stays home with their two children, the Orsecks go out to dinner only once a month. April even packs a brown bag lunch for Ben daily.

Yvonne Lowry quit teaching after the third of her four children was born. She and her husband Tom, a packaging designer, dipped into their savings to pay off their car loan. They also let their cleaning woman go and, of course, stopped sending their kids to day care. With hardly any effort, they slashed their expenses by $1,300 a month.

When Amanda and Neil Pinder both worked for her father's computer consulting company and had one son, careful shopping wasn't a priority. Then came triplets, and suddenly the Pinders had four kids under age two. Says Amanda, who's now a stay-at-home mom: "When I worked and had just one son, he had an outfit for every occasion. Now all four kids have a fairly sparse wardrobe." Amanda also used to spend more on each item, like the $90 winter coat she had to return because its zipper jammed. "Now I wouldn't pay more than $30 for a kid's coat," she says.

What will *you* find out by using the worksheet in this chapter to track *your* spending? You'll discover the following five crucial bits of information:

1. You'll learn how much money you'll save if you quit your job and simply cut out work-related expenses. Just think— you'll be able to kiss child care and commuting costs good-bye.

2. You'll see how much you spend on discretionary items, and you can plan to trim those expenditures through sheer will-power. If you eat out two or three times a week, for example, you can vow to reacquaint yourself with your kitchen. You might also cut back on the number of lattes you buy each week.

3. You'll see how much you spend on necessities like groceries, insurance, and health care. Having a handy record of these expenditures will help you figure out which ones you can cut—and by how much.

4. You'll find out what you do with (almost) all of the cash you pull out of automatic teller machines.

5. You'll know how much—if anything—you're saving now. That will be useful to know when you read about how to keep—or start—saving after you give up all or part of your second income.

You can use the worksheet on pages 9 and 10 to record your expenditures. Pencil in how much you now spend on thirty items from cable TV to wheels under the column labeled

"Current Amount." After you've finished this book, fill in the column labeled "Future Amount" to reflect spending cuts you plan to make.

I really want you to fill out this worksheet completely. So, I've included simple, line-by-line instructions. I don't ask for any numbers without telling you where to find them. And I swear that the whole exercise should take no more than a couple of hours. (You'll spend even less time on this project if you already track expenditures on a computer program.) A couple of hours may seem like a lot of time, but it isn't really when you consider that you're creating a road map to a saner and more satisfying family life.

If you're already using computer software like *Quicken* to record your monthly expenses, pull up your documents for the past twelve months. Add up how much you spend on different items, like child care, groceries, and utilities. Check your list against my worksheet to make sure you haven't missed anything. If you have, figure out how much you spend on those items by using the methods I suggest in this chapter. Then go on to Chapter 2.

If you don't know where your money goes, get ready to find out. First things first. Pick a time to do this project when you can really concentrate on it. If you already have kids, don't try to fill out this worksheet until after you've tucked them in for the night. Next, get settled. Gather the following documents and supplies, and brew a cup of coffee or tea to sip while you work:

- **A lined writing tablet.**
- **Two sharp pencils with clean erasers.**

- **Your checkbook registers for the past twelve months.**
- **Your credit card (American Express, MasterCard, Visa, department stores, etc.) statements for the past twelve months or annual summaries of charges.**
- **Statements for your brokerage, money-market, and savings accounts.**
- **Statements for your other investment accounts, if any.**
- **Your pay stubs and your spouse's.**
- **Your monthly mortgage statements or payment coupon books.**
- **Monthly statements or payment coupon books for your home equity, personal, or student loans.**
- **The last federal, state, and local income tax returns you filed.**
- **A calculator.**

Spread everything out on a desk or table. Now take the following four steps:

1. Copy the thirty categories listed on the master worksheet on pages 9 and 10 onto separate sheets of paper from your writing tablet. For example, label your first sheet of paper "Cable TV," the next sheet "Cash," and so on. You'll use the sheets to record how much you spent on each of the thirty items over the last twelve months. After you've recorded all of your expenditures, add up the amounts on each sheet to get a grand total. Then jot those numbers down on the master worksheet.

2. Flip through your check registers and record all payments

that belong under one of the thirty headings on your thirty sheets of paper. Every time you write down an amount, make a mark next to that entry in your check register. Alternatively, highlight the entry with a yellow marker. That way you won't count any payments more than once.

3. Comb through your credit card statements. Put all of your charges under one of the thirty headings on your thirty sheets of paper. For example, if your Visa statement from last January includes charges from Sears and Toys 'R Us, you can probably assume they represent holiday gifts. So enter them on the sheet of paper you labeled "Gifts." Check off or highlight all items you record.

4. Examine your savings and investment account statements. You may find that you wrote a check on your money-market account last summer to pay for that Caribbean cruise that you took. Check off or highlight all items you record.

Here's the master worksheet, followed by advice keyed to each item on it. For each type of expense, I tell you:

What types of expenditures you should include under this heading, unless it's self-explanatory

Where you're most likely to find records of such expenses, other than in your check registers or on your credit card statements

Which chapter of my book covers how to cut your spending on each item, assuming a whole chapter full of advice is necessary

Where Your Money Goes Annually

Expenditure	Current Amount	Future Amount
1. Cable TV	$	$
2. Cash		
3. Charitable gifts		
4. Child care		
5. Clothing		
6. Commuting		
7. Disability insurance		
8. Entertainment		
9. Finance charges		
10. Gifts		
11. Groceries		
12. Grooming		
13. Health insurance		
14. Homeowners' or tenants' insurance		
15. Household expenses		
16. Housing		
17. Life insurance		
18. Media		
19. Medical expenses		
20. Miscellaneous		
21. Pets		
22. Restaurants		
23. Savings		
24. Taxes		
25. Telephone		
26. Tuition		

Expenditure	Current Amount	Future Amount
27. Utilities	$	$
28. Vacations		
29. Vices		
30. Wheels		

1. Cable TV. Paying to bring the Rugrats into your home may be worthwhile if it keeps you from taking your whole clan to the movies once a week. There are plenty of other ways to save money on entertainment, however. I cover them in Chapter 12.

2. Cash. Thumb through your check registers and note every greenback you withdrew from ATMs. Chances are you can cut back your cash outlays on just about everything. You'll find lots of tips in Chapters 6, 8, 11, 12, and 13.

3. Charitable gifts. Check Schedule A of your 1040 federal income tax return if you itemize deductions. If you don't itemize, examine your check registers. If living on less than two incomes means you'll have to cut your cash gifts, give more of your time to worthy causes. Time is something you'll have more of.

4. Child care. You won't have to pay for day care anymore if you stay home, but you'll still need baby-sitters. Then there's preschool and summer camp. If you're a good citizen when it comes to paying caregivers, examine your check registers to figure out how much you spend. If you pay your sitter in—shh!—cash, multiply her weekly salary by the number of weeks per year she works. Add any special payments, like her Christmas bonus. Subtract the total from your cash expenditures (line 2 on this worksheet). Chapter 6 covers how to spend less on all types of child care.

5. Clothing. Count the cost of shoes, jewelry, and accessories, too. Don't go crazy trying to figure out if a $60 charge on your Macy's bill represents your son's sneakers or the toaster you bought to replace the one that died. Just record the amount under clothing (line 5) or household expenses (line 15), and move on. To find out how to spend less on just about everything, see Chapter 8.

6. Commuting. Tally up how much you spend on bus or train tickets, tolls, and parking fees. If you and your husband pay cash for these expenses, estimate your daily outlay, then multiply it by the number of days you commute each year. Subtract the total from cash (line 2). If you stop working or start working from home, you can erase your commuting costs. I saved more than $2,000 a year by cutting out my daily commute between New Jersey and Manhattan.

7. Disability insurance. This coverage kicks in if an accident or illness prevents you or your spouse from working. If either of you has group coverage at work, check your pay stubs to find out how much you pay for it. For individual policies, examine your check registers for premium payments. I cover cost cutting tips in Chapter 9.

8. Entertainment. Tote up how much you spend on tickets for concerts, movies, and sports events, health club dues, sports equipment, and toys. If you tend to pay cash for amusements, estimate your annual outlays. Let's say your family of three goes to the movies every two weeks. If tickets cost $8.00, multiply $24 (three tickets) by 26 (the number of times you go to the movies in a year) to get $624. If you typically spend $15 on refreshments every time you go, add $390 to $624 to get $1,014. Subtract that total from cash (line 2). Yes, you can have fun without spending a fortune; find out how in Chapter 12.

9. Finance charges. Check your credit card statements to see how much interest you pay on credit card balances. Also, examine statements from any home equity, personal, or student loans you carry. Don't include interest you pay on your mortgage or auto loans. For advice on cutting your interest costs, see Chapter 8.

10. Gifts. Check your credit card statements, although you may have to do some detective work. A $65 charge from Toys 'R Us, for instance, might include two bottles of bubble bath for your kids and $60 worth of birthday presents for their friends. Don't bother being precise unless your gut tells you that you're spending a small fortune on gifts. If that's true, thumb through your old calendars. It may jog your memory about what you bought your parents for their anniversary or your sister for her birthday. If you remember buying earrings for your sister's birthday, for example, check your credit card statements for a month or two after her birthday to figure out how much you spent. For suggestions on how to stop buying so much, see Chapter 8.

11. Groceries. Count the food and household supplies you buy at grocery, convenience, and gourmet stores. Examine your credit card statements if you ever charge groceries; flip through your check registers if you pay with checks or a debit card. If you usually pay cash, estimate your weekly bill and multiply it by 52. Subtract your annual total from cash (line 2). In Chapter 11, I tell you how to eat on the cheap.

12. Grooming. Tally your spending on haircuts, manicures, cosmetics, and dry cleaning. If you usually pay cash for these goods and services, estimate how much you spend annually and subtract it from cash (line 2). Then read Chapter 8.

13. Health insurance. If you've got group medical and dental insurance, check pay stubs to see how much you pay in premiums. If you buy coverage on your own, examine your check register. For cost-cutting advice, see Chapter 10.

14. Homeowners' or tenants' insurance. Check your mortgage statements if your lender sends a portion of your monthly payment to your insurer. If you buy homeowners' insurance directly, examine your check registers. The same holds true if you rent and buy tenants' insurance. For shopping tips, see Chapter 9.

15. Household expenses. Add up what you spent on your home over the past twelve months. Include big-ticket items like appliances and recurring expenses, like house cleaning. If you pay the teenager who mows your lawn in cash, estimate your annual outlay and subtract it from cash (line 2). Then see Chapter 8.

16. Housing. Examine your mortgage statements and check registers to figure out how much you spend to rent or own your home. Your mortgage lender may use a portion of your monthly payment to pay your real estate taxes, homeowners', and mortgage insurance. If so, record your annual tax bill on line 24 of this worksheet. Put your homeowners' insurance premium on line 14. To learn how to trim your housing costs or buy your first house, see Chapter 5.

17. Life insurance. Thumb through your check registers to find out how much you pay for your family's policies. If you or your spouse has group coverage at work, also check your pay stubs. Find out how to make insurance more affordable in Chapter 9.

18. Media. Tote up how much you spend on books, magazines, and newspapers. Don't forget all of the compact discs, computer software, and DVDs you buy. If your husband picks up a newspaper at the train station every morning, estimate the annual cost and subtract it from cash (line 2). Then check out Chapter 12.

19. Medical expenses. Add up how much you spend on visits to doctors, dentists, and other health care professionals. Count your outlays for drugs, contact lens supplies, and eyeglasses too. Don't forget that you get back some of the money you spend on medical care if you have health insurance. Look for checks from your health insurers on statements for your checking, savings, and investment accounts. Add up the reimbursements you received and subtract them from the amount you spent. Enter that number on line 19. I cover the high cost of keeping your family healthy in Chapter 10.

20. Miscellaneous. If you've got bills that don't quite fit under any other heading, put them here. A likely candidate: The fee you paid your accountant to complete your tax return. Most substantial miscellaneous expenses don't recur. If you paid a lawyer to draw up your will last year, for example, you won't have to do it again this year. One exception: union dues. If you or your husband pay them, check your pay stabs.

21. Pets. Tote up how much you spend on food and supplies, grooming, and visits to the vet. If you usually pay cash for Fifi's chow and coiffure, estimate your annual outlay and subtract it from cash (line 2). Or, if you buy pet food at the grocery store, subtract your annual outlay from your grocery bill (line

11). Assuming you love Fifi too much to even consider giving her away, there's not much you can do to cut the cost of owning a pet. Buy cheaper chow, or purchase it in bulk at a discount store. Let Fifi's fur go natural and dispense with trips to the beauty salon.

22. Restaurants. Count what you spend on takeout meals and lattes as well as at restaurants. (Don't include the money you spend on food while vacationing, however.) You probably charge meals at restaurants but pay cash for gourmet coffee and your kids' Happy Meals. Think about the food you and your family ate away from home during the past week. Estimate how much it cost, then project over a year to estimate your annual outlay. Subtract it from cash (line 2). Find some food for thought in Chapter 11.

23. Savings. Count any money that you socked away over the last twelve months and have yet to spend. Check the statements you got from your bank, broker, and mutual fund companies. Don't forget to check for withdrawals from your accounts to see how much you *really* saved. Have you purchased certificates of deposit or U.S. savings bonds over the past twelve months? Also, check your pay stubs to see how much you and your husband put into 401(k)s or other retirement savings plans. I tell you how to save for rainy days, retirement, and college in Chapters 13, 14, and 15.

24. Taxes. Check the last 1040 you filed to see how much you paid in federal income taxes. If you or your husband pays self-employment tax, look up how much you paid on your 1040. Examine Schedule A of your 1040 to find out how much you coughed up for state and local income taxes, real estate taxes, and personal property taxes. Check your pay stubs from the end of last year to see how much FICA tax you paid. (FICA pays for Social Security and Medicare.) If you don't itemize tax deductions, examine your mortgage statements or local tax bill to figure out how much real estate tax you pay. Look at your 1040A or 1040EZ to figure out how much federal income tax you pay. Dig out your state and local tax returns, and check your pay stubs for FICA payments. You'll be happy to read that Uncle Sam smiles upon families who live on less than two incomes. Read Chapter 4.

25. Telephone. Nowadays, gabbing can really add up to big bucks. Figure out how much you spend on local and long-distance calls, cellular service, pagers, and the Internet. Shop for a long-distance plan that fits your calling habits. Get rid of fancy features like call waiting and caller ID. And give up (or don't get) a cell phone. I know, I know. You carry a cell phone in case of dire emergency. However, admit it—you've used yours to call your mother from the mall about a spectacular sale, haven't you?

26. Tuition. Baby learns to crawl at Gymboree, while brother learns to count at preschool. Sister studies ballet, while Dad works toward a master's degree. Nowadays, we spend a small fortune improving our bodies and our minds. Fortunately, you can take tax deductions for some educational expenses. Read Chapter 4 for the details. I cover how to cut the cost of classes, camps, and college for kids in Chapters 6 and 15. And in Chapter 18, I explain how to get the training you need to get a good job when you're ready to return to work.

27. Utilities. You've got to pay for electricity, fuel oil or gas, and water. You may even have to pay someone to pick up your garbage and clean your septic tank. You already know you should turn the lights off when you leave a room. Your kids even do it, after you told them to about a million times. Being persnickety about lights is better than wasting energy, but it's not going to cut your bills to the bone. I thought I'd save a few bucks if I controlled the furnace and air conditioner in my house all day, instead of leaving it to a nanny. The most I ever saved was truly a few bucks—a whopping $39 a year.

28. Vacations. Figure out how much you spend on airfares, rental cars, hotels, and restaurants. You probably pay cash for admissions and incidentals, so add up the ATM withdrawals you made just before and during your vacations. Subtract the total from cash (line 2). For cost-cutting advice, see Chapter 12.

29. Vices. If you pay cash for cigarettes and liquor, estimate your weekly outlay and multiply by 52. Subtract your annual total from cash (line 2). Smoke a pack of cigarettes a day and you burn up at least $1,000 a year. That would pay for a nice vacation. Need I say more?

30. Wheels. Add up what you spend on loan or lease payments and auto insurance. Don't forget the cost of gasoline, maintenance, repairs, licenses, and fees. If you usually pay cash for gas, estimate your annual cost and subtract it from cash (line 2). To learn how to stop wasting money on wheels, see Chapter 7.

Once you've recorded all of your expenses, add up the entries on each of your thirty pages. Then pencil those numbers in on the worksheet.

The result may depress you. You probably spend lots of money on things your family really needs, like food and health care. And you probably also spend plenty on things you could live without but don't want to, like your dog and summer camp for your kids.

But believe me: you can cut virtually any expense if you really want to. Remember the Pinders, who've got four kids and one income? The first year that Amanda stayed home, they spent $12,000 more than Neil earned. Fortunately, they had savings to fall back on. Then, says Amanda, "we finally figured it out." They discovered they could cancel their mortgage insurance (to see if you can too, read Chapter 5). They gave up their cell phone and started shopping smarter for everything from clothes to groceries.

The Pinders' four little exemptions also give them a big break on taxes. You'll probably also cut the tax collector's take by quitting or cutting back on work—even if you don't have four kids. Turn the page to find out how.

CHAPTER 2

Tally Your Take-Home Pay

Now that you know how much you spend, it's time to figure out how much you make—after you pay taxes. You can't simply assume that your tax bill will drop by the same percentage your income does. Happily, you'll see a bigger decline in your tax bill than in your income. That's because Uncle Sam and the forty-one states that levy income taxes have especially ravenous appetites for second incomes. Most couples don't realize that taxes devour a bigger portion of their second income than their first because they mingle their tax deductions and credits on a joint return.

Once you consider taxes, you may be surprised at how much income you'll have if you quit your job or work only part time. Let's consider the case of Andy and Anna, a hypothetical yet typical couple. Andy and Anna both work full time. Together they earn $70,000 a year. Andy earns $45,000 and Anna makes $25,000. They spend $15,000 a year to send their kids to a day care center. Anna, who commutes to work by bus, spends $1,200 a year on bus tickets.

They claim four federal tax exemptions together worth $11,000. (Multiply four by $2,750, which is the value of each exemption in 1999). They also take the standard deduction, which is $7,200 in 1999 for married couples filing joint tax returns. As a result, their taxable income is $51,800. (Subtract $11,000 and $7,200 from $70,000.)

Before taking any tax credits into account, their federal tax bill is $8,915. However, Andy and Anna take a $960 child care tax credit and $1,000 in child tax credits. (Multiply two children by $500, which is the value of the child tax credit.) Consequently, they pay $6,955 to the federal government.

How much of their seemingly comfortable $70,000 income do Andy and Anna have left after they pay Uncle Sam, the day care center, and the bus company? Just $46,845.

Now let's say Anna quits her job. Andy's taxable income dips to $26,800 (Subtract $11,000 and $7,200 from $45,000.) His federal tax bill falls to just $3,024. Their day care costs and Anna's commuting expenses vanish, so they've got $41,976 left. That's only $4,869 less than they had when they both worked. Now, $4,869 isn't a small number. But it does work out to about $13 a day—an amount that most families could cut their spending by without feeling pinched.

Andy and Anna gave up a bit more than a third of their income, but slashed their tax bill by more than half. Their situation nicely illustrates something that most people don't realize. Uncle Sam loves old-fashioned families. The IRS treats families in which only one spouse works, or in which one spouse earns significantly more than the other, comparatively gently.

It's couples with roughly equal salaries that really get whacked with taxes. Those couples also face the challenge of giving up a greater portion of their income if one spouse stops working. Let's peek in on Andy and Anna's more affluent neighbors, Rich and Rita. Like Andy and Anna, they also juggle two full-time jobs and two preschoolers. However, Rich earns $65,000 a year and Rita makes $55,000. Rita rides the bus to work with Anna and sends her kids to the same day care center.

Rich and Rita claim four exemptions and take the standard deduction. As a result, their taxable income is $101,800. Once they take the child care and the child tax credits into account, they owe Uncle Sam $21,448. That leaves them $98,552 of their $120,000 gross income. Once they subtract day care and Rita's commuting costs from their net income, Rich and Rita have $82,352 left.

What happens if Rita stops working? She instantly cuts her family's expenses by $16,200 because she no longer commutes or needs child care. Rich's taxable income is $46,800. Uncle Sam's share of their income plunges from $21,448 to just $6,515. The couple gave up nearly half their income but cut their tax bill by about 70%. That's a thrill for sure, but can Rich and Rita survive on the $58,485 that Rich now takes home?

Yes—if they saved a substantial portion of their income when they both worked and don't mind saving less now.

Yes—if they spend a lot of money on expensive things that they could easily live without. When the lease on their Lexus is up, for instance, they could buy a cheaper car. They could cut out their annual trip to Bermuda, or cut down on restaurant and takeout meals.

Yes—if they have some savings to fall back on until their kids start grade school and Rita goes back to work full or part time.

If you doubt me, consider this: Some of the mothers I

surveyed who had quit their jobs had earned more than their husbands. (Indeed, about one in four working wives earn more than their husbands do.) Their families gave up *more* than half their income—and made it work. Why did they quit instead of their husbands? Simply because they thought it was the best choice for *them*. One woman whose husband offered to quit his job explained why they finally figured it would be better for her to do so. "My husband isn't a male chauvinist," she said. "And he'd never ask why dinner isn't ready yet if I told him I had a bad day. But I could see myself complaining to him if I came home from work and he hadn't made the beds properly."

Maybe Rich and Rita—or you and your husband—feel you can't cut your income by half or more without making wrenching changes to your lifestyle.

Or perhaps you don't want to stop working altogether even if you can afford to. That's why the worksheet on pages 24 and 25 has three columns, so you can calculate your family's after-tax income using different assumptions about how much you'll work and how much money you'll earn. For example, you could assume you'll have only your husband's income; work part time and make half your former salary; or work even less and earn a quarter of your old paycheck.

If you used computer software to do your last tax return, completing the worksheet will be a snap. Just call up last year's returns on your computer, save the documents, and print out copies if you like. Read the instructions that follow the worksheet. Then make necessary changes to the numbers on your last tax return and tell the computer to recalculate your tax bill.

Of course, you could also go to see your accountant, if you have one. That's what Danielle and Ken Leventhal did when Danielle was thinking about quitting her job as a computer instructor at a vocational school. Danielle and Ken, who's a school psychologist, liked what they heard from their accountant. Danielle now stays home with their sons, ages four and seventeen months.

While using a computer or asking an accountant to do the grunt work is easier, completing the worksheet by hand isn't a huge strain. It took me only thirty-five minutes. Start by gathering the following documents and supplies:

- **A writing tablet or a few sheets of blank paper.**
- **Two sharp pencils with clean erasers.**
- **The last federal and state income tax returns you filed.**
- **A copy of the federal income tax tables and rate schedules.** You can find them in Internal Revenue Service Publication 17, *Your Federal Income Tax*. Call 1-800-TAX-FORM for a free copy, or get the information you need from that publication by logging on to www.irs.gov. You can also find tax rates and tables in tax preparation guides like the *Ernst & Young Tax Guide*, *J. K. Lasser's Your Income Tax*, and the *H&R Block Income Tax Guide*. Look for them in your local library.
- **Copies of applicable state and local tax tables and rate schedules.** Look for them in the instruction booklets that came with your tax returns. If you threw the instructions away, check the reference section of your local library or find the information on your state government's Web site.
- **A calculator.**

A few words of warning before you begin: You can use this worksheet to *estimate* your after-tax income. *Do not* transfer numbers from the worksheet to the next tax return you fill out. Reason: I didn't incorporate every twist and turn of our tangled tax code in the worksheet. If I had, this chapter would swallow this book (as I would have swallowed cyanide while writing it) and you would stop reading right about now. In fact, you shouldn't even fill out this worksheet if you or your husband own a small business or pay the awful Alternative Minimum Tax. Call your accountant (you must have one!) instead and ask him or her to recalculate your tax liability.

Here's the worksheet. You'll find line-by-line instructions for it on pages 25 to 31.

How Much Money You'll Have Left After Taxes

	Scenario 1	Scenario 2	Scenario 3
1. Your income			
2. Your spouse's income			
3. Total income (Add lines 1 and 2)			
4. Adjustments to income			
5. Adjusted gross income (Subtract line 4 from line 3)			
6. Deductions			
7. Exemptions			
8. Taxable income (Subtract lines 6 and 7 from line 5)			
9. Federal income tax before credits applied			

	Scenario 1	Scenario 2	Scenario 3
10. Child tax credit			
11. Child care tax credit			
12. Federal income tax (Subtract lines 10 and 11 from line 9)			
13. State and local income taxes			
14. FICA tax on your income			
15. FICA tax on your spouse's income			
16. After-tax income (Subtract lines 12, 13, 14, and 15 from line 3)			

1. Your income. Pick a number, from zero to whatever fraction of your current income you think you can earn if you work part time. Be conservative. For example, when I started thinking about quitting my full-time job, I thought I could earn at least a fifth of my former salary as a part-time freelance writer. I did better, but I always slept at night knowing that we could pay our bills even if I hit a dry spell.

If you plan to work part time for a company that offers tax-favored benefits, subtract the contributions you intend to make from your pretax income to a 401(k) retirement savings plan and to flexible-spending accounts (FSAs) for child and medical care. (I'll discuss such plans in detail in Chapter 4.) Put your answer on line 1 of the worksheet.

2. Your spouse's income. Whatever he's earning now. If

your husband makes pretax contributions to a 401(k) or to FSAs, subtract his annual contributions from his gross income.

3. Total income. Technically, you should also include taxable interest, dividends, and capital gains here, but don't bother. If your family uses investment income from trust funds and such to pay its bills, you certainly don't need financial advice from me.

4. Adjustments to income. Check line 32 of your 1040 or line 17 of Form 1040A, and then make necessary adjustments. For example, if you made a tax-deductible IRA contribution last year but won't do so again this year, decrease your adjustments by that amount.

5. Adjusted gross income. Do what the worksheet says.

6. Deductions. This number is easy to get if you don't itemize. The standard deduction is $7,200 in 1999 for married couples filing jointly.

If you itemize, flip to Schedule A of your 1040. Let's examine each major deduction to see if you should adjust last year's numbers:

- **Medical and dental expenses.** You can take this deduction only if you have enormous out-of-pocket medical bills. Such expenses must exceed 7.5% of your adjusted gross income (line 5 of this worksheet).
- **Interest Paid.** Use the amount of home mortgage interest you reported on your last tax return unless you've moved or refinanced your mortgage since you filed your return. If that's the case, call your lender and ask approximately how much interest you'll pay over the next year.

- **Gifts to charity.** If you intend to give less because you'll earn less, decrease the amount on line 18 of Schedule A.

- **Casualty and theft losses.** I offer my condolences if you claimed this deduction last year. It's awfully tough to do, given that such losses must exceed 10% of your AGI.

- **Job expenses and miscellaneous deductions.** You probably didn't claim this deduction either, nor will you even after your income declines. That's because such deductions must exceed 2% of your AGI.

- **Property taxes.** Use the amount on line 6 of Schedule A unless you've moved since you filed your return. If you have, check the most recent real estate tax bill or statement from your town.

  If your state levies personal property taxes on cars and other possessions, use the amount on line 7 of Schedule A.

- **State and local income taxes.** If you're lucky, you live in one of the seven states (Alaska, Florida, Nevada, South Dakota, Texas, Washington, and Wyoming) that lack an income tax. You can also enter a zero on line 13 of the worksheet if you live in New Hampshire or Tennessee. Residents of those states pay tax on interest and dividends only.

  If you don't reside in one of those tax Shangri-La's, grab your state and local tax returns (which may be combined on a single return) and recalculate your tax bills using the appropriate tax tables. Don't despair; most of the numbers you'll need to recalculate your state and local taxes are the same ones you used to redo your federal tax return.

Once you've figured your state and local income tax liability, enter the amount on line 13 of the worksheet.

Next tally your deductions for state and local income taxes, property taxes, job expenses, miscellaneous deductions, casualty and theft losses, charitable donations, interest paid, and medical and dental expenses. Enter the total on line 6 of the worksheet if your AGI (line 5 of the worksheet) is $126,600 or less.

If your AGI exceeds $126,600, there's a limit on the itemized deductions you may claim. You must reduce your itemized deductions (not including medical and dental expenses or casualty and theft losses) by the smaller of:

1. 3% of the amount that your AGI exceeds $126,600, or

2. 80% of your itemized deductions that are subject to the limit.

For example, if your itemized deductions total $25,000 and your AGI is $130,000, you must enter $24,898 on line 6 of the worksheet.

Here's the math: $130,000 − $126,600 = $3,400

$$\$3,400 \times .03 = \$102$$

$$\$25,000 \times .80 = \$20,000$$

The smaller of $102 and $20,000 is the amount disallowed, so

$$\$25,000 - \$102 = \$24,898$$

7. Exemptions. Take one for each member of your family. Each is worth $2,750 if your AGI (line 5) is $189,950 or less. So, a family of four with an AGI of $75,000, for example, would enter $11,000 on line 7 of the worksheet. (You multiply $2,750 by 4.)

If your AGI exceeds $189,950, you must reduce your exemptions by 2% for each $2,500 or portion of that amount that your AGI exceeds the limit. And if your AGI exceeds $189,950 by more than $122,500, you can't take any exemptions. So a family of four with an AGI of $195,000, for instance, can enter $10,340 on line 7 of the worksheet.

Here's the math: $195,000 − $189,950 = $5,050

$$\$5,050 \div \$2,500 = 2.02$$

3 (2.02 rounded up) × .02 = .06

.06 × $11,000 = $660

$11,000 − $660 = $10,340

8. Taxable income. Follow the directions on the worksheet.

9. Federal income tax before credits applied. Use the federal tax tables or rate schedule to figure your bill before subtracting tax credits.

10. Child tax credit. You can take a $500 credit for each kid under age seventeen. However, the credit phases out for families with AGIs of $110,000 to $120,000. They lose $50 of the credit for every $1,000 or portion of $1,000 that their AGI exceeds $110,000. So a family of four with an AGI of $115,000 can claim a $750 credit.

Here's the math: $115,000 − $110,000 = $5,000

$$\$5,000 \div \$1,000 = 5$$

5 × $50 = $250

$1,000 − $250 = $750

However, families affected by this rule may lose even more of the credit to the Alternative Minimum Tax, a swamp that I promised not to dive into. If you must wrestle with the AMT, ask your accountant for help.

You may run into another complication. If you have three or more kids and the credit you've calculated exceeds your federal income tax liability, you may be able to get back a portion of the Social Security and Medicare taxes withheld from your paycheck. To see if you qualify, complete the worksheet on page 33 of the instructions for Form 1040.

11. Child care tax credit. If you plan to stop working, put a zero on line 11 of the worksheet.

If you intend to work part time, however, you can still enjoy this tax break. Many taxpayers don't realize that day care fees and baby-sitter's salaries aren't the only qualifying expenses. If you send your kids to nursery school, after-school care, or summer day camp so you can work, you can take a credit for a portion of those expenses. So find the Form 2441 (Child and Dependent Care Expenses) that you filed last year and redo it using new numbers for your income and child care expenses. If you were still childless when you filed your last tax return, get the form from the IRS, your local library, or a tax preparation guide.

12. Federal income tax. Follow the directions on the worksheet.

13. State and local income taxes. Enter the amount you got when you recalculated your itemized deductions.

14. FICA tax on your income. What's FICA tax? Why, Social Security, which may take the biggest bite of all from your paycheck. FICA tax pays for the checks that retirees receive. It also covers disability and survivor's benefits, plus Medicare. If you're an employee, you pay 6.20% on your earnings up to $80,400 in 2001 for Social Security. You also pay 1.45% on all of your earnings for Medicare. By the way, you do pay FICA tax on 401(k) contributions.

If you intend to stop working, enter a zero on line 14 of the worksheet. If you plan to work part time, put your FICA tax on line 14. Say you earn $15,000. Multiply $15,000 by .0765 to get $1,148.

Your FICA tax burden is heavier if you work for yourself. The math you must do is also more complicated. You pay tax on only (!) 92.35% of your self-employment income. But you must hand over 15.3% of the first $80,400 you make, plus 2.9% on earnings above that amount. So, if you make $15,000, you'll pay $2,119 in FICA tax.

Here's the math: $15,000 × .9235=$13,852.50

$13,852.50 × .153=$2,119

Uncle Sam does throw you a bone. You can deduct half the FICA tax you pay on line 27 of your 1040, thereby reducing your AGI.

15. FICA tax on your spouse's income. Follow the directions in number 14 above.

16. After-tax income. Follow the directions on the worksheet.

Voilà! You've completed the most brain-numbing chapter in this book. There's only one more worksheet to go, and it's a piece of cake.

CHAPTER 3

Figure Out What You Own and How Much You Owe

The worksheet in this chapter is the easiest one of all in my book to complete. You'll discover your net worth, which is the value of your assets minus your debts. You'll use the numbers on this worksheet as you read the rest of this book. The job should take you only an hour or so. What's the point? There are actually six:

1. You'll find out how big a cash reserve you've got to tap in case of an emergency.
2. You'll see how much money you've already saved for retirement.
3. Ditto your kids' future college costs.
4. You'll find out if you can handle your current credit card and other debts on less than two incomes.
5. You'll see if you have any assets, like life insurance, that you can borrow against if you need to.
6. You'll find out how your family's net worth compares to others. Do you read about twenty-five-year-olds making

millions at Internet companies and wonder if you're the only person left in America who isn't getting rich? Relax. You may have more than you think.

If you use computer software to track your assets and debts, tally your net worth, then print out the results. Check your list of assets and debts against my worksheet to make sure you haven't missed any. If you have, calculate the value of the items in question by using the methods I suggest in this chapter. Then go on to Chapter 4.

If you've never attempted to figure out how much you're worth, you can do it with pencil and paper. First, gather the following documents and supplies:

- **A lined writing tablet.**
- **Two sharp pencils with clean erasers.**
- **A recent issue of your local newspaper, or *The Wall Street Journal*.**
- **Your checkbook register.**
- **Your savings account register, or the last savings account statement you received from your bank.**
- **Your most recent money-market fund statements.**
- **Your most recent brokerage account statements.**
- **Your most recent mutual fund account statements.**
- **Records pertaining to any stocks, bonds, or other investments you own outside of your brokerage or mutual fund accounts.**
- **Records of any whole life insurance policies that have cash values.**
- **Your most recent statements from Individual Retirement Accounts and Keogh plans.**

- Your most recent statements from employer-sponsored retirement savings plans, like 401(k)s, 403(b)s, stock ownership, and profit-sharing plans.
- Records pertaining to your U.S. savings bonds.
- Records pertaining to your certificates of deposit.
- Records pertaining to stock options you hold.
- The most recent statements for your kids' savings and investment accounts, including Education IRAs.
- IOUs from relatives and friends.
- Sales receipts and other records you keep documenting the value of antiques, jewelry, and other valuables for insurance purposes.
- Your most recent credit card statements.
- Your most recent mortgage statement, or your payment coupon book.
- Your most recent statements, or payment coupon books, for auto, home equity, personal, or student loans.
- Your most recent statements for loans against investments (401(k)s, brokerage accounts) and life insurance policies.

A couple of caveats before you begin: Be as accurate as you can, but don't go nuts. You can call your stockbroker or mutual fund company, or check their Web sites, to find out what your account is worth today. If that sounds like too much trouble, however, use the value from your most recent statement. After all, your net worth fluctuates daily, with the prices of stocks and bonds. You're just taking a snapshot of your financial situation on a given day. Also, don't bother counting every penny you have. Round up to the nearest dollar, or to the nearest $50 or $100, if you prefer.

Here's the worksheet. In the instructions that follow it, I tell you which assets or liabilities to include under each heading. I also tell you how to calculate their value.

What You're Worth

Assets   *Value*

Liquid Financial Assets

1. Bonds $
2. Brokerage accounts
3. Certificates of deposit
4. Checking accounts
5. Children's savings and investments
6. IOUs
7. Life insurance cash values
8. Money-market funds
9. Mutual funds
10. Savings accounts
11. U.S. savings bonds
12. Stocks

Retirement Assets

13. Employer-sponsored retirement savings plans
14. IRAs
15. Keoghs

Other Assets

16. Residence
17. Other real estate
18. Valuables
19. Vehicles

Liabilities   *Value*

Liabilities

20. Auto loans $
21. Credit card balances
22. Home equity loans
23. Loans against investments
24. Mortgages
25. Personal loans
26. Student loans

Assets − Liabilities = Net Worth
$_____ − $_____ = $_____

Liquid Financial Assets

1. Bonds. Count corporate and municipal bonds, plus U.S. Treasury securities, that you hold *outside* of brokerage, mutual fund, or retirement accounts. Major newspapers list current prices for some bonds. Log on to www.investinginbonds.com to check municipal bond prices. If all else fails, call your broker.

2. Brokerage accounts. Check statements from brokerage houses for the value of your accounts. Alternatively, log on to your broker's Web site. Don't include the value of retirement accounts like IRAs and Keoghs on this line of the worksheet.

3. Certificates of deposit. Figure out how much CDs issued by banks and savings and loan associations will be worth when they mature. You may have to call your banker.

4. Checking accounts. See what your balance is on bank,

brokerage house, or credit union accounts that you write checks on.

5. Children's savings and investments. See how much your kids have in savings and custodial accounts. Don't forget Education IRAs, if they have them. To get savings account balances, look at passbooks or monthly statements. Call banks, brokerage houses, or mutual fund companies to get balances on custodial accounts and Education IRAs. Or, you can check their Web sites.

6. IOUs. If relatives and friends owe you money, pencil the loan amount on line 6 of the worksheet.

7. Life insurance cash values. If you've got cash value life insurance, there's a tax-deferred investment account in your policy that's worth something. To find out how much, check with your insurer.

8. Money-market funds. Check statements from your bank, broker, or mutual fund company. Alternatively, log on to their Web sites or make a few phone calls.

9. Mutual funds. Count all types of funds except for money funds (line 8). You may hold taxable or tax-free funds invested in stocks, bonds, or other types of financial assets. To find out how much your accounts are worth, follow the advice for line 8.

10. Savings accounts. Call your bank or check your most recent statement to find out how much you have stashed away.

11. U.S. savings bonds. To find out how much your savings bonds are worth, log on to www.treasurydirect.gov.

12. Stocks. Figure out how much shares you hold *outside* of brokerage, mutual fund, or retirement accounts are worth. A typical example: The ten shares of Disney stock that your uncle gave you for your tenth birthday. Find the current price in the newspaper, and multiply it by the number of shares you have. If you can't find the stock in the newspaper, call your broker.

Retirement Assets

13. Employer-sponsored retirement savings plans. Add up the value of your and your husband's 401(k), 403(b), stock ownership, and profit-sharing plans. Call the investment firm that manages your plan to find out how much your account is worth. Or, if the investment firm has a Web site, check it. Many investment advisers can tell you your account's value on a daily basis.

14. IRAs. Round up all of the traditional and Roth IRAs that you and your husband have opened over the years. Call banks, brokers, or mutual fund companies to find out how much your accounts are worth, or check their Web sites. Alternatively, look at the most recent statements you've received.

15. Keoghs. If you or your husband own a business or moonlight for extra income, you may have one of these tax-deferred accounts. If you do, check its value by checking with your bank, broker, or mutual fund company.

Other Assets

16. Residence. If you don't know how much your house is worth, ask a local real estate agent for a free price estimate. Or, browse the real estate listings on www.realtor.com to see how much homeowners in your town are asking for similar houses.

17. Other real estate. If you own a vacation home or rental real estate, follow the directions for line 16.

18. Valuables. If you own expensive antiques, art, or jewelry, check the appraisals you got for them when you insured them. Look at sales receipts for items you haven't had appraised. Don't bother trying to figure out how much your Beanie Babies are worth. Stick to stuff like the eighteenth-century oil painting that you inherited from your great-grandmother.

19. Vehicles. Figure out the current value of your cars, boats, motorcycles, and trucks, excluding any that you lease. You can check prices for used cars and trucks in *Edmund's Used Cars & Trucks: Prices and Ratings* or the *Kelley Blue Book Used Car Guide*, which are available in many libraries. Or do it electronically, at www.edmunds.com or www.kbb.com. Check the classifieds to see how much sellers are asking for used boats and motorcycles.

Liabilities

20. Auto loans. Figure out how much you still owe on all of your vehicle loans. For your loan balances, check your monthly statements or payment coupon books.

21. Credit card balances. Add up your outstanding balances, even if you plan to pay them all in full next week.

22. Home equity loans. Check your loan documents or call your lender to find out how much you owe on your home equity loan or line of credit.

23. Loans against investments. If you've borrowed against your brokerage account, 401(k), or life insurance policy, find out how much you still owe. For margin loans on your brokerage account, call your broker. For 401(k) loans, check with the investment firm that manages your plan. For insurance loans, talk to your insurer.

24. Mortgages. For outstanding balances, check statements or payment coupon books. Or, call your lenders.

25. Personal loans. Add up your outstanding balances on loans from banks, finance companies, family members, and friends. To figure out how much you still owe, check statements, payment coupon books, or IOUs. Or, call your lenders.

26. Student loans. To see how much you still owe, check statements or payment coupon books, or call lenders.

Once you've calculated your net worth, you can see how you stack up against other young families. It's not unusual for young families to have few assets. That was true when your parents were changing your diapers, and it's still true today. In fact, you've got plenty of company even if your net worth is negative. Fifteen percent of married couples in which one partner is under age thirty-five have zero or negative net worth. You don't have to be a spendthrift to fall into a hole. All you need is a big mortgage, which can cancel out the savings you've squirreled away.

Use the chart below to find the median net worth of households that match yours in age and annual income. (Half of all households has a net worth below the median amount; the other half has a net worth above the median.) Read across to find your age group. Read down to find your income range. Say, for example, that you're thirty-seven years old and earn

$50,000 a year. The median net worth for people like you is $40,857.

What We're Worth

	Age of Householder		
	Less than 35	*35 to 44*	*45 to 54*
Annual Household Income			
$0 to $12,852	$478	$970	$3,875
$12,853 to $23,556	$2,837	$4,742	$15,524
$23,557 to $35,940	$6,993	$17,315	$37,413
$35,941 to $55,620	$15,872	$40,857	$62,031
$55,621 and higher	$38,449	$91,349	$133,525

Source: U.S. Census Bureau, *Household Wealth and Asset Ownership: 1993*

Want to know how many other couples are as well off as you are? Check out the chart below. First, read down to find your age. Then read across to find your net worth. Say, for example, that you're thirty-three years old and have a net worth of $35,000. The chart shows that nearly 64% of households headed by people under 35 have a net worth between $1.00 and $49,999. (Percentages don't always add up to 100% due to rounding.)

You can also use this chart to figure out how well you're doing compared to households with similar incomes. Read down to find your annual household income. Then read across to find your net worth. Let's say you earn $50,000 a year and have a net worth of $250,000. Only 8% of households with earnings similar to yours are worth at least that much.

How Many of Us Are in the Same Boat

| Age of Householder | Negative–0 | Net Worth | | | |
		$1–49,999	$50,000–249,999	$250,000–499,999	$500,000+
Under 35	14.6%	63.5%	19.6%	1%	.8%
35 to 54	6.4%	36.8%	44.2%	8%	3.9%
Annual Household Income					
$0 to $12,852	25.3%	51.4%	21.0%	1%	.7%
$12,853 to $23,556	13.1%	50.1%	31.9%	3%	1.2%
$23,557 to $35,940	9.9%	49.0%	33.4%	5%	1.8%
$35,941 to $55,620	6.6%	43.0%	39.5%	8%	2.9%
$55,621 and higher	3.5%	23.1%	47.8%	14%	10.9%

Source: U.S. Census Bureau, *Household Wealth and Asset Ownership: 1993*

Now that you know how much you have, how much you spend, and how much of your income you keep after taxes, you're ready to slash your expenses. Start with your tax bill, since cutting it will give you tremendous pleasure. If you need another good reason to start with taxes, consider that for many families taxes are their biggest expense.

Part
Two

CHAPTER 4

Stiff the Tax Man

When it comes to cutting spending, what happier way to start than to slash the amount of cash you send to tax collectors? I know, I know—you'd rather have your wisdom teeth pulled than read about taxes. Believe me, writing about them isn't fun either. But you've got to understand how to trim your tax bill if you want to live comfortably on less than two incomes.

Nowadays taxes take a big bite out of the average family's income. Many families spend more on taxes than on their mortgage or anything else.

Could some families keep more of their money out of the tax collector's clutches? Absolutely, and so can you if you act on the advice in this chapter.

I promise I won't torture you a minute more than necessary. All of the tax-cutting tips in this chapter are for ordinary families with young children. I won't bog you down with tax code technicalities that affect only the super-rich. To save your sanity as well as your time, I start my explanation of each strategy with a one-sentence (okay, one tip did require *four paragraphs*) description of who can use it. If you don't match the target taxpayer, skip to the next section.

To further spare your brain from information overload, I've assumed that you and your husband file joint tax returns. You'll usually pay lower taxes if you file jointly, especially if you and your spouse earn disparate incomes. Still, tax laws are quirky. So compute your tax liability separately as well as jointly, just to be sure.

All of my tips reduce federal taxes. I don't directly address state or local taxes because you can usually trim them by cutting your federal tax bill. I've organized the strategies under five headings, starting with:

Strategies for Employees

Contribute to a Tax-Deferred Retirement Savings Plan

■ **Who can do it:** People who work for employers with 401(k), 403(b), or SIMPLE plans. (In case you're wondering, 401(k)s and 403(b)s take their names from sections of the federal tax code. And SIMPLE stands for Savings Incentive Match Plan for Employees.)

There's a good chance that you can contribute to one of these so-called salary reduction plans. About half of all firms with five hundred or more employees offer them, and not only to full-timers. Corporations have 401(k) plans. Charities, schools, and other tax-exempt organizations have 403(b)s. Small firms with no more than a hundred workers can offer SIMPLEs.

The money you contribute to such plans comes out of your salary before Uncle Sam helps himself to income taxes. (Except in Pennsylvania, state tax collectors also keep their hands off your contributions to salary reduction plans. However, you do pay FICA tax on your contributions.) The tax break is simply delicious. Let's say you're in the 28% federal tax bracket. If you put $4,000 in a 401(k), you cut your tax bill by a cool $1,120.

There's more. You don't pay taxes on your account until you start making withdrawals, presumably after you retire. Also, employers typically pitch in 50 cents for each dollar you contribute, up to an annual limit.

In 2000, you can stash up to $10,500 pretax in a 401(k) or 403(b), and up to $6,000 in a SIMPLE. Those amounts rise with the cost of living. However, your employer may place a lower limit on your contribution. Reason: By law, such plans can't favor highly paid executives over the Dilberts of this world.

So why do more than a third of employees who are eligible to fund such plans fail to do so? My guess is that many believe they can't afford to save for retirement *and* pay their monthly bills. I hope you won't feel the same way by the time you finish this book. Even contributing 1% of your pay is a start; you can always increase the amount as your income rises. There's simply no better way to save for the future while slashing your current tax bill. A contribution to an Individual Retirement Account (IRA) may not be tax-deductible, and besides, your boss won't match what you put in. Cash you slip into a bank savings account won't grow tax-deferred. Don't worry about getting your hands on your 401(k) money in case of an emergency. I'll explain how to do it if necessary in Chapter 14.

Pay for Child Care with Tax-Free Dollars

■ **Who can do it:** Parents who need child care so they can work or attend school full time, and whose employers offer dependent care flexible spending accounts (FSAs). Families with a full-time, stay-at-home parent don't qualify.

Nearly half of firms with five hundred or more employees offer dependent care FSAs. You can switch from full- to part-time work and still reap tremendous tax advantages from an FSA.

You don't pay income or FICA taxes on the portion of your pay that you stash in an FSA. (Except in New Jersey and Pennsylvania, your contribution is also exempt from state and local taxes.) You and your husband may together contribute up to $5,000 a year to FSAs, even if both of your employers offer them. (If either of you earns less than $5,000 a year, the lower income is the maximum you may contribute.)

If you continue to work part time, and both you and your spouse can contribute to dependent care FSAs, who should fund your FSA? The partner who earns less than the cut off for Social Security taxes, which will probably be you if you work part time. (In 2001, you pay Social Security tax on incomes up to $80,400. That amount goes up with inflation.) Every penny you put in your FSA will escape Social Security tax. By contrast, if your husband earns more than the Social Security cut off, some of his FSA contributions will already be exempt from Social Security tax.

The mechanics of funding an FSA are simple. Your boss asks you how much you want to contribute for the coming year, usually a month or so before the year begins. Your employer then deducts a prorated portion of your annual contribution from each of your paychecks. You can increase or decrease the amount deducted during the year only if your family experiences a birth, a death, or a divorce. You pay the bills for after-school care, baby-sitting, day care, day camp, or preschool. Then you file claims for reimbursement with your FSA's administrator. If you fail to ask for all of your money back by the deadline your employer imposes—typically April 15 of the following year—you lose it.

If that potential pitfall concerns you, relax. It's relatively easy to estimate how much you'll spend on child care. Say you plan to send your three-year-old to preschool so you can work part time. Ask directors of schools you're considering how much they charge. Base your FSA contribution on the lowest tuition and you'll be perfectly safe.

Don't worry that you won't have cash for groceries or gasoline if you contribute to an FSA. Just file claims for reimbursements from your account promptly after you write a check to your child's preschool or baby-sitter. (Psst—you can't use an FSA if your sitter hides her income from the IRS.) The only minor glitch is that your employer may limit paybacks to the amount in your account. Say your husband contributes $2,000 a year to his FSA to cover your son's preschool costs. What happens if you pay a $500 tuition bill in January, when your husband has only $152 in his account? Submit your canceled check to your FSA's administrator as soon as possible. At first, you may get a check for only $152. However, you'll receive the remaining $348 in installments equal to the amount that your husband contributes to his FSA each week. If he contributes $2,000 a year, he puts in $38.46 a week. So, he'll get his $348 back over nine weeks.

If your employer offers an FSA, you can use it and still take the dependent care tax credit described later in this chapter. In virtually every case, an FSA will give you a bigger tax break, so fund it to the max.

Pay Medical Bills with Tax-Free Dollars

■ **Who can do it:** People who work for companies with health care flexible spending accounts.

Nearly half of firms with five hundred or more employees offer health care FSAs, which work much like dependent care FSAs. You contribute a portion of your pretax pay to an account. You use the money to pay uninsured medical expenses. For example, you could use an FSA to cover your health plan's annual deductible. You could also use your FSA money for co-payments to doctors, or for eye exams, glasses, contact lenses, and orthodontia. Your employer may limit the amount you can contribute.

If you don't use your contributions, you lose them. That's tough, since medical expenses are harder to estimate than child care costs. Here's how my husband and I decide how much of his salary to contribute to his health FSA. First, we gather receipts for the uninsured medical expenses we had last year. We add up the bills, then subtract the amounts that were associated with freak accidents and illnesses.

Adjust Your Withholding

■ **Who can do it:** You and your husband *must* do it if either of you quits or cuts back on work.

Do nothing and you may have too much tax withheld from your pay. Sure, you'll get a refund when you file your tax return, but do you really want to give the government an interest-free loan? To change your withholding, fill out a fresh Form W-4, available from your employer. Also ask for the appropriate state and local forms. Check the worksheet you completed in Chapter 2 for many of the numbers you'll need to change your withholding.

Are you planning to quit your job during this calendar year? If so, ask your employer if you can use what's called part-year withholding. Your payroll department will calculate the amount of tax withheld from your paychecks based on your earnings over the number of months you plan to work during the year, instead of on your entire annual salary.

Strategies for Parents

Take the Child Tax Credit

- **Who can do it:** Parents with AGIs up to $110,000.

You get a $500 credit for each child under age seventeen. You lose $50 of the credit for every $1,000 or portion of $1,000 that your AGI tops $110,000. You can't take a credit for a kid who doesn't have a Social Security number. So, get that new baby a nine-digit ID, pronto.

Claim the Child and Dependent Care Tax Credit

- **Who can do it:** Parents who pay for after-school care, baby-sitting, day care, day camp, or preschool so they can work or attend school full time. Families with a full-time, stay-at-home parent don't qualify.

I hate to pooh-pooh any gift from Uncle Sam, but the size of the credit that most taxpayers can take is decidedly unspectacular. The credit equals 20% to 30% of your child care expenses, up to $2,400 for one child and $4,800 for two or more kids. The actual percentage depends on your AGI; the higher your earnings, the lower the credit you can claim.

The maximum credit you may take shrinks by a dollar for every buck you contribute to a dependent care FSA. For example, let's say you have two kids and put $5,000 in an FSA. You reduce your potential $4,800 dependent care tax credit to zero.

Minimize the "Kiddie Tax"

■ **Who can do it:** Anyone.

If your kids create tax headaches for you, congratulations! You've got this problem because you've saved a lot of money for college in your kids' names. That's great—up to a point. You see, kids under age fourteen pay tax on their unearned income at their parents' top marginal tax rate rather than at their own, presumably lower, rate. The first $700 of your child's investment income escapes tax, while the next $700 is taxed at his or her rate. (The $700 limits increase annually with inflation.) Your top marginal tax rate applies to your kid's unearned income above $1,400.

You can solve this problem quite simply. Choose investments for kids under age fourteen that throw off little or no taxable income. For instance, you could buy growth stocks that don't pay dividends. Or, you could buy municipal bonds. The interest they pay is exempt from federal tax. Keep one caveat in mind, however. You'll usually make less money from a tax-free investment than from a comparably risky taxable investment. So always weigh an investment's merits on an after-tax basis. (I explain how to do this later in this chapter.)

Take the Adoption Tax Credit

- **Who can do it:** Adoptive parents with AGIs up to $75,000.

You get a credit of up to $5,000 to pay attorneys' fees and other adoption expenses. The limit is $6,000 if you adopt a child who has special needs. The credit phases out if your AGI is $75,000 to $115,000. The credit expires after the year 2001 for all but special needs kids.

Strategies for Investors

Contribute to a Tax-Deductible IRA

- **Who can do it:** The rules are dizzying, so you'll have to read the following four paragraphs to determine if you, your husband, or both of you qualify.

1. Neither you nor your spouse can participate in a retirement savings plan at work. Congratulations! You may each contribute up to $2,000 to an IRA. And both of you may deduct your entire contribution.
2. You and your spouse participate in retirement plans at work. You have a 1999 AGI of $51,000 or less. Another winning

couple! You may each stash up to $2,000 in an IRA. And both of you may deduct your entire contribution.

3. You and your spouse participate in retirement plans at work. Your AGI is between $51,000 and $61,000 in 1999. (That range will go up gradually until it becomes $80,000 to $100,000 in 2007.) You win too! Well, sort of. The portion of your IRA contribution that's tax-deductible shrinks as your AGI grows. So, a couple with retirement plans at work and an AGI of $61,000 or more in 1999 can't deduct their IRA contributions.

4. Your husband participates in a retirement plan at work. You stay home with the kids full time or work so little that you earn less than $2,000 a year. (Or your husband stays home while you work.) Either way, you and your husband play the IRA game under different rules. Let's say your husband's the one with a job. If your family's 1999 AGI is $51,000 or less, he can put up to $2,000 in an IRA and deduct his full contribution. His deduction phases out if your AGI is between $51,000 and $61,000. Meanwhile, *you* can contribute up to $2,000 to a fully deductible IRA if your family's 1999 AGI is $150,000 or less. (You can use your husband's earnings, if necessary.) Your deduction phases out if your AGI falls between $150,000 and $160,000.

Of course, you gain more than a tax deduction by contributing to an IRA; money in your account grows tax-free until withdrawal. So, if neither you nor your husband contributes to a retirement savings plan at work, stash as much cash as you can in tax-deductible IRAs. Reluctant to contribute to an IRA because you think you'll need all the money you make to pay your bills? If you have savings outside tax-deferred retirement accounts, use some of it to pay bills so you can fund an IRA. Also, remember that you have until April 15 of the following year to earn money to contribute to an IRA for the previous tax year.

What if one or both of you can contribute to a retirement savings plan at work? Fund your employer-sponsored plan to the hilt. If you've still got money left over to invest, then open an IRA.

Make Tax-Free Investments

■ **Who can do it:** Anyone can, but not everyone should.

Are you and your spouse in the 28% federal tax bracket or above? (You are in the 28% bracket if you file jointly and had a taxable income between $43,050 and $104,050 in 1999.) If so, you may earn more after taxes from a tax-free bond or mutual fund than a comparably risky taxable bond or fund.

Let's say you're shopping for a money-market fund. A tax-free money-market fund is yielding 3.50%. A taxable money fund is yielding 4.5%. Here's how to figure out which is better for you.

1. Subtract your federal tax bracket from 1. If you're in the 28% bracket, subtract .28 from 1 to get .72.
2. Divide the return you can expect from the tax-exempt fund by your answer on line 1. In this example, divide .0350 by .72 to get .0486, or 4.9%. This is the return you need from a taxable fund to match the after-tax yield of a tax-free fund paying 3.50%.
3. Compare your answer on line 2 to the yield of the taxable

investment you're considering. In this case, you're slightly better off with the tax-exempt fund because the taxable version yields only 4.5%.

Strategies for Students

Deduct Student Loan Interest

- **Who can do it:** Married couples with AGIs up to $60,000.

You may deduct up to $1,500 in 1999. The maximum you can deduct goes to $2,000 in 2000 and to $2,500 in 2001 and thereafter. The deduction phases out for married couples with AGIs of $60,000 to $75,000. Also, you can only deduct interest you pay during the first five years that payments are due. So, if you're in year six of your payback schedule, forget about this tax break.

Deduct Continuing Education Expenses

- **Who can do it:** People who take college or vocational courses and have AGIs up to $80,000. Education tax credits phase out for married couples with AGIs of $80,000 to $100,000.

If you can't imagine going back to school while your children are young, think again. Perhaps your husband's employer will offer to pay half the cost of an MBA for him. Maybe you'll take a few computer courses at a nearby community college to freshen your job skills while you're home with your kids. (Frankly, you'd better stay sharp if you plan to reenter the job market someday. See Chapter 18.)

There are two types of education tax credits: HOPE scholar-ships and lifetime learning credits. You're more likely to qualify for the latter than the former. (I'm talking about you using these credits instead of your children because I assume that your kids are much too young for college.) That's because you can apply the lifetime learning credit to tuition and fees for undergraduate, graduate, or vocational courses. By contrast, HOPE scholarships go only to students in their first or second year of study leading to a bachelor's degree or vocational cer-tificate. By the way, an individual can't claim both credits in same year.

You can take a lifetime learning credit for 20% of the first $5,000 you pay in tuition and fees. The maximum credit a family can take is $1,000. After 2002, you can take a credit for 20% of the first $10,000 you spend.

If you do qualify for a HOPE scholarship, you get a credit for the first $1,000 and for half of the next $1,000 you spend on tuition and fees. The maximum credit a student can take is $1,500. So, if both you and your spouse qualify, you can take $3,000 in credits.

Strategies for Entrepreneurs

Contribute to a Keogh Plan

- **Who can do it:** People who are self-employed.

The advice I'm about to give applies to sole proprietors. If you or your husband own a business that has employees, talk to an accountant about setting up a retirement plan. Your op-tions are much too complex to cover here.

If you're just starting out on your own, however, a Keogh plan or SEP should fit your needs nicely. (SEP is short for Simplified Employee Pension.) There are different types of Keoghs. If your business has little or no track record, consider a profit-sharing defined contribution plan. With this type of Keogh, you can contribute little or nothing to your account if you make very little money during the year. If you have a great year, on the other hand, you can make a big contribution. You can contribute whichever amount is lower: $22,168 or 13.04% of your net self-employment income up to $170,000. (The $170,000 limit will rise with inflation.) Net self-employment income is the money you earned from your business after expenses, minus your SEP or Keogh contribution and half the self-employment tax you paid. As you can see, a Keogh is a much better deal than a tax-deductible IRA.

A SEP works much like a profit-sharing defined contribution plan Keogh, but entails less paperwork. It's also ideal for entrepreneurs who don't plan ahead. Here's why: You must set up a Keogh by the end of the tax year. However, you have until the due date of your tax return for that year (including extensions) to contribute to your account. You can set up or contribute to a SEP, however, up to the due date of your tax return (including extensions) and still take a tax deduction for the previous year.

Deduct Home Office Expenses

- **Who can do it:** People who use a room or part of a room in their home *exclusively* and *regularly* for business. Translation from the legalese: You can't claim your family room as your home office if your kids play and watch TV in it.

If you qualify, you can deduct a portion of the mortgage interest or rent payments you make. The same goes for repairs, real estate taxes, homeowners' or tenants' insurance, and utilities. You can also depreciate the purchase price of your house, but only the portion you use for business.

You'll have to figure out the best way to calculate the deductible percentage of your housing expenses. You can either divide the number of rooms in your office (typically one) by the total number of rooms in your house. Or you can calculate the square footage of your office, then divide it by the total square footage of your house.

One caveat: When you sell your house, the portion that you used as your home office may not qualify for other tax benefits. For more details, see IRS publications 523 and 587.

Deduct Health Insurance Premiums

- **Who can do it:** Self-employed people who buy insurance for themselves and their families.

You may deduct 60% of the premiums you pay in 1999. Your deduction goes up gradually until it reaches 100% in 2003.

Pay Estimated Taxes

- **Who can do it:** You *must* do it if you trade a full-time, salaried job for part-time consulting work or start your own business.

When you don't receive a paycheck every week, it's easy to forget that you still owe taxes on your earnings. If you and your husband have too little withheld throughout the year, the IRS will penalize you. Generally, tax penalties apply if you fail to pay at least 90% of your tax liability during the year. To comply, get Form 1040-ES from the IRS and compute the quarterly estimated tax payments you must make based on your projected earnings.

If you're starting a business, it's tough to figure out exactly how much estimated tax you should pay. That's why many people play it safe and use an alternative method to satisfy the IRS. They make estimated tax payments equal to 100% of their prior year's tax bill.

I've said all I'll say about cutting your taxes. Now it's time to move on to another money-eating monster—your house.

CHAPTER 5

Cut Your
Housing Costs

Families who long to live on less than two incomes have one of two problems when it comes to shelter. Some already own homes that are plenty roomy for raising kids, but shoulder mammoth mortgages as a result. Others are still renting, and wondering how they'll ever scrape up enough money to buy a place big enough to accommodate their kids' bikes, books, and Barbies.

My husband and I have problem number one. We bought our spacious four-bedroom colonial before we had kids. We figured we'd eventually need enough space for two kids and a live-in nanny. Two kids and two nannies later, I wanted to quit working full time, stop hiring nannies, and turn the nanny's room into a guest bedroom.

There was only one hitch: Our same old high mortgage payment still came due each month.

Our mortgage lender hasn't yet threatened to foreclose, however, so we obviously found a way to keep the home we love despite our lower income. You'll be able to do the same if you follow the advice in the first part of this chapter.

If you don't yet own a home, the second section of this chapter will tell you what you need to know to buy a super starter home on less than two incomes.

If You're Already a Homeowner

Can You Still Afford Your Mortgage?

To find out, pretend you're trying to qualify for your current mortgage all over again, but this time on one income instead of two. You may discover that you're well within the safety zone, perhaps because you didn't take out the biggest mortgage you could have qualified for when you bought your house. Or maybe the income of your family's main breadwinner has risen since you purchased your place.

To see where you stand, grab a piece of paper, a pencil, and a calculator. Then jot down the following numbers:

1. Your monthly mortgage payment, including interest and principal. (If you pay a monthly premium for mortgage insurance because you made a down payment of less than 20% of your home's purchase price, also add in that amount.)

2. Your monthly payment for real estate taxes and homeowners' insurance.

3. Your family's monthly income, before taxes. If your income includes an annual bonus, divide it by twelve and add it to your base pay.

Now multiply your income (line 3) by 0.28. (You multiply by 0.28 because most lenders will let you spend about 28% of your gross income on housing.) If the number you get is higher than your current monthly housing expenses (lines 1 and 2 added together), you can stop worrying. Even the most button-downed banker would conclude that you have enough money to keep making your mortgage payments with no sweat.

If you didn't make the grade, try to pass this makeup test: Multiply your income by 0.36. (You multiply by 0.36 because most lenders will let you spend about 36% of your gross income on housing and other debts.) Subtract from your answer the total of all monthly payments you make on long-term installment debts other than your mortgage. Take into account auto and student loans plus other debts that'll take you at least ten more months to pay off. If the answer you get is higher than your present monthly housing expenses, you can relax. Making your mortgage payments shouldn't be a problem if you tighten your spending on other items. It still makes sense to cut your mortgage payment if you can, however, so read on. Of course, if you didn't pass either the 28% or the 36% test, you've *got* to read on.

The Amazing, Shrinking Mortgage

Refinancing your mortgage is a great way to cut your monthly payment. When you refinance, you simply pay off your existing mortgage by taking out a new loan at a lower interest rate. You should generally consider refinancing if you can satisfy the so-called two-and-two rule. First, the rate on a new mortgage must be at least two percentage points lower than the rate on your existing loan. (Don't despair if interest rates haven't fallen at least two points since you bought your house, however. This rule doesn't apply if you can refinance without paying points, which is sometimes possible. I'll explain what points are later in this chapter.) Second, you must plan to live in your house for at least two more years. Move sooner, and your mortgage interest savings aren't likely to offset the refinancing costs you'll incur.

Can't remember the interest rate on your current loan? Check your monthly mortgage statement, call your mortgage lender, or dig up your loan documents (you should have filed them somewhere).

To find current mortgage interest rates, check the business or real estate section of your local newspaper. Many newspapers publish the rates that local lenders charge. Or, log on to a Web site that lists current average rates, like www.hsh.com or www.bankrate.com.

If rates have fallen since you got your loan, use the calculators on www.hsh.com or www.financenter.com to figure out if you should refinance. Or, grab a sheet of paper and do the math yourself. Follow these steps:

1. Write down the amount of your current monthly mortgage payment. Subtract any part of the payment that covers your homeowners' or mortgage insurance premiums or your property taxes.

2. Jot down what your new monthly mortgage payment will be after refinancing. To get this number, check the newspaper or one of the Web sites I mentioned earlier for the going rate on thirty-year, fixed-rate mortgages. Then use the table below to estimate your new payment. For example, say you need a $150,000 loan and can get one at 8%. Read across the table from left to right to learn that you'll pay $7.34 a month for each $1,000 that you borrow. Next divide $150,000 by $1,000 to get 150. Finally, multiply 150 by $7.34 to get your new monthly mortgage payment of $1,101.

Monthly Mortgage Payment Table

Interest rate	Monthly payment for each $1,000 borrowed
7.00%	$6.65
7.25	6.82
7.50	6.99
7.75	7.16
8.00	7.34
8.25	7.51
8.50	7.69
8.75	7.87
9.00	8.05
9.25	8.23
9.50	8.41
9.75	8.59
10.00	8.78

Source: HSH Associates

3. Write down the amount you'll pay in closing costs for the new loan, including points, application, appraisal, attorney, title search, and other fees. Points are interest that you pay to the lender in a lump sum when you take out the loan. One point equals 1% of the amount you borrow. So if the lender charges two points on a $150,000 loan, you'll pay $3,000 in points. In general, the more points you pay, the lower the interest rate you can get. Other closing costs vary depending on which part of the country you live in; brace yourself to cough up about 2% to 6% of the amount you borrow. For a rough estimate of how much you'll pay in closing costs, check the loan documents for your existing mortgage.

4. Subtract line 2 from line 1 to find out how much you'll save on your monthly mortgage payment by refinancing.

To figure out how many months you'll have to remain in your home to recoup the cost of refinancing in lower monthly mortgage payments, divide line 3 by line 2. For example, assume you now pay $1,317 a month for a $150,000 mortgage at 10% interest (line 1). Say you can get a new loan for the same amount at 8%, thereby reducing your monthly mortgage payment to $1,101 (line 2). Figure you'll spend about $6,000 on points and other closing costs (line 3). Refinancing will save you $216 a month (line 1 minus line 2). To determine how many months it'll take to recoup what you paid in points and other closing costs, divide line 3 by your monthly savings of $216. The answer is almost 28 months, so refinancing is a good deal for you if you expect to stay put for more than two years.

So far I've discussed only fixed-rate mortgages. It may make sense for you to trade a fixed-rate loan for an adjustable rate mortgage instead. The trick is finding the right type of ARM at an interest rate lower than what lenders are charging for fixed-rate loans. If you're trying to live on a reduced income, steer clear of ARMs with annually readjusted interest rates. If interest rates rise, your mortgage payment will balloon—and that's the last thing you need when you're trying to survive on less than two incomes.

Instead, check out ARMs with interest rates that remain unchanged for three, five, seven, or even ten years, then move up or down each year for the balance of the loan's term. A five-year ARM might be a terrific option if, for instance, you plan to stay home with a newborn, then return to work after your baby starts school.

Shop Smart for a Mortgage

You don't need to call dozens of lenders in your area to find the lowest interest rates, points, and closing costs. Why bother, when you can pay HSH Associates (800-873-2837; www.hsh.com) to do it for you? Each week, HSH surveys 2,500 to 3,000 lenders nationwide. Borrowers like you buy this data from HSH, as do newspapers, magazines, and lenders who want to know what their competitors are up to. HSH doesn't make loans, accept referral fees or commissions, or sell links on its Web site to lenders. It just publishes information— the kind you need to find the cheapest loan. You can get HSH's report for your area for $11 by e-mail. For $23, you get the report plus an extremely useful fifty-six-page booklet on how to shop for a mortgage.

Nowadays about half of all borrowers hire mortgage brokers to help them find loans, but I don't think that's a smart move. Mortgage brokers promise to steer you to lenders offering the lowest rates, for fees equal to 1% to 2.5% of your loan amount. So you pay them a lot for research you could have done yourself or paid HSH a modest fee to do for you. Another reason to bypass mortgage brokers: borrowers have alleged in lawsuits that some brokers steered customers to high-rate lenders who paid them kickbacks.

What about applying for a mortgage online through E-Loan (www.eloan.com), GetSmart.com (www.getsmart.com), or other similar firms? Give one or two a try, if you don't mind answering questions about your situation before you find out anything about the mortgages you might qualify for. I also think you should still order a report from HSH. Why? Because online lenders match you up with a limited number of lenders that they've cut deals with. And those lenders may not be the ones offering the lowest rates in your area.

Ditch Your Mortgage Insurance

You can trim $25 to $100 or more from your monthly budget if you drop your mortgage insurance. You probably have mortgage insurance if you put down less than 20% of your home's purchase price. To protect him if you default on your loan, your lender makes you buy an insurance policy. There's nothing in it for you. The mortgage insurance payments you make don't reduce your loan principal, nor can you take a tax deduction for them.

Amanda and Neil Pinder had forgotten that they even had mortgage insurance until the birth of their triplets. Then Amanda quit her job and they began looking for ways to cut their expenses. They got their lender's permission to cancel their policy because their equity in their home exceeded 20%. "We saved $125 a month," recalls Amanda.

If you got your mortgage after July 29, 1999, your lender must automatically cancel your mortgage insurance once you have 22% equity in your home. Your lender will calculate your equity based on the price you paid for your house. So let's say you took out a $100,000 mortgage. When your loan balance falls to $78,000, you can stop paying mortgage insurance.

You can get rid of your mortgage insurance quicker, however. Your lender will probably let you drop your policy once you have 20% equity in your home. Moreover, your lender will calculate your equity based on the current market value of your house, not its purchase price. So, keep track of where you stand, especially if home values have been rising in your area. Subtract the amount you have left to pay on your mortgage (check your monthly mortgage statement for this number or call your lender) from the current market value of your home. (If you don't know how much your house is worth, ask a local real estate agent.) If your equity exceeds 20% of your home's value (the price it would sell for multiplied by 0.20), send a letter to your lender explaining why you no longer need mortgage insurance. Then be prepared to prove it by hiring a professional appraiser to validate your house's value. Typical cost: $250.

Trading Down

The American dream is all about moving up. Sure, some retirees sell big houses and move to condos. But everyone else is striving to move from an apartment to a starter home to their dream house. If you worry that the Joneses will label you a loser if you trade down, skip this section. Read it later if you finish this book and feel you still need to dramatically slash your expenses. If you don't give a hoot what your neighbors think, read my four rules for trading down without tears right now:

1. Do it only if you plan to live on a greatly reduced income for a long time. That's because trading down costs money and involves a lot of inconvenience. You'll probably have to pay a commission to the real estate agent who sells your old home, and you'll also have to hire a mover and pay closing costs to get a mortgage for the new home you buy. As a result, trading down is pointless if you plan to go back to work full time in a couple of years or if you feel confident that your spouse's income will continue to rise.

2. Don't trade a palace for a pigsty. You'll save big bucks on your mortgage payment, but you'll be miserable. And you probably won't feel better until you spend thousands of dollars on repairs and redecorating.

3. Don't leave a lovely neighborhood for one with problems. It's tempting to trade a large, expensive house in a quiet suburb with super public schools for an equally impressive house that's cheaper because the town it's in has seen better days. Sure, new settlers may eventually reverse the neighborhood's decline, but can you afford to send your kids to private school while you wait for a turnaround?

4. Think hard before moving to the sticks. This strategy is trendy today because it usually costs less to buy a new house in a developing town than it does to purchase an older house in an established suburb. But you may spend a large portion of the money you save on housing on increased commuting costs. You should also ask yourself if your family would be happy if you stay home while your spouse sees the kids only on weekends because of a killer commute.

Buying Your First Home

Yes, You Can Do It on Less Than Two Incomes

Contrary to popular belief, the average American Joe *can* afford to buy a house today even if his wife stays home with the kids. The idea that you need two incomes to buy a house comes from journalists who live in and around New York City. In that neck of the woods, fifty-year-old Cape Cods *do* routinely sell for $200,000 and up. But prices aren't nearly as high in most other sections of the country. Indeed, the median price of an existing home nationwide is $135,400, which means that half of all homes sell for less than that.

If you think I'm exaggerating Joe's prospects, crunch some numbers along with me. Let's assume that Joe grosses $30,000 a year, or $2,500 a month. Since he isn't wallowing in debt, he can spend about a third of his income, or $825 a month, on housing. Joe will probably spend about 20% of that amount on property taxes, homeowners' insurance, and household repairs. So, he can afford loan payments of about $660 a month. The table below shows how big a mortgage he can get at various interest rates.

Amount of 30-Year Fixed-Rate Mortgage

Monthly payment	Interest Rate			
	7%	8%	9%	10%
$600	$90,226	$81,744	$74,534	$68,337
700	105,263	95,368	86,957	79,727
800	120,301	108,992	99,379	91,116
900	135,338	122,616	111,801	102,506
1,000	150,376	136,240	124,224	113,895
1,250	187,970	170,300	155,280	142,369
1,500	225,564	204,360	186,335	170,843

Source: HSH Associates

Since Joe can swing a monthly mortgage payment of $660, he can borrow $81,744 at 8%. Of course, he must also come up with a down payment. If he can scrape up a 20% down payment, he can spend $98,093. How did I get that number? Multiply $81,744 by 1.20. (You multiply the mortgage amount by 1.20 because the number you're after is the mortgage amount plus a 20% down payment.)

Ah, ha! You may be thinking—a guy like Joe probably doesn't have $16,349 in savings. Can he really save that much money on his salary? Yes, though I admit it won't be a snap. Assuming Joe's savings earn 5¼%, he'd have to sock away $210 each month to have his down payment in three years. That means he must save $2,520 a year, or roughly 8½% of his income. To figure out how long it'll take you to save a down payment, log on to www.financenter.com and find ClickCalcs. You can also use calculators on a number of Web sites to estimate how expensive a house you can afford to buy. Try www.hsh.com, www.realtor.com, or www.financenter.com.

Oddly enough, retirement accounts are great places to save for a down payment. In an IRA, your savings grow tax-free until you make a withdrawal. Plus, the 10% tax penalty on early withdrawals doesn't apply to amounts of up to $10,000 to help pay for the purchase of a first home.

The best IRA for you depends upon your income and whether you or your spouse has an employer-sponsored retirement plan. For all of the details, see Chapters 4 and 14.

If you still don't feel confident that you'll be able to scrape up a fat down payment before your hair turns completely gray, read the next section of this chapter.

Special Deals for Cash-Strapped Buyers

Saving a substantial down payment may not be a realistic goal for you if you have a low income, especially if you live in an area where rents and house prices are high. If you feel closed out of the housing market, check out these alternative paths to home ownership:

1. Consider a low-down-payment (3% to 5%) mortgage backed by the Federal National Mortgage Association (www.fanniemae.com) or Federal Home Loan Mortgage Corporation (www.freddiemac.com). For details, check Fannie Mae's and Freddie Mac's Web sites. Alternatively, call Fannie Mae at 800-732-6643 or Freddie Mac at 800-972-7555.

2. Look into Uncle Sam's offerings. For an overview, log on to the Department of Housing and Urban Development's Web site (www.hud.gov). Click on "Own a Home," then "Federal Mortgage Programs." (You can also call HUD at 800-569-4287.) You may be able to get a Federal Housing Administration loan for 3% down, or even less. If you or your husband is a veteran, find out about the Department of Veterans Affairs Home Loan Program (800-827-1000).

3. Check out state or local programs for first-time home buyers. Down payments typically range from zero to 5%. Interest rates are usually lower than what banks and other private lenders charge. Call local and state housing agencies for more information. You can find their telephone numbers in the government pages of your phone book.

How to Find the (Almost) Perfect Starter Home

Notice I didn't say *perfect* starter home? That's because there are no perfect homes in *any* price range. If there were, why do millionaires invariably remodel the kitchens and bathrooms shortly after they move into their mansions? Except for a small percentage of people with deep pockets who can afford to build custom-designed homes, we all have to compromise.

My husband and I looked at about seventy-five houses before we bought our first. (The average buyer looks at just thirteen, says the Chicago Title Corp.) Some people (especially foot-sore real estate agents) might think that my husband and I went overboard, but I don't. It pays to look at lots of houses because what's offered within a fairly narrow price range varies tremendously. The basics are pretty much the same: starter homes usually have three bedrooms and one or one and a half bathrooms. What differs is the floor plan, condition, yard, and neighborhood. My husband and I saw homes that were clean enough to pass the fussiest mother-in-law's white-glove test. But we also looked at a place with fresh cat urine on the living room carpet and greasy automotive parts strewn all over the basement floor.

The house we finally bought was far from perfect. It had just one bathroom, which was on the second floor. About a quarter of the houses in the neighborhood desperately needed paint jobs or other exterior repairs. On the plus side, the town's schools were sound, there was a pleasant park within walking distance, and our house was in excellent condition. We lived there six years, then sold the place for nearly 40% more than we paid for it within a week of putting it on the market. To find a first house that you'll enjoy living in and be able to sell for a profit when you decide to move, look until you find a place with the following attributes:

1. Solid schools. Ask educators to name the top public school systems in the U.S. and you'll get a list of mostly wealthy suburban districts. It's easy to understand why. Most parents in such districts are well educated. They demand the same for their kids, and they can afford to pay high property taxes to fund good schools. So, you can always buy one of the cheapest houses in a wealthy school district. If that's not palatable, you can hunt for a town with more affordable real estate that still has super public schools. They do exist and an education research company called SchoolMatch (www.schoolmatch.com) can help you find them in your area. SchoolMatch's search service identifies school systems in your area that most closely match your criteria. The service is free over the Internet.

You can also scout school systems on your own. That's because thirty-six states require local districts to publish annual report cards. Reports typically include attendance and dropout rates, test scores, class size, spending, and college attendance rates. Identify three or four towns that you like, then call their school superintendents for copies of their report cards.

2. Good neighbors. There are two questions you should try to answer about a neighborhood before you move in: Is it safe, and is it child-friendly?

To get a sense of a neighborhood's safety, visit its shopping area at night. It's a bad sign if most of the people you see are young, male, and aimlessly hanging around in groups. You can rest easier if you see families with young children or elderly couples out for ice cream or a walk. If there's a store that sells a local newspaper that covers the neighborhood or town, buy a copy and look for the crime column. Many local newspapers publish weekly lists of calls to the police, including the names of streets where crimes occurred. Stay away from neighborhoods troubled by burglaries and robberies.

Figuring out if a neighborhood is child-friendly is a bit more challenging. Look for signs of young families, like tricycles in driveways, soccer balls on lawns, or playhouses in backyards. If you're house hunting during the school year and can spare some time on a weekday, drive through the neighborhood after school lets out to see if there are many kids around.

3. Peace and quiet. Let someone else buy a house that abuts a highway or is within spitting distance of a train station. Even if the roar of cars or clatter of trains doesn't drive *you* crazy, it will surely turn off most potential home buyers when you try to sell the place. While buying a house on a quiet residential street is your best bet, don't pass up a terrific house because it's on a heavily trafficked avenue. Make sure, however, that its price reflects the fact that it's not on a quieter street. Ask your real estate agent for recent sale prices of comparable homes on busy streets in the same town.

4. Condition and quirks. A handyman's special will always be cheaper than a similar house in good condition. Yet its price may not be low enough given the money it would take to replace the leaky roof, update the ancient electrical system, or gut the grimy kitchen. If you fall in love with an ugly duckling because it has potential, ask a contractor to estimate the cost of repairs *before* you bid on the place.

You should also be wary of cream puffs. If you find an exquisitely decorated house that's priced fairly, snap it up. But don't overpay for a place that'll be as ordinary as a dozen others on its block once the seller strips it of her Oriental rugs and extravagant window treatments.

As for quirks, avoid houses with oddball attributes that keep you puzzling for hours over how you would fix them. For example, when we were looking for our first home, my husband and I came very close to buying a 1920s brick, three-bedroom colonial. There was nothing extraordinary about that house—except for the fact that you had to pass through the first-floor bathroom to walk out the back door. My husband and I spent hours discussing how we'd fix the problem by moving either the back door (an expensive proposition) or the bathroom (a very expensive proposition). Then we came to our senses and withdrew our bid after concluding "Why buy this place anyway? It's too weird!" So if something about a house strikes you as incredibly bizarre, keep shopping; there's something better out there. It may take you another week or even another month of looking to find it, but when you do, you and your family will be happy to call it home.

What if you shop and shop and find nothing you can afford that you like better than the apartment you're currently renting? *Don't force yourself to buy!* Sure, homeowners get a tax break and build up equity. But they also spend a bundle on maintenance and repairs, especially if they must settle for the least expensive house in a neighborhood. Think about it: If you buy a house, you'll also have to purchase a lawn mower, hedge clippers, a hose, a rake, maybe even a snow shovel. If your neighbors fuss over their lawns, you'll soon find yourself shamed into buying fertilizer, seed, and weed killer for your patch of green.

Your building superintendent won't fix your leaky faucet any-more; you'll have to spend $65 an hour on a plumber instead.

There's nothing more to say if your apartment is big enough for your family and you can afford it on less than two incomes. You'll eventually need a bigger place if your family continues to grow, however. One solution: Find a larger apartment in a less expensive neighborhood. If that's as unappealing as skimping to buy a small house in some distant suburb, look hard for a bigger apartment in the same building or complex. Your land-lord may give you a break on the rent because he already knows you're reliable and neat. And you won't have to spend money on Realtor's fees.

Bob and Tamara Kent were living in a studio apartment in Manhattan when they were expecting their first child. They couldn't afford the available two-bedroom apartment in their building. But that unit was perfect for a neighboring couple with a second child on the way. The family of four moved into the two-bedroom, while Bob and Tamara snapped up the apart-ment they left behind, a one-bedroom with a dining area that had been turned into a child's bedroom. Says Bob: "We kept our ears to the ground and stayed on friendly terms with our build-ing's superintendent." Indeed, if you're a renter, the Christmas gift you give your super may be the most important investment in housing that you make.

CHAPTER 6

Spend Less on Child Care

If you're now pregnant with your first child, you can't imagine the relief that parents who quit or cut back on work feel when those bills for full-time day care stop coming due. Even in areas where the cost of living is low, child care isn't cheap—$260 a month or so is as little as you can expect to pay. In high-cost regions, monthly fees exceed $700, and dwarf tuition at some state colleges.

Even $700 a month seems like a bargain to parents who hire live-in nannies because they work long hours or have tough commutes. Nanny salaries start at about $350 a week and climb as high as $800. And base salary is just the beginning. There's also overtime, vacation, holiday, and sick day pay; FICA and unemployment taxes; employer-paid health insurance; room and board; use of a car; auto insurance; *and* a year-end bonus equal to one or two weeks' salary. Despite such perks, the demand for nannies far outstrips the supply. Faced with finding an elusive Mary Poppins, many parents run to nanny placement agencies for help. If the agency finds a nanny for them, they pay a placement fee of $800 to $3,000.

It would be wonderful if *all* of your child care expenses disappeared when you quit or cut back on work.

Unfortunately, they won't. If you plan to work part time, you can't eliminate child care from your budget—unless you have a relative who's willing to help you for free. As anyone who's tried to make a five-minute phone call with a toddler hanging on her leg knows, you can't care for kids and work at the same time.

There is a bright side, however. You can still qualify for child care tax breaks if you switch from full- to part-time work. Parents who need child care so they can work even part time, or attend college or vocational school full time, may be able to use a dependent care flexible spending account to pay for child care with tax-free dollars. (For more about child care FSAs, turn back to Chapter 4.) You may also claim the child and dependent care tax credit on your federal income tax return if you work part time or go to school full time. (For details, see Chapter 4.)

Even if you plan to stay home full time, you'll probably still spend some money on child care. Sure, you and your husband could rent videos every Friday night, but how long could you stand being a prisoner in your own home? You'll probably want to hire a baby-sitter at least once or twice a month, if not every week. And while children can certainly thrive without ever setting foot in a preschool or summer camp, you may want to send yours just because all of the other kids in your neighborhood go. Or, you may believe, as more and more parents do, that preschool is good preparation for today's more academic kindergartens. Today about a third of all three- to five-year-olds attend nursery school, up from just 4% in 1965.

So, if you intend to work part time, read this entire chapter. The first section covers how to get the part-time child care you need at a price you can afford. The second section tells you how to cut the cost of preschool, summer camp, and baby-sitting. Those of you who plan to stay home full time should skip to the second section.

How to Find Part-Time Child Care

I knew that my full-time, live-in nanny would have to go when I quit my full-time job to freelance part time. (Fortunately, she was ready to leave, having earned a bachelor's degree, and taken up accounting.) The cost of keeping her would have been prohibitive, and we'd probably have been tripping over each other all day long. So I sat down and did what you should also do if you're thinking about working part time. I figured out what kind of part-time child care would be appropriate for each of my two children over the next five years. (I looked five years ahead because by the end of that period my youngest would be in grade school.) I thought about how many hours a week I'd need child care, and whether I'd work fewer hours during the summer, when schools are closed. Then I called about a dozen day care centers, nursery schools, and summer camps so I could estimate how much child care would cost for each of the next five years.

After you complete this exercise, you may find that you'll net only a few dollars an hour if you work part-time when your children are too young for grade school. Unless you can get free child care courtesy of a relative or friend, it won't pay for you to work part time. Instead, consider staying home full time until your kids are ready for full-day kindergarten or first grade, even if you must dip into your savings to swing it. If you work part time starting when your kids are in grade school, you'll still need to pay for child care during the summer, of course. But that's only three months out of twelve.

If working part time makes sense for you now, ask yourself the following questions to help you choose the best type of care for you and your kids:

1. **How old are your children?** You obviously can't send an eight-month-old to preschool. And it's not a good idea to hire a baby-sitter who doesn't drive if your eight-year-old desperately wants to join a traveling after-school soccer team.

2. **How many hours will you work?** Toil just ten hours a week and your mother may be thrilled to care for your three-year-old twins—gratis. Ask her to mind them twenty hours a week and she may politely decline. Even if she's too nice to say no, you probably shouldn't impose on her to such an extent.

3. **How flexible can you be?** Your answer will depend on whether you're self-employed, and what kind of work you do. I can be extremely flexible because I take on only as much freelance work as I want. I can also write any day, any time. I wrote much of this book while my kids slept. I also worked while my second grader was in school and at a half-day summer camp. My three-year-old attended half-day nursery school and half-day summer camp. She also napped

for ninety minutes or so some afternoons. I could usually take off when my daughters' schools and camps weren't in session. If you can't do the same, you'll have to stitch together backup child care for the days your kids have off and you don't.

Once you've figured out your needs, check out care child options in your area. Here are some strategies to consider, listed from the least to most expensive, plus advice on how to cut costs:

- **Work when your spouse is home.** Lots of couples who juggle two full-time jobs do this. It's a time-honored way to save money and impart parental values. If spouses rarely see each other, however, shift work can strain a marriage. Having one parent work part time reduces the stress. Registered nurse Beth Auletta and her husband Brian, an engineer, have used this strategy successfully since their twin boys were born ten years ago. Beth switched from full-time work to part-time shift work at the same hospital. She also had two more kids, now ages nine and seven. "When my kids were young, I usually worked weeknights or Saturdays," Beth says. "Now that all of my kids are in school, I typically work 10 A.M. to 2 P.M. on weekdays one or two days a week during the school year. I can get them on the school bus and be home before they are."

Best for which kids: All ages.
Best for which husbands: Please forgive my sexism, but this isn't a good child care choice if Dad is the type who

must ask where the milk is *every time* he opens the refrigerator.

Cost: Free.

Upside: Your sitter won't quit and will (hopefully) share your child-rearing values.

Downside: If you put in a lot of hours at work, you won't have much private time with your husband. Remember Elana Skinner, the child life specialist who quit her job because she didn't want to leave her son in day care? About six months after she resigned, she got an offer to go back to work twenty hours a week on evenings and weekends only. It sounded ideal. She'd spend all day with her son, then go to work when her husband was home to take over the child care duties. She enjoyed her job, but did it for only nine months. "My husband and I realized that it was a real drain on our relationship. We never had any time alone together," Elana says. "I was ready to become a full-time stay-at-home mom."

- **Get help from other family members.** Asking your mother, mother-in-law, or sister to care for your kids ten or fifteen hours a week isn't nearly as big an imposition as full-time caregiving. Lindsey Warren didn't even have to ask her mother for help when she quit her full-time job in the accounts receivable department of a big company after the first of her five children was born in 1990. To supplement her husband Bob's income as a parts manager for a car dealership, Lindsey went back to cleaning houses, which is what she did to help pay her way through college. "My mother, who'd been a stay-at-home mom, volunteered to watch my daughter while I cleaned," recalls Lindsey. "She wanted me to be able to earn some money so I could stay home with my baby most of the time."

Some people use more than one relative to baby-sit, but I don't think that's wise. If you send your son to your mother's house on Mondays, your mother-in-law's on Tuesdays, and your sister's on Wednesdays, he won't have any one place to call his home away from home. Chances are his caregivers will all have different rules regarding snacks, television, and other important topics. Grandma Number One lets him eat an entire bag of M&M's, Grandma Number Two allows him just ten, and Auntie insists he eat an apple instead. What a challenge it will be for you to get him to follow your rules when you're home!

> **Best for which kids:** All ages.
> **Best for which relatives:** Younger is better than older, especially if your kids are very young and frisky. Homebodies will enjoy themselves more than grandmas who'd rather be shopping or coffee-klatsching.
> **Cost:** Free or nominal, though you obviously owe a family caregiver any favor she asks of you.
> **Upside:** Your kids are with someone you love and trust.
> **Downside:** Your relative may take the job because she feels compelled to help you out, not because she enjoys caring for kids.

- **Barter baby-sitting with another parent who works part time.** A brilliant strategy in theory, but tough to pull off. Your needs have to mesh with hers, and your kids must peacefully coexist. I surveyed more than 100 parents for this book and didn't run across anyone who'd ever done it.

Best for which kids: All ages, but it's easier with toddlers and preschoolers because they usually aren't terribly fussy about whom they play with.

Best for which adults: Both parents must truly enjoy baby-sitting *and* give it their all when it's their turn. If you sneak in business calls when you're supposed to be playing Mom to the brood, you can bet that your friend's kids will rat on you.

Cost: Free.

Upside: Your children get to play with other kids in an unstructured setting. You get free child care without imposing on relatives.

Downside: No child care arrangement lasts forever, but this one is particularly precarious. What if your friend's work hours change, or your kids clash?

- **Get a part-time job with on-site child care.** Admittedly, you're more likely to find a needle in a haystack than on-site child care if you confine your job search to corporate America. (Only about 8,000 companies nationwide offer it.) So look elsewhere, like Kathy Shannon did. Kathy worked full time as a bank teller before she had her first daughter; her husband Patrick is a truck driver. Always interested in fitness, Kathy passed practical and written exams to become a certified fitness instructor and personal trainer. She then found part-time work at health clubs that offered free on-site child care to attract and keep instructors as well as members. Kathy often used on-site child care centers at the gyms she worked at when her two daughters, now ages ten and nine, were preschoolers.

Best for which kids: Infants, toddlers, and perhaps preschoolers—if you don't work so many hours that they become bored with the surroundings.

Cost: A few bucks an hour at most; sometimes free.

Upside: Your kids are close by.

Downside: Older kids won't want to hang out with babies and toddlers in a day care center.

- **Use part-time day care.** Many centers and family day care providers offer part-time hours, typically three or four full days per week, or five mornings a week. If you've ever used full-time day care, you know you should put your child's name on waiting lists well in advance of when you'll need care. Slots fill up quickly at well-regarded centers, and few part-time openings are available because it's easier for providers to maximize their income by filling all of their openings with full-timers.

Best for which kids: Toddlers and preschoolers. It's virtually impossible to find part-time day care for infants.

Cost: Home day care providers charge $3.00 to $5.00 an hour; day care centers are usually more expensive, charging up to $8.50 an hour. Some centers offer part-time hours and reduce their fees accordingly. Don't expect the same from home day care providers, warns Eileen Mulhern, a former news service editor who freelanced part time from home while her two children were young.

"I paid my caregiver for a full week's work even though my kids were at her house only part time," Eileen recalls. "Other providers I checked out also wanted me to pay for a full week."

Upside: Researchers say that quality day care increases kids' verbal and social skills.

Downside: Good day care is tough to find.

- **Work while your kids are in grade school.** Parents who work part time cheer the day when their youngest turns five and can go to public school—free. Their child care problems are suddenly solved! Well, for at least nine months out of the year, and from about 8 A.M. to 3 P.M. And let's not forget Christmas, winter and spring breaks, plus teacher conference and sick days. If you, like me, live in an area where natives aren't used to severe winters, your kids will also get to stay home whenever more than an inch of snow falls.

Of course, there are solutions. Parents who can't take summers off can hire college kids to baby-sit or send their kids to camp. If you must leave for the office before 8 A.M. or work past 3 P.M., you can hire a baby-sitter or send your kids to a before- or after-school program sponsored by their school or the local Y. Typical cost: About $70 a week.

Then there's the challenge of half-day kindergarten, which is still surprisingly common. Here are your options if you work more than two and a half hours a day:

1. **Divide your child's day between public school kindergarten and a private preschool or day care center.** To

use this strategy, you'll have to find a way to get your kid from school A to school B.

2. **Combine kindergarten with a half-day enrichment program offered by your school system.** This is usually easy to pull off because both classes are often in the same building, or the school district provides busing. Availability varies, as do prices. The tab can easily run $30 a day. Despite their name, don't expect enrichment programs to give your kid a leg up on his peers. If such programs emphasized academics, parents whose kids attend school only half a day would complain.

3. **Send your child to a private, full-day kindergarten.** First, find out how much it'll cost. If it makes sense for you, apply early for admission. Be prepared to pay tuition of $5,000 and up.

Best for which kids: Age five and up.

Cost: Free at public schools; private school tuition varies.

Upside: You can finally stop worrying that your kids aren't learning while you're at work.

Downside: You've got to find backup child care if you or your spouse can't take off when school is closed.

- **Send your child to preschool.** When my firstborn started first grade, I figured I'd send my two-year-old to preschool for two hours each weekday morning. After school, we'd play and have lunch together. Then she'd nap, and I'd have at least ninety more minutes a day to write. Naturally, daughter #2, unlike her older sister, didn't nap consistently. So, if you think this strategy sounds good, have a backup plan just in case your little darling doesn't cooperate.

Preschool teachers usually get even more days off than grade school teachers do, so be prepared to find lots of alternative child care. Before you choose a preschool, check to see if it's closed most of the same days that your school age kids will be home. Also, bear in mind that summer camps usually don't take children under three.

Best for which kids: Three- to five-year-olds, though some nursery schools enroll children as young as eighteen months.

Cost: Varies widely, depending upon the number of days per week that your kid attends, where you live, and whether parents help out in the classroom. Nine-month, five-day programs often cost $3,000 or more. For cost-cutting tips, see the next section of this chapter.

Upside: Kids who go to good preschools are usually ready and able to tackle the three R's in kindergarten.

Downside: The price is steep, especially if you need additional child care.

- **Hire a part-time baby-sitter to come to you.** On an hourly basis, a part-time sitter can cost more than a full-time, live-in nanny. And once you start paying a sitter a lot of money, taxes come into play. If you pay your sitter $1,200 or more in 2000, you must also pay half of her Social Security and Medicare taxes. (The amount that's exempt from tax rises with inflation.) You must also pay federal unemployment tax and probably state unemployment tax too. What's more, you can't wait until you file your tax return to pay nanny taxes. You've got two choices: File quarterly estimated tax payments, or increase your withholding. You can read all of the mind-numbing details in IRS Publication 926, "Household Employer's Tax Guide." If you can't deal with another tax form, you can get help from a nanny tax preparation firm. Throwing in the towel will cost you another $350 or so a year.

Best for which kids: Okay for all ages, and often your only option for infants.

Cost: About $4.00 to $15 an hour, depending upon where you live, whether your sitter is a teenager or an adult, and how many kids you have. If you hire a part-time sitter through a nanny placement agency, also factor in the agency's fee.

Upside: The sitter comes to you, preferably in her own car.

Downside: Unless you hire a teenager, this is an expensive proposition. If you do find a willing and able teen, chances are you'll soon have to look for another, and then another, as they quit to join the high school yearbook staff, get a better-paying job at the Gap, or become bored.

How One-Income Families Can Cut Child Care Costs

Even if you don't work for pay at all, you'll still have some child care costs. You'll need baby-sitters occasionally, and you may want to send your kids to preschool or summer camp. Here's how to save on all of those things:

What to Do About Preschool

When I was young, it seemed that only rich kids went to nursery school. The rest of us watched *Romper Room* on TV. That's changed, but children from affluent families are still much more likely to go. The Carnegie Corporation reports that fewer than half of three- to five-year-olds from families with annual incomes of $40,000 or less are enrolled in preschool, compared to 82% of children from families that earn more than $75,000 a year. You *could* keep your kids at home to watch Barney, who is, after all, just Miss Sally in a purple dinosaur suit. But if you'd rather not, here's how to send your kids to preschool for less:

- **Hunt for free public preschool.** Most states offer free public preschool programs, but usually limit enrollment to kids from low-income families. Still, it's worth a two-minute phone call to your school district's administrative office to find out if your town offers public preschool. You may be pleasantly surprised. Take Paramus, New Jersey, for example. This affluent New York City suburb perhaps best known for its shopping malls offers free preschool for four-year-olds. Classes meet three days a week for two and a half hours. The program is open only to residents, of course, who rush to sign up for a limited number of slots.

- **Join a cooperative nursery school.** Co-ops hold costs down by putting parents to work as unpaid teacher's assistants, secretaries, and even janitors. Stay-at-home mom Barbara Gervolino, whose husband Rick operates a catering truck, sent both of her daughters to a co-op preschool. She now pays $890 a year to send her four-year-old to school three half-days per week. Some regular nursery schools in her town charge more than $2,000 for the same number of hours. Barbara helps in her daughter's classroom two days a month. Her duties include serving snacks, sweeping the floor, and scrubbing the bathroom. Co-op parents also must make a major contribution once a month; Barbara cleans the school's kitchen. In addition, she and Rick are required to work at the school's annual fund-raising flea market.

■ **Send your kids to preschool two or three days a week instead of five.** On a per-day basis, five-day schedules are usually the least expensive. However, you'll save 20% to 35% out-of-pocket if you send your children to school two or three days week.

Cut the Cost of Summer Camp

Nowadays camps cater to aspiring astronauts, soccer stars, computer jocks, and noncompetitive nature lovers. Most boast price tags that'll knock your Birkenstocks off. Private day camps generally cost $300 to $500 a week, and often require minimum stays of four weeks. If you want an air-conditioned bus to pick up and drop off your child, add another $60 or so per week. If you want your kid to stay overnight, prepare to pay $500 to $800 a week.

Of course, you can forget about camp and send your kids out to play in the backyard. If you live in an affluent neighborhood that's camp-crazy, however, watch out. Your kids may go the entire summer without ever seeing any other kids in their backyards. You may be able to solve that problem if your town features a recreation center, however. Although she lives in a town where many four-year-olds board those air-conditioned buses for full-day camps, Barbara Gervolino takes her kids to the town pool. Cost of a season's pass for a family of four: $180.

If you'd like to send your kids to camp, however, consider these cost-cutting strategies:

- **Find out if your town runs a day camp.** If it does, you'll probably breathe a sigh of relief when you hear the price. My second grader attends our town's half-day, six-week camp, which costs only $185. It's nothing fancy: Arts and crafts, swimming, brown-bag lunches, and old-fashioned games. Campers put on a talent show and take field trips to the fire station, county zoo, and an indoor ice skating rink.

- **Try a nonprofit camp.** To find them, check Ys and religious denominations. Typical cost: $60 to $150 a week for day camps; $250 to $300 a week for overnight stays.

- **Organize a backyard camp.** This takes some work, but it's an inexpensive way to give your kids a taste of summer camp right in your own neighborhood. Here's how it works: A dozen families who live near each other get together and agree to hire a camp director and an assistant. Ideally, the director could be a schoolteacher who has the summer off. You could hire a college student or a mature high school student as the assistant. Parents get together with the director and dream up ideas for activities that kids can do in their own backyards, like arts and crafts, old-fashioned games, or sports lessons. The kids move to a different backyard every week, so all of the families play host. The cost varies depending upon the director's and assistant's salaries, which depend on their experience and the number of hours and days that camp is in session. You also have to factor in the cost of art supplies and snacks, of course. Still, $50 a week per kid should cover it.

Start a Baby-sitting Cooperative

Wouldn't you love to leave your kids with a trusted *adult* sitter and go out with your husband—free? You can do it by joining with other parents to start a baby-sitting cooperative. In a co-op, members take turns watching each other's kids. No money changes hands. Instead, parents exchange chits or tokens good for baby-sitting time. You can save money and stop worrying about leaving your kids with inexperienced (and sometimes unreliable) teenage sitters.

Starting a co-op is simple. All you need is someone who believes in the idea and isn't afraid to organize a meeting of parents who already have something in common. For example, they might live in the same neighborhood, attend church together, or send their kids to the same preschool or grade school.

A couple who attends my church put out a call to fellow parents, and arranged a pizza party for interested families. Seventeen families joined the co-op. Each filled out a sign-up sheet, giving their name, address, telephone number, children's names and ages, and the days and times when they're able to baby-sit. One member used her computer to print chits good for a half an hour of baby-sitting time. Each family got six chits to start. Since then, co-op members have called each other when they needed sitters, and paid each other with the chits. At the rate it's going, the co-op will probably peter out only after the initial members' kids are old enough to become baby-sitters themselves.

CHAPTER 7

Stop Wasting Money on Wheels

Are you spending way too much on the gas-guzzlers that live in your garage? Probably. Car prices have increased at a greater rate than incomes for more than a generation. While it's true that cars are safer and more rust-resistant than ever, sticker prices have also soared because cars are fancier. Power windows and CD players, once luxury options, are now standard on many models. Big, bulky vehicles that gulp gas are in style. Soccer moms now feel the need to drive gussied-up all-terrain vehicles on smooth suburban streets.

Parents have it tough. We don't want to spend a fortune on transportation, yet we'd rather not drive one of the smallest, cheapest cars on the market. Even if you *can* squeeze your family into a two-door subcompact, do you feel comfortable ferrying your most precious cargo in a vehicle that folds like an accordion in government crash tests?

Don't fret. You can drive a safe, reliable car without sinking deep into debt. Here's what to do:

Figure Out How Much Car You Can Afford

Do you have enough cash in your savings account or money-market fund to pay cash for a car? If you're one of the few who do, buy your next car with cash. The reason is quite simple: Unlike houses, cars begin to depreciate as soon as you drive them off the dealer's lot. Why pay interest to purchase a depreciating asset if you don't have to?

If you can't pay cash the next time you need to buy a car, follow the advice in this chapter. If you do, and you drive your current car for at least ten years, you'll surely be able to pay cash for your *next* car. Merle and Drew Traylor, who've lived on only Drew's income since they had their second child seven years ago, worked their way up to paying cash for their cars. They vowed to keep their cars for at least six years. They also established a separate savings account at their credit union for new car purchases, which they add to monthly. And they stick to used cars. They now drive a 1990 Ford Taurus station wagon and a 1996 GMC Safari minivan. When the Traylors bought them, both had only 50,000 miles or so on their odometers.

If you need to borrow, figure on putting at least 20% down—more if possible. If you make a down payment of 20% or more, many lenders will shave a percentage point or so off their regular auto loan rate. Remember that you may be able to raise a portion of your down payment by selling or trading in your old car.

Also, assume you'll get a thirty-six-month loan—forty-eight months at most. By making a hefty down payment and choosing a relatively short loan term, you'll pay less interest over the life of the loan. Let's say you borrow $15,000 at 8%. A sixty-month loan would cost $304.15 a month, or a total of $18,249. Pay $470.05 a month on a thirty-six-month loan instead, and you'll spend only $16,921.80. Paying off the loan in three years instead of five costs an additional $165.90 a month, but saves $1,327.20 overall. When you're ready to apply for a loan, you can ask lenders to do the same kind of comparison for you. Or you can do it yourself using the loan payment calculators on www.bankrate.com or www.autosite.com.

Here's an easy way to determine how much car you can afford: Add up how much you can put down and work from there. Let's say you can make a $4,000 down payment. That works out to 20% of $20,000, which leaves you $16,000 to finance. Get the going rate for auto loans from the business section of your daily newspaper, or log on to www.hsh.com or www.bankrate.com. You can then use the loan payments calculator on the latter Web site to find out what your monthly payment would be on a thirty-six- or forty-eight-month loan. Flip back to the worksheet you filled out in Chapter 1 to review your other expenses. If the payment on even a forty-eight-month loan seems too high given your other obligations, you can either:

Postpone purchasing a car until you scrape up a bigger down payment.

If you have two cars, wait until you've paid off the loan on the one you intend to keep before replacing the other. You'll be able to handle a larger monthly payment on a new auto loan as a result.

Shop for a less expensive new car than you initially thought you would. The next section of this chapter explains how to buy a vehicle that'll fit your family's needs *and* your budget.

Buy a used car. I'll tell you how later in this chapter.

Why haven't I mentioned leasing as an option? After all, leased cars comprise a third of all new vehicles on the road today, up from fewer than 3% fifteen years ago. Lease and you can drive a more expensive car than you could afford to buy. That's because, compared to buying a car, leasing requires low or no down payment and lower monthly payments.

So, what's not to like about leasing? Just this: When you lease, you aren't building equity in an asset that you can eventually sell or trade. Instead, your monthly payments cover merely the decrease in the vehicle's value over the term of your lease. The bottom line: If you typically keep cars for more than three years, you're better off buying. (If you want to compare the cost of buying vs. leasing yourself, log onto www.lease source.com or www.autosite.com.) Besides, if you change cars more frequently, you can't be serious about saving money on wheels. Next time a Lexus or Lincoln Navigator blows by you on the highway, don't feel envious. The driver probably isn't nearly as rich (or as smart) as you imagine. Why do I say that? Leasing accounts for about six in ten luxury vehicles on the road.

Find a Vehicle That Fits Your Family and Your Budget

Okay, admit it: The typical family with a couple of kids doesn't really need a 5,290-pound Ford Expedition that seats nine and gets only thirteen miles to the gallon. In truth, even a minivan is overkill. Buy a vehicle that's only as big as you need on a *daily* basis. If Grandma and Grandpa come to visit for a week, you can always rent a van to accommodate the whole clan. If you think you need something bigger than a five-passenger sedan to haul your son's basketball team to and from practice, let me ask you this: Do you really want the job anyway?

The extra money you'll spend on gas if you buy one of the behemoths that are so popular today really adds up. My Toyota Camry sedan gets about twenty-three miles to the gallon and I drive about 15,000 miles a year. If I traded my Camry for an Expedition, I'd spend about $500 more a year on fuel.

The cost of gas is just the beginning. The bigger and more luxurious a vehicle is, the more it'll cost to insure. Then there's the federal luxury tax, which in 1999 is 6% of any amount over $36,000 that you pay for a vehicle.

If you can't afford to buy an SUV but are thinking of leasing one for safety's sake, think again. Sure, it's true that you're much less likely to get hurt in a crash if you're driving a heavy-weight SUV instead of a subcompact. The most enormous SUVs are generally quite safe. It gets considerably more complicated when you look at smaller SUVs, however. In fact, some mid-size, four-door sedans do better in crash tests than some mid-size SUVs. Check for yourself on www.dot.gov (click on National Highway Traffic Safety Administration) or www.hwysafety.org. Or peruse *Consumer Reports'* annual auto issue.

Also, bear in mind that crash test results apply only to drivers and passengers wearing seat belts. Ensconced in two tons of steel, some folks get complacent. The directors of my kids' preschool felt compelled to send home a memo reminding parents to buckle their kids in. My children and I always use seat belts, but I see plenty of mothers who let their kids wander around their enormous SUVs unrestrained.

So please keep an open mind when shopping for a car. You may be surprised to find that you can get what you need without spending as much as you thought you'd have to. Of course, the purchase price of a car isn't the only expense you should consider. You should also compare how much it'll cost to maintain and insure comparable models. IntelliChoice, a research company, calculates the cost of owning new cars and trucks over the next five years. IntelliChoice's analysts tally up how much you're likely to spend on insurance, maintenance, repairs, gasoline, and other items. They also project how much a vehicle will depreciate. For $4.95, you can download reports on as many as six different vehicles from the firm's Web site, www.intellichoice.com. You can also find the company's data in *Kiplinger*'s and *Money*'s annual auto issues. To find out if a vehicle is likely to break down a lot, see *Consumer Reports'* annual auto issue.

Once you've narrowed your choices to six or fewer vehicles, take your whole family to an auto show. You can examine cars, trucks, and vans from many manufacturers without pressure from pushy salespeople. Have your whole gang climb into models that interest you. If you hate the dashboard or your kids look like canned sardines squeezed into the backseat, cross the model off your list. When you're down to two or three models, arrange to test-drive them at local dealerships.

Get Financing

There are two good reasons to line up an auto loan before you talk to car dealers:

You'll know exactly how much you can afford to spend. You'll be able to compare the best rate you find to a dealer's financing offer.

Check advertisements in your local newspaper for banks with low auto loan rates. Call two or three of those lenders, plus the bank you usually do business with. If you belong to a credit union, also call it. Ask all of the lenders for their annual percentage rate (APR) for car loans. Once you've identified the best deal, fill out an application. Assuming you win approval, tuck your loan documents into your pocket or purse, *then* go shopping for a car. If a dealer offers you financing, ask for the APR and make sure you're comparing apples to apples. Many of the incredibly low rates touted on television commercials for cars are good on only twenty-four-month loans.

Should you borrow from your 401(k) retirement plan instead of a bank to buy a car? No way. Why mess with your retirement savings to purchase a depreciating asset? (To read more about the downside of borrowing from your 401(k), see Chapter 14.)

If you own a house, what about taking out a home equity loan or line of credit to finance a car? The interest you pay will usually be tax-deductible, unlike interest on a traditional auto loan. Thanks to this tax break, you'll usually save a few hundred dollars by taking out a home equity loan instead of a car loan. That's true only if everything else is equal, however.

Often, it's not. Home equity loans often carry up front costs, like appraisers' fees. Depending upon your tax bracket, those fees may erase your tax savings. To find out if a home equity loan is worth considering, log on to www.financecenter.com, click on calculators and plug your numbers into the program that compares auto and home equity loans. To me, the potential tax savings aren't great enough to compensate for the fact that you risk losing your home if you can't keep up with your loan payments.

Do One More Round of Research

Now you're ready to figure out how much you should expect to pay for the vehicle you want. Thanks to the Internet, it's a snap to find out how much dealers must pay for the car or truck you want, including options. You can get these so-called invoice prices free by logging on to www.edmunds.com, www.kbb.com, www.carprices.com, www.autosite.com, or www.carpoint.com. You can also get invoice prices by mail or FAX from *Consumer Reports* (800-888-8275 or 800-258-1169). Getting information the old-fashioned way will cost you $12, however.

You can also find out which models manufacturers are eager to move off dealers' lots. To find out about rebates and sales incentives, log onto www.edmunds.com, www.carprices.com, www.autosite.com, or www.carpoint.com. You can get the same type of information in the weekly *Automotive News*, which you may find in your local public library. Alternatively, you can pay $7.00 to download *CarDeals*, a biweekly newsletter from the nonprofit Center for the Study of Services (www.checkbook.org). If you prefer to order a copy by phone, call 800-475-7283.

Drive a Hard Bargain

Now you're ready to call or visit dealers in your area. Tell them you're talking to their competitors, and ask how small a markup they'll accept over invoice price for the vehicle you want. Always bargain up from the invoice price, not down from the inflated sticker price that's pasted in a car's window. Make sure all of the quotes you get are "out-the-door" prices, which include all charges except state and local taxes and registration fees. Dealers will sell most new cars for about 4% above invoice price. Luxurious or wildly popular models often go for up to 8% above invoice price. If you can live with last year's model or an unpopular car that carries a rebate, you can expect to pay invoice price or less.

If you want to include a trade-in in the deal, don't bring it up until the dealer has given you a firm price on the new car. Better yet, sell your old car through the classifieds or to a different dealer. (I explain why in "Keep Your Cars at Least Ten Years" on page 108.)

Finally, don't be duped into giving up the discount you negotiated before you close the deal. Car dealers try to make up the profits they lose to savvy shoppers by selling overpriced add-ons. Be on guard when the salesperson passes you along to the manager. Just say no when he or she tries to sell you rustproofing, a dealer-installed alarm system, or an extended warranty. Those items can inflate the price you bargained for by $2,000 or more.

Or Get a Hired Gun
to Haggle for You

If you haven't the time or stomach for bargaining, you can get someone else to do it for you. You'll probably pay more for your car than you would have had you negotiated skillfully yourself. But you'll definitely get a break off the sticker price. One option is to order through a no-fee buying service. The buying service refers you to a dealer in your area who agrees to charge you a discounted, nonnegotiable price. The buying service makes money by collecting referral fees from dealers in its network. You can find buying services on the Internet at www.autobytel.com, www.autoweb.com, www.autovantage.com, www.carpoint.com, and www.autoconnect.com.

If you hate haggling so much you're willing to pay someone to do it for you, consider hiring an auto broker. Brokers like AutoAdvisor (800-326-1976, www.autoadvisor.com) and CarQ (800-517-2277, www.carq.com) charge $227 to $475 to negotiate for you. All you need to do is sign the sales contract. If you don't want to spend that much, those brokers as well as CarBargains (800-475-7283, www.carbargains.org) will get price quotes for you from about five local dealers for fees of $165 to $175. It's then up to you to do the rest.

What to Do When
You Want to Buy Used

In the 1950s and 1960s, used car salesmen were the butt of jokes and Americans bought only one used car for every new one they purchased. Nowadays, guys in expensive suits sell "pre-owned" Jaguars, and we purchase three used cars for every new one. Even folks who can afford to buy new are choosing used instead. And why not? You can save 25% to 40% by purchasing a three-year-old car instead of a new one, since new vehicles suffer their biggest drop in value during their first three years. Cars are also more reliable than ever. The typical car on the road today is more than eight years old, up from six and a half a decade ago. It didn't surprise me that lots of parents who answered my survey drive used cars.

Shopping for a used car is much like shopping for a new one. Start by figuring out how much you can afford to spend, zero in on the models that fit your family's needs, arrange for financing if you need it, do some research on prices, then jaw with dealers. One word of warning: Lenders typically charge a percentage point more for used car loans.

Of course, when you buy a used car, you must assess its condition. It's handy if you or your mate is mechanically inclined. Most of us aren't amateur auto mechanics, but we can all read what experts have written about various models. *Consumer Reports* lists lemons in its annual auto issue. You can also log on to www.intellichoice.com to get free information on recalls and consumer complaints.

Unless the used car you want is a "pre-owned" luxury model that comes with a fresh warranty, it's worth paying an independent auto mechanic $100 or so to check it out. (Where on earth do you find an independent mechanic who knows what he's doing? I can only tell you to ask relatives and friends for recommendations.) You should also ask the seller for a detailed, written history of checkups and repairs. You're most likely to get one if you're buying from a fastidious private owner.

If you're buying from a dealer, ask him to run the car's Vehicle Identification Number (VIN) through his computer to check if the car has ever been totaled. If you're dealing with a private owner, get the VIN from the vehicle's dashboard and do the sleuthing yourself. It'll cost you $12 to get the information over the Web at www.carfax.com. If you use the phone (888-422-7329), you'll pay $20.

It's easier than ever to determine how much you should pay for a used car. You can check used car prices for free by logging on to www.edmunds.com, www.carpoint.com, www.intellichoice.com, www.autoweb.com, www.carprices.com, www.autosite.com, or www.kbb.com. Luddites can page through *Edmund's Used Cars & Trucks: Prices and Ratings* or the *Kelley Blue Book Used Car Guide* at their local libraries.

While you're at it, check www.edmunds.com, www.carprices.com, www.carpoint.com, www.autosite.com, *Automotive News*, or *CarDeals* to find out if the new version of the used vehicle you're interested in carries a rebate or other sales incentive. Why bother if you're buying a used model? Because a rebate on the current model will push down prices for its used cousins.

There are also more places than ever to shop for a used car. You can compare asking prices by scanning newspaper classified ads placed by private owners, or by checking Web sites like www.autoweb.com, www.carpoint.com, or www.autoconnect.com. As always, you can find used cars at new car dealerships and used car lots. (Avoid used car dealers who move from town to town. That's a sign that the local Better Business Bureau or Chamber of Commerce had something uncomplimentary to say about them to consumers who asked.) If you hate bargaining, you can visit auto superstores that feature nonnegotiable prices. You can even use a no-fee Internet buy-ing service, www.autobytel.com, to get a price quote on a used car from a dealer in your area.

Keep Your Cars at Least Ten Years

Imagine the joy of driving a vehicle for years after you've paid off the loan on it. And just picture how much money you can sock away for your next car after those loan payments stop. Nowadays it's no big deal to drive a car with 100,000 miles on its odometer. My husband and I still have the first car either of us ever purchased, a 1984 Toyota Tercel hatchback. We paid off the loan on it years ago, and don't carry collision coverage anymore. We no longer drive it long distances because we bought a four-door sedan after our first child was born. My husband drives the Tercel to the commuter bus station on weekdays, where it sits surrounded by late model BMWs and SUVs. My husband jokes that our daughters will learn to drive in it, and he may be right. I lost count of the number of parents I surveyed who said they had at least one ancient car. Glenda Vogel, a former pediatric nurse who stays home with her two-year-old daughter, wins the award for having the oldest ancient car—a 1974 Plymouth Valiant. Her husband Paul drives it daily—and unlike my husband, Paul has a long commute!

There's one potential problem with hanging on to a car for years, however. Get emotionally attached to your car, and you may repair it when you should let it be or even junk it. I had to restrain my husband, who affectionately calls the Tercel "the Baby," from taking it to a *body shop* when it developed a rust spot on the passenger's door.

If you decide to unload an old car while it's still got some life in it, you'll get the most money by selling it yourself to an acquaintance or through the classifieds. If you lack the time or patience to deal with hagglers or deadbeats, sell to a car dealer. Of course, you'll get the wholesale price rather than retail, but it'll be less of a hassle. It's best to sell to a dealer other than the one you're buying your new car from. If you've bargained hard enough to get a great price on your new car, the dealer will probably try to make up for some of his lost profit by offering you a low-ball price on your old car.

Consider Becoming a One-Car Family

If you're going to take up the Ozzie and Harriet lifestyle, why not go all the way? It's easiest to pull off if you live in the center of a big city, but it's possible elsewhere too. Plenty of older houses in inner-ring suburbs have one-car garages, reflecting the fact that Dad once walked to the bus or train station or got a lift from Mom and the kids. In real life, Ozzie and Harriet Nelson lived in Teaneck, New Jersey, a classic inner-ring suburb where many residents still commute to New York City by bus. Heck, *we* could live without our Tercel. My husband could easily walk to the bus station in about 15 minutes. Annual savings: $175 for parking at the station, $645 for insurance, and about $550 for gasoline, maintenance, and repairs. Hmmm . . . enough to pay for a nice vacation.

CHAPTER 8

Cure Your
Credit Card Habit

Two out of three people who'll read this book carry the burden of a credit card balance. If you're one of them, you know that debt brings worries. If you're thinking about quitting or cutting back on work, you're probably worried about whether you can without sinking even deeper into debt. And if you've already given up some income to spend more time with your kids, you may fret that you'll always owe money to MasterCard.

To all of you who are wondering if you can indeed quit or cut back on work, I say go ahead and do it. There's no reason to think that you need two full-time incomes to pay off your debts. After all, you've got two full incomes now and you've still managed to run up a credit card balance. The key to getting out of hock is having a repayment plan and sticking to it. Part one of this chapter will show you how to stop piling on additional debt and pay off your outstanding balances. As for you who are wondering if you did the right thing when you quit your job or switched to part-time work, relax. You too need a plan to help you make the transition from free to controlled credit card spending.

The remaining third of you who've started this chapter are probably wondering if you should bother reading any further. After all, you don't have any bad credit card habits to break. You use plastic like cash, and pay your bills in full each month. Congratulations, but please don't stop reading. If you haven't yet quit or cut back on work, consider this: You just might *develop* a problem paying your credit card balances off each month after your income drops. Plenty of former two-career couples do, as they continue to run up charges on one income that they barely paid off when they enjoyed two paychecks. That's why I've dedicated the second part of this chapter to folks who don't carry credit card balances and want to keep it that way. So skip ahead to "How to Stay Debt-Free" on page 120, but don't get smug. Remember that credit card issuers are always dreaming up ways to get people like you to start paying interest, or at least annual fees.

How to Dig Yourself Out of a Credit Card Hole

There's debt and then there's *debt*. Some people are in so deep that they pay their electric bill late so they can scrape up enough cash to make minimum payments on a wallet full of plastic. I hope you're not one of them, but if you are, don't despair. You'll probably need help to get out of debt, and I'll tell you where to find it.

Then there are folks like Barbara and Rick Gervolino, who live on one income and can't seem to get rid of the $2,000 balance on their credit card. The Gervolinos certainly aren't in over their heads; other than their mortgage, that credit card balance is the only debt they have. But it would be nice if they didn't have to pay $260 in interest this year just to maintain their balance.

Depending upon how much they charge this year, the Gervolinos may spend considerably more on interest payments. Why? Because credit card issuers usually don't give cardholders who carry balances a grace period before interest starts accruing on new purchases. So interest begins mounting the minute that you charge an item, or at least as soon as the merchant posts the charge to your account a day or two later. The typical grace period, on the other hand, gives you about twenty-five days from the closing date of your card's billing cycle to pay your bill without incurring interest.

So, even if credit card debt isn't ruining your life, it's still worth vanquishing. Here's how:

- **Transfer as much credit card debt as possible to a low-rate card.** Skip this step if all of your credit card debt is already on a low-rate card. If you aren't so lucky, don't just wait for offers from card issuers to land in your mailbox. Use one of these services to scour the nation for the low-rate (and preferably no fee) card that's right for you:

1. **Bank Rate Monitor's** Web site (www.bankrate.com) lets you search for the best deals on balance transfers. You can also target cards with no annual fees, low interest rates, and long grace periods.
2. **CARDWEB'S** Web site (www.cardweb.com) highlights low-rate and no-fee cards. If it isn't easy for you to get on the

Internet, spend $5.00 for CARDWEB's monthly *CardTrak* newsletter (800-344-7714; P.O. Box 1700, Frederick, MD 21702).

3. **Bankcard Holders of America,** a nonprofit consumer advocacy group, sells its list of low-rate credit cards for $4.00. Write to 524 Branch Drive, Salem, VA 24153.

■ **Once you've zeroed in on the best deal, call the issuer and ask these questions:**

1. **How long does your low rate last?** Beware of ultra-low teaser rates that double after they expire in six months or so. There's nothing wrong with taking a teaser rate; just be prepared to switch cards again shortly before it skyrockets. Also ask when the clock starts ticking. Ideally, you want a rate that stays low for a specified period that begins when you open your account.

What if a card issuer won't tell you exactly what interest rate you'll get until *after* you fill out a credit application? That happens. The issuer will check your credit history. If it's sterling, you'll get the low, advertised interest rate. If it's blemished, you'll pay more. If you don't want to risk having the rug pulled out from under you, apply for credit only from issuers that state your rate up front.

2. **Which charges does your rate apply to?** Some issuers apply the low rate only to the balance you transfer from another card. They hit you with a higher rate on any cash advances you take or new purchases you make. Worse, some issuers *force* you to take out a cash advance immediately,

then insist that you pay off your transferred balance before you can direct payments to your high-cost cash advance.

3. **Must I pay a transaction fee for transferring my balance to your card?** Sometimes it's worth paying a small fee to transfer your balance to a low-rate credit card, but be careful. Some card issuers slap you with fees as high as 4% of the balance you shift.

4. **Does a grace period apply to my balance transfer?** Some issuers start charging you interest the moment you switch your balance to their card. Try to find one that gives you a little breathing room.

5. **How long will it take to complete my balance transfer?** Two to four weeks is typical, but some issuers take up to eight weeks. Keep making payments on your old cards until you've learned—in writing—that your transfer is complete. Then send letters to your old card issuers to let them know you're closing your accounts and cutting up your old credit cards.

6. **Must I pay an annual fee?** Obviously, the ideal card has a low rate and no annual fee. If you can't find—or can't qualify for—a low-rate, no-fee card, go for the lowest rate you can get, whether or not you have to pay a fee. After all, you can pay a $20 annual fee and still save $103 if you pay off a $2,000 balance over eleven months with a card that charges 9% interest instead of one that charges 18%. To run your own numbers, log on to www.financenter.com. Click on "Credit Cards," then on "ClickCalcs."

- **Once you've zeroed in on the best deal, make a few phone calls.** If you belong to a credit union, call it. One out of three Americans belong to credit unions, and 88% of them belong to one that issues credit cards. You may find a card with an interest rate that's a half of a percentage point or so lower than the norm for bank-issued cards.

Next call your current card issuers and ask if they'll match the best offer you've found. If one will, transfer your balances to it. It'll be less of a hassle than opening a new account. If none of your current card issuers will give you a great deal, open a new account and transfer as much of your balance from other cards as you can to it.

- **Determine how much money you can spend on debt elimination.** Flip back to the worksheet you completed in Chapter 1. How much can you slash your spending on nonessentials like dinners out, movie tickets, or clothing for yourself and your spouse? Consider cutting back to basic cable TV service or stretching out the time between haircuts. Call your sister long distance every other week instead of every week. Be realistic. Don't tell yourself you'll suddenly find a way to spend half as much on groceries. You won't, so don't set yourself up for disappointment.

If you're saving some money, should you stop and use that cash to pay off your credit card instead? Yes, if you're putting money in a 4% money-market fund while paying 18% on your MasterCard. No, if the only money you save goes for retirement. If you stop contributing to your 401(k), for instance, you'll miss out on tax-deferred growth. You'll probably also forgo extra income, since most employers match their employees' contributions.

- **Draw up a plan to eliminate your debts.** Once you figure out how much money you can spend each month paying off your debts, figure out which debt you want to erase first. Some people pick the smallest amount, so they can quickly pay at least one of their bills in full. You'll save more money on interest payments, however, if you pay off your highest-rate credit card first. Make the required minimum payments on all of your other cards, then put the rest of the money you've earmarked for debt elimination toward the balance on your most expensive card.

You can use the Internet to figure out how long it'll take you to ditch your debts—and how much you'll pay in interest. Log on to www.bankrate.com, click on "Calculators," then click on "Calculate the Real Cost of Your Debt." Or go to www.financenter.com, click on "Credit Cards," then "ClickCalcs," and finally on "What Will It Take to Pay Off My Balance?" The chart below shows how long it would take to pay off a $2,000 balance at 13% interest at six different monthly payment amounts. It'll take six long years if you make only the minimum payment of $40 a month, or 2% of the balance.

How to Erase a $2,000 Balance

Monthly payment	Number of years to pay off balance/ total interest paid
$179	1 year/$144
95	2 years/ 282
67	3 years/ 426
54	4 years/ 575
46	5 years/ 730
40	6 years/ 891

Source: Bank Rate Monitor

■ **Jump-start your payback plan.** If you can't afford to make hefty monthly payments so you can pay off your balance quickly, consider raising cash or raiding your savings so you can reduce your balance with a big lump sum payment. Hold a garage sale, or sell a big-ticket item that you rarely use, like that canoe that's collecting dust in your garage.

If you have savings outside of tax-deferred retirement accounts, use a portion of your cache to pay off your debt. Try to maintain an emergency cash reserve equal to three months income, however. (What, no reserve? See Chapter 13.)

■ **Stop using credit cards until you pay your balance off.** This is the toughest step to take, but you've got to do it. If you don't, you'll just keep piling up more debts and more interest. That's what's happened to Diane and Gary Porter. Diane stays home with their seventeen-month-old son. They don't usually stay in one place for long, however, because Gary is in the Coast Guard. The Porters recently got a consolidation loan from their credit union to pay off $10,000 in credit card debt. They also bought a house. The loan repayments are going fine. In fact, the credit union deducts their $379 monthly payment from Gary's paychecks. Meanwhile, however, the Porters continue to use their two credit cards to buy things for their new house, including a lawn mower, a weed trimmer, paint, and shutters.

Please don't fall into the trap that the Porters did. Instead, get out your credit card statements for the last six months or so. Comb through them to figure out which necessities you normally charge, like prescription drugs, diapers, and shoes for your kids. Start paying for those items with cash, checks, or a debit card that siphons money directly from your checking account. Put your credit cards somewhere inaccessible, like in a box within a box in your attic. Tucked away, you won't be tempted to dig them out unless a real emergency strikes. With any luck, you'll have paid off your balance before your car's transmission dies or some other domestic disaster occurs.

- **Get help if you need it.** Some people desperately want to pay off their credit card debt but just can't because their credit history isn't good enough to get them a low-rate card. If you do your best to draw up a debt elimination plan only to find that it'll take you many years to get rid of your balance, get help from a nonprofit credit-counseling agency. These organizations will negotiate with your creditors to reduce your interest rate or waive late fees. They can also consolidate your debts into one monthly payment, which you send to them and they dole out to your creditors. You pay little ($10 a month is typical) or nothing for their help. They make money by charging your creditors up to 15% of what you repay them.

Find out if one of these respected debt-counseling services can help you:

1. The National Foundation for Consumer Credit (800-388-2227, www.nfcc.org) is a network of 1,450 nonprofit agencies nationwide that offer confidential budgeting, credit, debt counseling, and debt repayment plans. Check their Web site or call their toll-free telephone number to find an agency in your area.

2. American Family Debt Counseling Centers (888-565-9250, www.credit-america.com) offer debt counseling at local nonprofit agencies or over the phone.

Don't confuse nonprofit counseling services with shysters who call themselves credit repairers. Those guys promise to erase blemishes on your credit record and even get you more credit. Some charge hundreds of dollars, then do nothing. Others get you another credit card or a debt consolidation loan, but use a false identity to do it.

Why haven't I suggested that you take out a loan to pay off your debts? Banks and finance companies say that's the smartest solution on TV, radio, and Internet ads, but I disagree. At first glance, borrowing from your 401(k) or against your home equity seems very clever. After all, you pay interest to yourself when you borrow against your retirement fund. However, you'll probably lose out on some tax-deferred growth while your loan is outstanding. If your account is earning around 10% and you take out an 8% loan, for example, you'll lose 2%. (For more reasons why borrowing from a 401(k) isn't a great idea, see Chapter 14.)

Please, please, please, do not consolidate credit card debts into a home equity loan or line of credit. Sure, you'll get a lower interest rate and be able to deduct interest payments on your tax return. But you risk losing your house if you continue to live beyond your means and can't pay off your loan as planned.

You *can* get rid of credit card debt without taking on even more debt. You must stop piling on new debt, however, and you must stick to a repayment schedule. Do that and you'll become debt-free. Once you are, you'll want to keep living that way. Read the rest of this chapter to find out how you can.

How to Stay Debt-Free

Whether you've vowed to dig yourself out of debt or never been in hock, one thing's for sure: Trading some or all of your income for more time with your kids makes it tougher to keep the credit card balance bug away. You'll have to be more careful about spending, and pay more attention to the terms your credit card issuers extend. Here's what to do:

- **Before you pull out your plastic, ask yourself: "Do we really need this?"** That's advice from my friend Eileen Mulhern, a former news editor who freelanced for nearly ten years after she had kids. (Eileen got a full-time job when the younger of her two children entered third grade.) Eileen and her husband Bill, a newspaper columnist, still ask themselves that question before they buy anything. That's not to say they live a Spartan existence. They've got plenty of food in the refrigerator, rugs on their floors, curtains on their windows, and more kids' books and art supplies than the typical nursery school.

By the time you get your monthly credit card statement, it's easy to forget exactly what you charged. Skim your statements from the last three or four months to refresh your memory. I did, and discovered that only a third of our credit card expenditures were necessities, like mail-order prescription drugs, dentist appointments, and new glasses for my husband. So, even if I cut out only half of my discretionary credit card purchases, I'd cut my monthly bill by about a third.

How can we all start consuming less? Buying less is a bit like eating less; if you don't keep potato chips or candy in your house, you'll probably snack less than someone who does. And you'll probably buy less if you spend very little time eyeing items that you might be tempted to buy. So don't flip through catalogs that you get in the mail. You won't see anything you need, but you may see something you want. Don't browse for "bargains" on the Internet. And don't go shopping unless you need to. When you do, make your trip a targeted one. For instance, if your kids need sandals for summertime, visit your favorite kids' shoe store shortly after your kids have had a meal or snack. (That way they can't bamboozle you into believing that they'll die unless you buy them a drink or a snack.) Purchase one pair of sandals for each kid, get pretzels or balloons from the salesman, then hop back in your car and drive directly home.

What if the local mall is the only place you can go to get out of the house, especially during the winter? Try curbing your urge to splurge by using the twenty-four-hour cooling-off method. Normally, you see it, you want it, and you whip out your plastic to buy it. Try this instead: Vow that you'll come back to the store tomorrow to buy the object of your desire. Chances are you won't return twenty-four hours later. You'll have decided you really don't want the item. You won't be able to go to the mall because your daughter has a dental appointment. Or the sale will have ended, and you'll decide you don't want the item badly enough to pay full price for it.

- **Shelve your snobbism.** Yvonne Lowry, the former teacher who quit working after the birth of her third child, changed her shopping habits. "I've become less snobbish about everything from discount stores to cosmetics to haircuts," she says. "I'll never pay $17.50 for a lipstick again!" If you gravitate to designer labels, consider trading down to a lower-priced brand the next time you need a lipstick or a pair of jeans.

Granted, you'll occasionally find that it pays to buy a pricier brand. For instance, I no longer buy kids' clothes in discount stores because I found that the typical $6.00 T-shirt usually wore out after just one summer. A better-made $12 T-shirt from a mail-order company or department store usually lasts four summers. Each of my daughters can wear it for two years. And after my little one outgrows the shirt, it's usually still in good enough condition to donate to charity.

- **Get your spouse on board.** Some of the women I surveyed told me that they've become very careful spenders, but their husbands have not. I can sympathize. When I told my husband that only a third of our credit card purchases were truly necessary, he replied, "What do you consider an unnecessary expense, other than the CDs I buy?" Now, I don't think that my husband and those other guys are particularly profligate. I suspect instead that they're innocently clueless. Their wives (me included) quit their full-time jobs and completely took over the domestic sphere. These guys never even *see* the bills that come in, let alone write the checks for them.

It makes more sense to sit down with your spouse and work out a spending and saving plan together. That's what April and Ben Orseck did. They agreed not to spend more than $5.00 on recreational items like compact discs, video games, or restaurant meals without first consulting each other. "It works because my husband usually decides not to buy yet another CD rather than ask me. When he actually does ask me, I of course say yes," says April.

- **Save so you can buy big-ticket items with cash.** Want a new sofa or stereo system? Shop around to see how much the one you want costs, then put money aside each month for six, nine, or as many months as it'll take to raise cash to pay for it. I know that sounds awfully old-fashioned. Nevertheless, you've got to admit that it makes more sense than charging an expensive item today, then paying interest on your purchase for six, nine, or even more months.

You can also use this strategy to avoid carrying a balance after those bills for Christmas, Hanukkah, or Kwanzaa gifts roll in. Lindsey and Bob Warren contribute to a Christmas Club (remember those?) at their bank each month. They know they could earn more on their savings by stashing it in a higher-yielding account, but they got into the habit of making Christmas Club deposits years ago. It's an easy way to save and it sure beats paying interest on a credit card balance in January, February, and March.

Controlling your spending is the first step to using credit wisely. The second is making sure you're getting the best deal from your credit card issuer. Here's how to do that:

- **Cut up all but one of your cards.** Okay, all but two if you can't find one that has no annual fee *and* a low-interest rate. Why bother hunting for a low-rate card if you never carry a balance? My motto is never say never. You never know when an emergency might cause you to carry a balance. I hope it never happens, but you should be prepared if it does.

Why bother cleaning out your wallet if you don't have a problem with credit? Three good reasons:

1. **It's easier to track your spending if you and your spouse charge everything to one card.**
2. **There's less temptation to spend more than you earn simply because you have less credit available.**
3. **It's less of a hassle to report one lost or stolen credit card than a purse full of them. (By the way, if you're paying a service to report lost or stolen cards for you, cancel your contract immediately. You can do the job yourself.)**

Don't worry that you and your spouse need cards in your own names in case you ever need to qualify for credit on your own. Just make sure that the one card you carry is in both your names. That way you're both responsible for the bills, and you'll both build a credit history.

Start by closing your department store credit card accounts. Those cards generally have the highest interest rates and least lenient terms, and nowadays department stores take Visa and MasterCard anyway. As an added bonus, you'll receive less junk mail from department stores.

■ **Find the best card for you.** Use the services listed on pages 112 and 113 to find a card that looks good. Then call the issuer and ask these questions:

1. **Is this a teaser rate?** When those too-good-to-be-true rates expire in a few months, your interest rate may double. Since you don't have a balance, ignore teaser rates. Just get the best permanent rate you can find.

2. **Which method do you use to calculate interest?** Choose a card that uses the average daily balance method. That means the issuer computes interest charges over a month-long billing cycle. Stay away from cards that use the two-cycle method, meaning that the issuer calculates interest based on your average daily balance over the last two months. With a two-cycle card, you'll pay two month's worth of interest if you pay your balance in full one month but carry a balance the following month.

3. **Will you penalize me for paying off my balance every month?** Some card issuers hit you with an annual maintenance fee if you don't incur a specified amount in finance charges over the year.

Once you've found the perfect card, call the issuers of the nationally accepted cards you currently carry and ask if they'll match the best deal you've identified. Then decide which card to make your one and only and cut up all the others. Now, just four more tips on using plastic like a pro:

- **Never use those so-called convenience checks that your card issuer sends along with your billing statement.** Those time bombs typically work like cash advances. There's generally no grace period, so you start accruing interest as soon as you write one. Plus, they typically have higher interest rates than your card does.
- **Don't overspend to earn rewards.** Instead of charging

stuff you don't need just to earn enough points for a one-way ticket to Florida during hurricane season, stick to your spending plan and buy your own airline tickets. You'll have more control over when and where you travel. Whatever you do, don't run up a balance on a reward card; they typically carry interest rates five percentage points or more above low-rate cards.

- **Enjoy your grace period to the hilt.** You've got some breathing room between when you charge an item and when you start incurring interest on it. Grace periods used to last as long as thirty days, but they've been shrinking and are now as short as twenty-five or even twenty days. Check your billing statements to see how long your grace period lasts and when your current cycle started. Then spread your purchases out, waiting until the next billing cycle begins before you add another expensive item to your balance.

Don't dawdle when it's time to pay your bill, however. If you miss your due date, you'll have to cough up a late payment fee of $29 or so. Many card issuers will also raise the interest rate as high as 25% on your balance, if you have one.

- **Don't exceed your credit limit.** Back in the old days, store clerks wouldn't let you use your card if they checked and found that you were over your credit limit. Nowadays they let you charge away. Then your card issuer slaps a fee of $25 or so on your next bill for your transgression. Check your billing statement to see how high your limit is, then be careful not to exceed it during the course of a billing cycle.
- **Watch for changes in your card agreement.** Credit

card issuers are free to change interest rates, shorten grace periods, and increase late-payment fees. And many issuers have been making lots of changes lately because many credit card businesses are changing hands. So, once you've got a card that perfectly fits your needs, keep reading the fine print your issuer sends you to make sure it stays that way.

CHAPTER 9

Disaster-Proof Yourself

If your family is going to live comfortably on less than two incomes, you can't afford to be an insurance victim. That means you can't just let an insurance agent sell you whatever coverage pays him a fat commission. Instead, you've got to shop for insurance like a smart consumer.

The stakes are high. Most families spend a bundle on life, auto, and homeowners' insurance. Your family's main breadwinner may also have to buy disability insurance. In this chapter, I'll explain how to figure out how much insurance your family really needs. I'll also tell you how to buy the coverage you need without busting your budget.

Spend Less on More Life Insurance

The Four-Letter Word You Must Know

No, it's not a word you shouldn't repeat in front of your kids, though shopping for life insurance may cause you to blurt out a few of those, too. The four-letter word I'm thinking of is *term,* which is the only type of life insurance that young families should buy. Term is pure, unadulterated insurance. If you die with a term policy in force, your survivors collect a death benefit.

By contrast, *cash value* life insurance gives you a death benefit *and* an investment account that grows tax-deferred. Some insurers also pay dividends to your account, based on their financial performance. When you buy term insurance, your annual premium increases as the years go by. That's not the case with cash value insurance. Why not? Because the insurer can use the cash that builds up in your policy to cover an increasing portion of your death benefit. There are three main varieties of cash value life insurance: whole, universal, and variable life.

If you already know that term is the way to go, skip to the section of this chapter titled "The Best Term for You." If you need convincing, read on.

Money is the main reason to buy term instead of cash value life insurance. A thirty-five-year-old man who doesn't smoke can buy $500,000 worth of term insurance for about $350 a year. He could easily pay more than $5,000 a year for the same amount of cash value coverage. Choosing term seems like a no-brainer. Yet, insurance agents still sell plenty of cash value insurance. Here are the sales pitches they use—and the reasons why you shouldn't fall for them:

■ **Cash value coverage is permanent, term is temporary.** True enough. When you buy a term policy, you insure your life for a specified number of years—typically one to thirty. You probably won't be able to buy term once you reach age seventy. When you buy a cash value policy, you can usually keep your coverage until you hit 100.

But who says you'll need life insurance when you're 100— or even sixty? Consider this: Will you still need a four-bedroom house after your kids leave the nest? Or will a two-bedroom condo suit you better? Likewise, will you still need life insurance after you've paid off your mortgage and sent your kids to college? Insurers have a little secret about the *real* permanency of cash value insurance: Only half the people who buy it still hold their policies after seven years, and only a quarter keep them twenty years.

Besides, nearly all term policies are *convertible*. That means you can convert them to cash value coverage within a specified period. Of course, you will pay a higher annual premium if you do so.

- **With term, all you get is insurance.** That's right, and that's why you get far more coverage for your money than you do with a cash value policy. You buy life insurance to re-place income lost because of a breadwinner's death. To buy less insurance than your family needs because you can't afford the proper amount of cash value coverage is just plain dumb.

Also, cash value insurance won't make you rich. Even if you hold a policy for twenty years, you'll earn less than 6%. And that's according to the nonprofit Consumer Federation of America, not some mutual fund company that wants the money you'd otherwise invest in insurance. Yes, that's better than what money-market funds have recently paid. However, you usually lose money for the first few years that you pay into a cash value policy. In fact, returns are generally pitiful for at least the first *fifteen years* that you hold a policy. That's because a big chunk of your premium ends up in the salesperson's pocket.

- **You can't borrow against a term policy.** True, but borrowing against a cash value policy may not be the best way to raise cash. (I discuss loans from insurance policies and other sources in Chapter 13.) You may pay a low rate. There's a downside if you die before repaying your loan, however. Your insurer will deduct the unpaid balance from the death benefit your survivors receive.

The Best Term for You

There are two basic types of term insurance:

- **Annual renewable term,** or ART for short, stays in force for only one year. However, you can renew your coverage each year without filling out a new application or taking a medical exam to prove that you're still healthy. Premiums start low and rise as you age. They typically increase rapidly after you reach age 50. If you're healthy, however, you can always switch insurers to get a lower rate. That's what Bill Mulhern did when the annual premium on his $100,000 policy shot up to $750. He switched to USAA Life, which sold him the same coverage for $320. (I'll tell you more about this low-cost insurer later in this chapter.)
- **Level premium term** remains in force for five, ten, fifteen, twenty, twenty-five, or even thirty years. If you still want

coverage after the term ends, you'll have to take another medical exam. Your premium stays the same for the length of the term you choose. One caveat: Some insurers sell a brand of level premium term that isn't what it seems. For example, they might reserve the right to raise premiums on a twenty-year level term policy after only five years. Read a policy's fine print to make sure you're getting what you want.

Level premium term may cost slightly more than ART during the first few years that you own a policy. However, at the end of the term you will have typically paid less over time than you would have had you purchased ART year after year.

Should you buy ART or level premium term? In general, go for level premium if you plan to hold your policy more than five years. But think hard about whether you'll still need insurance after the term is up. If you do and the results of your new medical exam aren't flawless, you'll pay dearly to continue your policy or to buy a new one.

How Much Insurance Is Enough?

The answer depends on who you're insuring.

- **Your kids don't need life insurance.** They don't earn income to help pay your mortgage, do they? So there's no reason to insure their lives. An insurance agent may argue that you should insure your kids in case they suffer an illness or injury and can't get insurance later. Don't worry. Only 4% of all applicants for insurance don't qualify for coverage, says the American Council of Life Insurance, a trade group. And most of those unfortunate folks are middle-aged or older adults with medical problems. Moreover, fewer than 10% of all applicants must pay increased premiums because of health conditions.

What about using cash value insurance to save for college? There are better ways to save for your children's education, and I discuss them in Chapter 15.

What if you or your doting parents have already bought life insurance for your kids? Be sure to read the section of this chapter titled "Should You Dump Your Old Policy?"

- **You may be able to go bare if you're a stay-at-home parent.** You can go without insurance if you're certain that a relative will step in after your death and care for your kids until they're old enough to care for themselves. You also don't need coverage if your husband earns enough to pay for child care. If neither situation describes your own, perhaps you need enough life insurance to pay for day care or a baby-sitter. But also consider that some expenses will disappear if you depart, like clothing, food, and a car for you.
- **Breadwinners need lots of insurance.** I know that sounds terribly vague, but truth is, there's no way to figure out *precisely* how much *you* need. (By the way, if you plan to work part time, you and your husband both need insurance.)

God knows, people have tried. Back when we were kids, a life insurance agent sat across the kitchen table from your dad and told him he needed a policy worth five times his income. Your father might have wondered why the multiplier was five instead of four or six, but he probably kept quiet and followed the guy's advice.

Then came the first generation of personal finance gurus. These experts urged consumers to figure out for themselves how much coverage they needed. They published detailed worksheets in books and magazines. Many of the worksheets were truly ingenious. I have one that runs for thirteen pages, plus six more pages of tables and explanatory notes. Few people, if any, ever finished filling one of these worksheets out. Instead, they called an insurance agent and *begged* for a policy worth five times their income.

Now we're in the digital age. You can buy insurance on the Internet. You can also use calculators on the Internet to quickly estimate your insurance needs. However, you still won't find out *exactly* how big a policy you need. How come? Simply because each calculator asks you to plug in different numbers. They also use varying formulas to compute your insurance needs. It's not surprising that you get wildly different results.

I used five popular Internet calculators to find out if my husband had enough life insurance. One program said he had *too much* insurance. Another said that his coverage was $6 *million* short. The three other programs also said he needed more insurance, but not $6 million worth. So, what's the problem with these calculators?

- **You've still got to make some wild guesses.** Do you think you can accurately estimate what your monthly living expenses will be once your kids finish college and leave home? Some Internet calculators ask you to take a guess.
- **You may not get credit for moves you've already made**

to secure your family's future. Some Internet programs fail to ask about your savings or investments. That's a big flaw because you could tap them if your family's bread-winner died. Some programs ignore Social Security sur-vivor's benefits. That's another big mistake because such payments can be substantial. Let's assume that a breadwin-ner earns about $30,000 a year and dies when he's thirty-nine. If he has a wife and two or more kids under eighteen, they can collect as much as $22,020 a year. To find out ap-proximately how much your family would collect, check your Social Security Statement. The Social Security Adminis-tration has sent statements each year to all workers twenty-five and older since October of 1999. If you haven't received your free copy, call the agency toll-free at 800-772-1213 and ask for Form SSA-7004. Or, log on to the agency's Web site (www.ssa.gov).

- **You can err by making your family's breadwinner more valuable dead than alive.** How could that happen? Easy. Let's say you currently can't afford to save much for your kids' college education. Then you log on to an Internet calculator that asks if you'd like to send your kids to private, four-year colleges. Of course you'd *like* to, so you say yes. Naturally, the calculator says you need a ton of insurance. If you buy lots of insurance, you'll have even less money left in your budget, so you'll probably *never* increase your college savings. If you live to a ripe old age, your kids will have to work their way through college, take out student loans, and search for scholarships. If you die prematurely, however, your entire brood will have enough money to go to Harvard. Odds are, of course, that you'll live to see your kids graduate colleges that they'll pay for themselves.

So what should you do? Run your numbers through a couple of good Internet calculators, just for curiosity. My favorites are QuickQuote's Term Life Estimator (www.quickquote.com) and InsWeb's Life Insurance Needs Analyzer (www.insweb. com). Whatever they conclude, figure on carrying life insurance equal to at least six to eight times your annual income. Don't take my word for it. Insurance experts at the Consumer Federation of America think you can safely use that rule of thumb instead of spending hours filling out worksheets. Use the bigger multiplier if you lack group life insurance through your employer. Use the smaller multiplier if you have group life insurance equal to at least two times your salary. The CFA assumes that the surviving spouse spends all of the income and gradually draws down the principal that insurance provides.

If you filled out the worksheets in Chapters 1 and 3, you have almost all of the information you'll need to figure out how much life insurance you and your spouse need. You'll need to find only the face values of insurance policies that you and your husband already have. So, pull any individual policies that you and your husband own out of your file cabinet. Also, call your employer's human resources department to find out how much your group coverage is worth.

Getting a Good Deal

How high a premium you'll pay for insurance depends on a lot of things. Insurers consider your age, sex, weight, driving record, health, your immediate family's health history, and your hobbies. (Gardeners pay less than scuba divers do.) Some insurers are pickier than others are. There's no way to know for sure if you'll qualify for an insurer's lowest rate, highest rate, or something in between until you take a medical exam.

You'll usually get the lowest rate only if you're in excellent health. You also can't have a dangerous job or hobby. And it helps if your parents haven't suffered from heart disease or other serious ailments. How much can you save if you qualify for the preferred rate instead of the standard rate? If you're thirty-five to forty-five years old, you can save about 25% to 30% on a $250,000, ten-year level term policy.

If you smoke, you'll pay premiums roughly double that of nonsmokers. If you have a chronic disease like diabetes or epilepsy, you'll pay higher rates than healthy people do. Some companies will be more willing than others to quote you an affordable price.

To get accurate price quotes, shop with the following information at your fingertips:

- **Your height and weight.**
- **Your medical history.**
- **Your driving record.**
- **Your immediate family's medical history.** You don't need your father's cholesterol count, but you do need to know whether your grandfather died young of heart disease.

If you think you're in good health, shop for a preferred-rate policy. What happens if you take an insurer's medical exam and find out that you have high blood pressure or some other health problem? Don't grab a more expensive policy from the same insurer. Instead, shop around some more. Another insurer may give people with your health condition a better price.

Most people should use all four of the methods described below to shop for term insurance. If you know you're high-risk, however, place your bets mainly on method three.

1. Get free price quotes over the Internet or telephone. Lots of insurance agencies sell policies over the Internet. To increase your odds of finding an inexpensive policy, try agencies that sell policies from 100 or more insurers. Some agencies provide quotes online; others mail a list to you within a week or so. Most will also give you quotes over the phone. Get quotes from two or three of the following services. If you have questions about the policies they recommend, ask to speak to a licensed insurance agent over the phone.

- **AccuQuote** (800-442-9899, www.accuquote.com) offers policies from more than 250 companies. To get a quote, you'll need to answer a series of detailed questions about your health, job, hobbies, and driving record.
- **ConsumerQuote** (800-552-7283, www.consumerquote.com) has more than 300 insurers in its database.
- **1stQuote** (800-583-0231, www.1stquote.com) features more than 150 companies.
- **InstantQuote** (888-223-2220, www.instantquote.com) doesn't ask you to answer personal questions online. Instead, people who don't think they'll qualify for preferred rates fill out an application, which the service then presents to various insurers.
- **ITECH Corporation** (800-400-4832, itechusa.com) features more than 155 insurers in its database.
- **MasterQuote of America** (800-337-5433, www.master quote.com) sells policies from more than 300 companies.
- **NationsBanc Insurance Services** (888-294-2265,

www.nationsbank.com) features policies from more than 100 insurers.

- **Quotesmith** (800-556-9393, www.quotesmith.com) has more than 300 companies in its database. You don't have to answer a lot of detailed questions to get quotes from this service, which instead provides underwriting criteria for each policy it highlights for you. You then check to see if a particular insurer might reject you, or charge you higher than standard rates.

2. Call companies that don't use agents. You can buy policies from some insurers over the phone. Or, you can buy from a financial planner, who earns less from the sale than an insurance agent. So-called low-load insurers do business this way. Two of the best known are USAA Life (800-531-7015) and Ameritas Life (800-745-6665, www.ameritas.com).

3. Call an agent or two. Ask independent insurance agents in your area if they can beat the best price you get from the Internet quote services. Be sure to call an independent agent or two if you have a health problem. An experienced agent should know which companies are best for people with your health problem. For a list of agents in your area, log on to the Independent Insurance Agents of America's Web site (www.iiaa.org).

Also, call an agent who works for Northwestern Mutual Life. That advice comes from James Hunt of the Consumer Federation of America. Hunt, who once served as Vermont's insurance commissioner, is one of the most knowledgeable experts in the country. He says that Northwestern boasts competitive rates on term insurance. Its cash value policies are also top-notch, if you ever decide to convert. Check your

local Yellow Pages for an agent in your area, or log on to www.
NorthwesternMutual.com.

4. Price group coverage. Your college alumni group
probably offers group life insurance to its members. You may
also be able to buy additional group coverage through your employer. Call clubs you belong to and read all of the solicitations
that land in your mailbox. But shop for individual insurance,
too. Group coverage isn't always a bargain.

Before You Buy

Make sure that an insurer has the money to make good on
its promises. Various firms rate insurers' financial strength. Look
for companies with ratings of at least double A from Standard
& Poor's or Duff & Phelps, at least A+ from A. M. Best Company, and at least Aa from Moody's Investors Service. Many
Internet quote services provide ratings. Standard & Poor's and
Duff & Phelps post ratings on the Insurance News Network's
Web site (www.insure.com/ratings). To get Best's ratings on
line, log on to www.ambest.com. For Moody's ratings, go to
www.moodys.com. If you'd rather read a book, see if your library has annual reports from the rating companies.

Should You Dump Your Old Policy?

By all means, if you have term insurance and discover you
can buy cheaper coverage from another insurer. Ditch your
old policy, but be careful when you do it. Don't let your old
policy lapse until you've purchased a replacement and have it
in your possession. Also, shop for a new policy a month or two
before the next premium is due on your old policy. Why? Some

insurers don't refund prepaid term insurance premiums, so you won't get your money back if you drop your coverage shortly after you paid your premium.

If you've got cash value insurance, don't drop it without consulting an actuary. The actuary you need is James Hunt. He charges $45 to analyze one policy, and $35 for each additional policy. For details, call the Consumer Federation of America at 202-387-0087. If you're ready for a little fun after worrying about insurance, take Hunt up on this special offer. He'll evaluate your policy for free if you spend at least two nights at the Lakeview Inn (802-533-2291, www.hcr.net/lakeview) in Greensboro, Vermont. What's the deal? Hunt's son and daughter-in-law run the place.

Breadwinners Also Need Disability Insurance

What would happen if your spouse got seriously ill or had an accident and couldn't work for months? Most of us couldn't live on our savings alone for very long. We also need disability insurance. This type of coverage pays you a portion of your former income if you can't work because of an illness or injury. Don't confuse disability insurance with workers' compensation. You can collect workers' compensation only if you get hurt on the job or get sick because of your work. By contrast, you can collect disability benefits whether disaster strikes you at work, at home, or even on vacation.

Most workers have some disability coverage, thanks to Social Security. You can collect benefits if you suffer from a physical or mental impairment that will eventually result in death or that prevents you from doing substantial work for at least one year. (The government decides what substantial work is case by case.) You can start collecting after five months of disability if it's apparent that your condition will last longer than a year. Your salary and the number of years you've worked determine how much you receive. The payments you get rise with inflation. A thirty-nine-year-old who earns about $30,000 a year and has a spouse and two kids can collect up to $1,425 a month. To find out how much you or your husband would get, check your Social Security Statements.

You may also get coverage through your employer. Employers in Hawaii, New Jersey, New York, and Rhode Island must by law provide coverage for up to twenty-six weeks. In California, most employers must furnish coverage for up to fifty-two weeks. Employers don't have to be more generous, but some are. Nearly half of medium and large companies provide benefits for at least five years.

In general, you must be disabled three to six months before you can collect benefits. You can collect up to 60% of your income. However, you can't collect more than $5,000 a month.

You usually can't collect benefits from all sources worth more than 60% to 70% of your former salary. Insurers figure that you would have little incentive to go back to work if you got more.

So, do you or your husband need to buy disability insurance on your own? The answer is generally no unless you're self-employed *and* you earn big bucks. You won't be able to get by on Social Security alone.

You'll need big bucks to afford a good policy from a strong insurer that pays benefits until you reach age sixty-five. Your husband should figure on spending about 2% of his income for

Cadillac coverage. That's about $2,000 a year if he makes $100,000. If you're the breadwinner, expect to pay a bit more. Premiums depend on your age, sex, occupation, and the percentage of your income that you want to replace. Insurers charge women more because they say they file more claims.

How to Cut Costs

Given the high cost of coverage, you may decide to skip it—especially if you think you could go back to work and support your family if you had to. If you really want to buy, however, the best way to cut the cost of comprehensive coverage is to choose a long waiting period. You usually can choose to start collecting benefits after you've been out of work from 30 to 365 days. Pick the longest possible waiting period your family could stand. You can save about 30% by waiting 180 days instead of the standard 90 days.

Where to Shop for Disability Insurance

Don't expect to get instant price quotes over the Internet or phone. This type of coverage is way too complicated. Indeed, even the definition of disabled varies from policy to policy. (Some pay benefits if you can't do your usual job. Others pay only if you can't do *any* type of work.) You'll have to call local agents. Put Northwestern Mutual Life and USAA Life on your list of companies to call, advises the Consumer Federation of America. I mentioned both companies earlier in this chapter.

How to Save on Auto and Homeowners' Insurance

No More Gut-Wrenching Decisions

After grappling with life and disability coverage, it's a relief to buy auto and homeowners' insurance. Your state, your mortgage lender, and whoever you borrowed from to buy your car often tell you what kind and how much coverage to buy. You can save time by shopping for both types of coverage as a package, which might save you as much as 15%.

Keep a few things in mind as you shop. Prices change frequently. Therefore, it's worth shopping every other year if you can find the time. Irene Ryerson's husband Don calls competing companies to compare prices *every* year. "It's time consuming but worth it," Irene says. Don't switch insurers if the best quote you find saves you less than $50 a year, however. It's not worth the hassle, and some insurers may peg you as a higher-risk if you have a history of policy hopping. (On the other hand, some companies offer discounts of 5% to 10% to long-time policyholders. So if you've been with the same company three years or longer, ask for a rate cut.) Also, don't jump to a small, no-name insurer that offers the lowest rates without first checking its rating for financial strength and for consumer complaints against it. In theory, you can call your state insurance commissioner's office to check for complaints. (Look for the telephone number under the state government listings in your local Yellow Pages). In reality, however, you may get an interminable busy signal. If you have access to the Internet, log on to www.insure.com and check your state's page for information on consumer complaints. If you still can't find out anything about an obscure insurer, ask friends, relatives, and business associates if they can recommend the company. If no one can, don't risk switching your business to the firm.

How to Get a Good Deal on Auto Insurance

Follow these five steps:

1. **Prepare to shop.** Get out your insurance policy and car registration documents. Get a sheet of paper and on it note the makes and models of your cars, their ages, and their vehicle identification numbers. Be prepared to answer questions about you and your husband's driving records and commuting habits. Estimate how many miles each of you drives each year.

2. **Drop collision and comprehensive coverage on old cars.** If you own a car free and clear that's worth $1,000 or less, don't bother insuring it against collision, theft, or vandalism. You won't get more than the car's depreciated value minus the cost of repairs. You can look up your vehicle's current value in the *Kelley Blue Book* (www.kbb.com), which is available in most libraries.

3. **Go for higher deductibles.** Let's say you hike your deductible for collision from $250 to $500. You'll save up to 30% on that coverage.

4. **Ask for discounts.** Most insurers give you a break if your car has air bags, antilock brakes, or an alarm system. Some companies offer special deals to members of fraternal groups.

5. **If you're buying a new car, choose a sensible model.** I know, I know, this is something your dad did when he was

bringing up babies. But buying a fuddy-duddy car still pays off. You'll pay lower premiums if you drive a car that's relatively inexpensive to repair and uncool in the eyes of thieves. For information on collision repair costs and a list of vehicles that crooks crave, check www.insure.com.

Where to Shop for Auto Insurance

The Internet isn't a fertile hunting ground yet. Indeed, it may never be. That's because auto insurance policies vary greatly from state to state. In addition, prices range widely even within the same state. You can get some auto insurance quotes from QuoteSmith (800-556-9393, www.quotesmith.com).

Some states publish sample auto insurance rates. To find out if your state does, call your state's insurance office or log on to www.insure.com. You can use such a list to eliminate very high-priced insurers, but you can't rely on it entirely. Rates are often a few years old. Plus, the hypothetical examples used to generate sample rates may not match your situation.

As a result, you'll have to do most of your research on the phone. Start with companies that don't use agents. Direct sellers of auto insurance include Amica Mutual (800-242-6422, www.amica.com), Electric Insurance (800-227-2757, www. electricinsurance.com), Geico (800-861-8380, www.geico.com), Nationwide Direct (888-634-7328, www.ndirect.com), and 21st Century Insurance (800-211-7283, www.21stcentins.com).

Then call a few agents to see if they can beat the best price that you find. Be sure to call State Farm, which is the biggest auto insurer. Also check Allstate. While you're at it, call at least one independent agent who represents more than one company.

Sound like too much trouble? You can pay *Consumer Reports* to do research for you if you live in one of twenty-seven states (Alabama, Arizona, California, Colorado, Connecticut, Florida, Georgia, Idaho, Illinois, Louisiana, Michigan, Minnesota, Mississippi, Missouri, Nevada, New Jersey, New Mexico, New York, North Carolina, Ohio, Pennsylvania, Tennessee, Texas, Utah, Virginia, Washington, and Wisconsin). You'll get a list of up to twenty-five of the best deals you qualify for. Cost: $12 for the first car, $8.00 for each additional vehicle. For more information, call 800-224-9495 or log on to www.consumerreports.org.

How to Get a Good Deal on Homeowners' Insurance

First things first. Find out if you now have *guaranteed replacement cost* coverage. That means your insurer will pay whatever it costs to rebuild your home. (There's often a cap, however.) With such a policy, your insurer typically raises your coverage amount and your premium annually to keep pace with rising construction costs. (By the way, the amount of coverage you get shouldn't include the value of your land. If your house burns down, the land will still be there.) It's also a good idea to cover the replacement cost of your personal belongings, not their cash value.

If you don't have guaranteed replacement cost coverage, find out how much it would cost to get it. You may not be able to. Such coverage is sometimes tough to get for older homes loaded with architectural detail or for houses in high-risk areas. When you shop for a cheaper policy, make sure you get price quotes for guaranteed replacement cost coverage.

Here's another thing to think about if you have a high net worth. You may want more liability protection than your auto and homeowners' policies provide. If so, buy an umbrella policy. You'll pay only $200 to $300 a year for a $1 million policy. Shop for an umbrella when you shop for car and home insurance. You'll get a discount if you buy everything from the same company.

You can cut costs by making these moves:

1. **Increase your deductible.** You'll save about 12% if you hike it from $250 to $500. Going up to $1,000 saves as much as 24%. Does a $1,000 deductible seem a bit much? Well, bear in mind that insurers sometimes drop policyholders who file frequent claims—even if the claims are tiny. So you might as well take on a big deductible and save on premiums.
2. **Ask for discounts.** You can shave your premium if you have smoke detectors or a burglar alarm, for example.

Where to Shop for Homeowners' Insurance

Don't expect much from the Internet. You can find a few quotes through InsureMarket (800-695-0011, www.insuremarket.com) and InsWeb (www.insweb.com).

Your state may publish sample rates, as some do for auto insurance. To find out, call your state's insurance office or log on to www.insure.com.

Your best bet is the good old telephone. Call companies that sell directly to consumers, including Amica Mutual, Electric Insurance, and 21st Century Insurance. (See page 146 for their phone numbers and Internet addresses.)

Call a few agents as well. Major companies in the field include Allstate, State Farm, Zurich, Nationwide, and Citigroup.

The Insurance You Shouldn't Buy

Policies that cover only one disease, like cancer, are bad buys. So are policies that cover one cause of accidental death, like flight insurance. Don't buy credit insurance if you're worried about dying or becoming disabled before you can pay off your mortgage, car loan, or credit card balance. It's cheaper to buy life or disability insurance, which serves the same purpose. It's also inadvisable to buy a home warranty on a new home. Who's going to stand behind the warranty if the builder goes bust? Stick to life, auto, and homeowners' insurance, shop carefully for it, and you'll have done your duty.

CHAPTER 10

Keep Your Family Healthy

A few years ago, insuring your family's good health didn't take much effort. You got a job with an employer who paid all or most of your health insurance premiums. You went to any doctor you wanted to see, whenever you felt sick. You sent your medical bills to your insurance company and got a check back for most of the money you spent. I don't know about you, but I almost get misty-eyed when I reminisce about how simple it all used to be.

But the old way of doing things got too expensive, and in swept managed care. Now nearly eight in ten Americans and their dependents who get health insurance through their employers belong to HMOs or other types of managed care plans. For many of these people, nothing about getting sick or trying to stay well is simple anymore. They've got to shop for health plans and doctors, and follow lots of rules to ensure that their families get the best care at the lowest cost.

And those folks are the lucky ones. Self-employed people

have to do all that *and* pay for costly individual insurance out of their own pockets.

This chapter will help you make the best of an often confusing situation whether you get health insurance through an employer or will have to buy it yourself if you quit your job or cut back to part-time work. In the first section of this chapter, I take a quick look at the different types of health care plans available today. I also explain basic health insurance concepts, like deductibles and copayments.

In part two, I tell you how to choose a health care plan if you've got a choice. This section is also worth reading if you must buy individual coverage and are healthy enough to get affordable price quotes from multiple insurers.

In the third section of this chapter, I explain how anyone with a managed care plan can hold down their health care expenditures and still stay healthy.

I devote the last section of this chapter to the special concerns of families who must buy health care coverage on their own. If quitting or cutting back on work means that your family will lose its group health insurance, please skip ahead to "How to Buy Health Insurance on Your Own" on page 165 right now! Individual policies can be so costly that you may not be able to pay the premiums if you stop working. That doesn't mean that you can't pursue your dream of staying home with your kids. It also doesn't mean that you're destined for bankruptcy court if you've already quit your job and the clock is ticking on the group insurance coverage you've continued under federal COBRA regulations. You've got options, and I tell you what they are. The only option you *don't* have is waiting until the last possible moment to solve your problem.

What Health Insurance
Looks Like Today

There are three basic types of health care plans offered today. If you get your coverage through an employer's group plan, you may not be able to choose among all three types. The same is true if you must buy individual coverage because the number of insurers who sell health plans and the type of coverage they offer varies from state to state. That said, here's a quick look at the main types of insurance you may encounter:

- **Indemnity or fee-for-service plans** let you visit any doctor or hospital you wish. You pay a monthly fee, or *premium,* to belong to the plan. You pay your own medical bills until you spend a specified amount on services covered by your plan. That amount is your *deductible.* Deductibles typically range from $250 to more than $1,000 a year. They may apply to individuals, or to your entire family. After you meet your deductible, your insurer pays a portion of the costs it covers. Your policy might pay 80% while you pay 20%, for instance. Your portion is your *copayment.*

  Most health care plans place an annual limit, or *cap,* on your expenditures. Once you reach it, your insurer pays all expenses covered by your policy. Caps typically range from $1,000 to $5,000. Premium payments don't count against the cap.

  Many plans also place a *lifetime maximum cap* on the amount *they* will pay. It's important to know what this limit is in case you or a member of your family becomes seriously ill.

- **Health maintenance organizations** let you use only doctors and hospitals that they contract with. You pay a monthly premium to belong to an HMO. You probably won't have to meet a deductible.

Some HMOs operate like clinics, and you see whichever doctor is on duty when you're sick. Other HMOs let you select a *primary care physician,* or *PCP,* from a list. When you visit your PCP, you pay a small copayment of $5.00 to $15.00. If you need to see a specialist, like an allergist or a cardiologist, your PCP must give you a written *referral* to one who contracts with your HMO. If you decide to see a doctor outside of your HMO, you'll have to pay the whole tab yourself.

- **Preferred-provider organizations** let you use any doctor or hospital you wish. You pay less if you use health care providers who belong to the PPO's network, however.

PPOs typically work like this: You pay a monthly premium to belong to the plan. You pick a PCP from its list. Whenever you visit your PCP, you pay a modest copayment, typically $15 or less. If you need a specialist, your PCP can refer you to one in your PPO's network. When you visit him or her, you'll also pay just $15 or so. If you go to a doctor outside of your PPO, however, you'll have to make a bigger copayment after meeting an annual deductible. PPOs typically place annual caps on your expenditures, as well as lifetime maximum caps on their payments.

How to Pick the Best
Plan for Your Family

The decision boils down to cost vs. benefits. If you get health insurance through an employer, you can switch plans during your company's annual *open enrollment period.* In general, the more flexibility you demand to pick your own doctors, the more money you'll spend on health care. It's impossible to predict exactly how much more you'll spend if you choose a PPO instead of an HMO, however, because you never know how often you'll feel the need to visit a doctor who's not in your PPO's network. Once you choose a plan, you're usually stuck with your choice for one year.

You can go nuts trying to weigh the pros and cons of three or four health care plans. I've tried to simplify the process by giving you two brief charts to fill in. The first chart gives you space to pencil in the cost of up to four different plans.

How to Compare Costs

	Plan #1	*Plan #2*	*Plan #3*	*Plan #4*
Monthly premium				
Annual deductible (inside the plan's network)				
Copayment (inside the plan's network)				
Annual deductible (outside the plan's network)				

	Plan #1	Plan #2	Plan #3	Plan #4
Copayment (outside the plan's network)				
Annual cap on your expenditures				
Lifetime maximum the plan will pay				

The second chart lets you rate the doctors, benefits, and reputation of the plans you're considering. Fill in this chart with stars (*), check marks (✓), and Xs (✗). A * means you like what the plan has to offer. A ✓ means you can live with what the plan offers. An ✗, of course, means thumbs down.

How to Compare Benefits

	Plan #1	Plan #2	Plan #3	Plan #4
Doctors				
Benefits				
Reputation				

Here's an example. Let's say you're choosing between two PPOs. The first plan includes your gynecologist, your husband's physician, and your kids' pediatrician in its network. You plan to continue seeing all three doctors, and are thrilled that you can do so for only $15 per office visit. So you give the doctors in plan #1 a * rating. The second PPO, on the other hand, includes none of your current doctors. You'd have to pick three new ones, so you give plan #2 an ✗ rating for its doctors.

Of course, it's rarely that easy to determine if one plan is better than another. You'll usually need to do a bit more research. Here are the questions you need to ask about a plan's doctors, benefits, and reputation. Look for answers in the *summary plan description* that details what the plan covers and lists its doctors. If you can't make sense of the booklet, ask a counselor in your employer's benefits department for help. Still stumped? Call the plan's toll-free customer service telephone number.

What You Need to Know About a Plan's Doctors

Ask yourself these questions:

- **Are any of our family's doctors in the plan's network?** If some or all of them aren't, how do you feel about finding new doctors? (For more about that process, read on.)
- **Can I pick a specialist to be my PCP?** Many plans permit women to use a gynecologist as their PCP. Children get to use pediatricians as their PCPs. Some plans permit your PCP to give you a referral good for multiple visits to a specialist who's in your plan's network. For example, every three months my husband visits an endocrinologist who specializes in diabetes. He cuts the cost of those visits by going to his PCP first. He pays her $15 for an office visit, and she gives him a referral good for six visits to his endocrinologist, who's also in our PPO. When he uses his referrals to see the specialist, he pays only $15 for a checkup. If he went directly to the specialist without first seeing his PCP, he'd have to pay $47 for the same service.
- **Do my doctors intend to stay in the plan?** I've lost count of how many PCPs my husband and I have had. We

dropped one; the others quit the plan. Fortunately, our daughters' excellent pediatrician has stuck with the plan, which is why we have too. Ask your doctors if they intend to stick around. They may not, if they're unhappy with the plan's reimbursement rates or tangled bureaucracy. Also, ask your employee benefits counselor or the health plan's customer service representatives how many PCPs have left the plan during the past three years. Compare the turnover rates of the plans you're considering.

- **What happens if my obstetrician quits the plan when I'm six months pregnant?** Some plans permit you to keep seeing your old doctor for a specified period. The same holds true if a physician who leaves your health care plan is treating you or a member of your family for a life-threatening illness.

If you've got to choose one or more new doctors from a plan's network, where do you start? Ask these questions:

- **Do I know anyone who can recommend any of the doctors on the plan's list?** Little did the inventors of e-mail know how often office colleagues would use it to swap information about doctors in their company's health care plans.
- **Is the doctor's office convenient to my home?** Imagine having to drive for forty-five minutes to get to the pediatrician's office while your toddler screams with pain from an ear infection. Not a pleasant thought, is it?
- **Is the doctor accepting new patients?** Don't assume the answer is yes. Call his or her office and ask. If the answer is no, go back to step one and start your search again.
- **Which hospitals can the doctor admit patients to?**

Don't assume that a hospital belongs to a health care plan just because a doctor who has admitting privileges there is in the plan's network. Our pediatrician can admit patients to the hospital in our town as well as to another one that's about twenty minutes away from our home. Only the hospital farther from us belongs to our PPO.

- **Does the doctor have excellent credentials?** Look for a doctor who's board-certified. That means she's finished an approved residency program and passed an exam sponsored by a board of experts in her specialty.

- **Does the doctor have a clean record?** Ask your state's medical licensing board. You can find its telephone number in the government blue pages of your telephone book. Alternatively, log on to the Web site of the Federation of State Medical Boards of the United States (www.fsmd.org). Some state insurance departments will tell you if a doctor has been disciplined for poor care, or in some cases, criminal conduct. Look for the phone number of your state insurance department in the government blue pages of your phone book. Or, log on to www.insure.com.

What You Need to Know About a Plan's Benefits

Of course, it's impossible to know what kind of medical services your family will need six months or a year from now. So, the best advice I can give is to pick a comprehensive plan. Here are the questions you should ask:

- **Does the plan pay for preventative care?** Most managed care plans cover immunizations, pap smears, and routine checkups for your kids.

- **Does the plan pay for alternative health care?** If you see an acupuncturist or a chiropractor, find out if the plan will pay for such services.

- **To what extent does the plan cover outpatient mental health services, home health care, and rehabilitation therapy?** None of these services may be important to you now, but what if you fall down the stairs and need physical therapy?

- **Does the plan cover treatments that help kids develop properly?** Most plans don't cover speech therapy, for instance.

- **What are the plan's rules regarding emergency room visits?** Most plans require you or your PCP to call their toll-free telephone number before rushing to the hospital, or within a specified period after you go home. If you forget to follow the rules, you get stuck with the bill. Also, find out what happens if your husband gets sick while traveling on business, or if your son breaks his arm while you're vacationing far from home.

- **What are the plan's rules regarding prescription drugs?** Many plans are cutting back on coverage. Look at the bright side, however. At least you've got insurance for drugs. Many people with individual health insurance policies don't.

Find out what your copayment is for prescription drugs. Ask if you must fill prescriptions through a mail-order company or at one of the pharmacies that's contracted to work with the health care plan. If you buy the same drug repeatedly, find out if a ninety-day prescription is a better deal than getting a thirty-day supply. Also, ask if the plan covers the cost of your kids' vitamins. If you or a member of your family takes a specific drug, find out if it's included in the plan's *formulary*, or list of covered drugs. If it isn't, ask your doctor if he or she can recommend an equivalent drug that *is* covered.

- **Does the plan cover dental care?** Employers often offer only one dental plan, which is separate from any of the health care plans they provide.
- **Does the plan cover eyeglasses and other vision services?** Like dental plans, vision plans are usually separate from health care plans. It's important for you to know what's covered, and how often you can visit your optometrist.

What You Need to Know About a Plan's Reputation

Sure, you should ask your friends, relatives, and coworkers if they're satisfied with their health care plans. However, you should also do a little more digging. Here's what to find out:

- **Is the plan accredited?** The National Committee for Quality Assurance rates managed care plans. Most plans have yet to try to earn this respected group's stamp of approval, so don't reject a plan just because it isn't accredited. It's a bad sign, however, if a plan *has* tried for accreditation and failed. To find out a plan's standing with the NCQA, call the plan's customer service number, or ask your employee benefits manager. Or, contact the NCQA (800-839-6487 or 888-275-7585, www.ncqa.org).
- **Can I get a report card for the plan?** Some employers work with the NCQA to produce report cards that consumers can use to compare the performance of managed

care plans. Among other things, the report cards reveal how satisfied current plan members are.

Government agencies in at least six states rate managed care plans. To see if your state offers consumers any help, log on to www.insure.com.

- **Is the plan financially healthy?** Why should you care? Simple. If your plan can't pay the doctors in its network, they'll probably bolt. Companies that rate the financial solvency of life insurers now also examine health care plans, but the business is in its infancy. Still, you should ask your employee benefits manager or a plan's customer service representative if the plan has been rated by A. M. Best, Standard & Poor's, or Weiss Ratings. Also, keep your eyes and ears open for news reports about managed care plans that do business in your area.

Once you pick a plan, breathe a sigh of relief until it's time to do it again next year. *Yes, you've got to shop every year.* Plans change constantly, and so do the doctors in their networks. Meanwhile, here's how to get the most out of the plan you've got:

How to Play the System

To get the medical service your family needs without paying a penny more than necessary, you've got to be patient, persistent, and a stickler for details. I've made some mistakes in the past that have cost me money, and I'm trying hard not to repeat them. Savvy consumers should all pledge to:

- **Follow all rules regarding referrals to specialists.** Don't expect your PCP to explain your plan's ins and outs to you. You've got to figure it out yourself. For example, a referral from your PCP may be good for only one visit to a specialist. If the specialist tells you to come back, you'll have to get another referral from your PCP if you want to pay the specialist the low copayment that your health care plan has negotiated with specialists in its network.

    Referrals are usually good for only a certain number of days. If you make an appointment with a specialist for the day after your referral expires, you'll pay a higher fee.

- **Read your plan's rules regarding emergencies as soon as you get home from the hospital.** I know that's not the first thing on your mind after your toddler has taken a tumble down the basement steps, but you've got to make it a priority. Otherwise, how would you remember that you've got only forty-eight hours to call your pediatrician so she can confirm that rushing to the emergency room was the right thing to do?

- **Figure out in advance how much it'll cost you to see a doctor who's not in your health plan's network.** That way you can decide if it's worth the extra expense to venture out of the network. Let's say that your current gynecologist doesn't belong to your health care plan, but you want to continue seeing him. Like most insurers, yours will pay 80%

of the *usual and customary* fee for an office visit or medical procedure if you see a doctor who isn't in the plan's network. If your gynecologist charges more for an annual checkup than your plan's usual and customary rate, you'll pay more than 20% of tab. Assume your doctor charges $135 while your insurer's usual and customary fee is $100. You might think that your share of the bill is $27. Wrong. It's actually $55. You pay 20% of the $100 usual and customary rate, plus the $35 difference between that rate and your doctor's fee. What's more, only $20 of the $55 counts toward your deductible.

- **Keep detailed records.** File health insurance claims in a folder by the date that you sent them to your insurer. Check the file every couple of weeks to make sure that your plan is paying your claims promptly.

Whenever you call your plan's toll-free customer service number, take notes. Always jot down the names of representatives you speak with.

- **Use a health care flexible spending account if you can.** Many large employers offer health care FSAs. (For more about how FSAs work, turn back to Chapter 4.) If your spouse's company does, he can contribute a portion of his pretax salary to an FSA. You may use the money in your account to pay out-of-pocket medical expenses. For instance, you might use money in your FSA to cover your deductible, copayments, or services and supplies that your health care plan doesn't pay for, like eyeglasses. The government doesn't limit your annual contribution, but your employer may.

The only downside is that you lose your contributions to an FSA if you don't use them. Don't let that scare you. Just take some time to add up what you spend on health care during a typical year. That's what Holly and Mike Schuler do. Holly, a former financial analyst, stays home with their two kids, Kevin, three, and Kerry, six months. Mike, a sales manager, contributes to the health care FSA that the insurance company he works for offers. "We set aside part of Mike's salary before paying taxes on it, and get reimbursed at the end of the year," says Holly.

- **Fill in any holes in your plan with free services.** Rosemary and Malachy O'Brien get health insurance through the bank that Malachy works for. Their plan doesn't cover all of the cost of childhood immunizations, however. So, they take their four daughters to their county's health clinic for free vaccinations. Rosemary, a former speech pathologist, found out about the program from other moms. She also got flyers advertising it from the hospital after she delivered her girls. How else can you find out about free programs like the one the O'Briens use? Ask your pediatrician, call your county, state, and local health departments, and keep your eyes open for newspaper articles and ads.

- **Be persistent if your plan won't pay for something you think it should.** Complain in writing if your insurer denies a claim that you have good reason to believe it should pay. First call your plan's customer service department and ask if you must fill out a formal grievance form. If you don't, send a letter describing your complaint, along with any relevant documentation, to your plan's medical director and customer service department. Mail a copy to your employer's benefits department. (After all, your employer decided to do business with the plan.) Also, send a copy to your state insurance department. If your state has an agency that oversees managed care plans, send a copy of your letter to it too.

If your plan's internal review panel turns you down, some states let you appeal to an independent panel. I hope you never get into a tiff that serious with your health insurer. More likely, you'll suffer some small annoyances. If those nuisances add up, of course, consider switching plans the next chance you get.

How to Buy Health Insurance on Your Own

If your family gets group health insurance through your employer, you'll save yourself a lot of stress—and money—if you look into how much individual coverage will cost *before* you quit your job. It's impossible for me to say if you'll be appalled or appeased by the price. The type of coverage you can get and the price you'll pay depends on where you live, your age, and how healthy you and your family members are.

If you're lucky, you'll learn that you can afford to buy health insurance on your own. However, chances are that your coverage won't be as comprehensive as it was under a group plan. The Gervolinos, whom we first met back in Chapter 6, are in that situation. Rick, thirty-nine, operates a catering truck. Barbara, thirty-seven, takes care of their two daughters. Fortunately, all of the Gervolinos are healthy. They asked a friend who's an insurance agent to find them a comprehensive yet affordable policy.

What they got was coverage for catastrophic costs, not routine care. Each of the Gervolinos must meet an annual deductible of $2,000. So Rick and Barbara pay their daughters' pediatrician $75 for a checkup. If they belonged to a group plan, they'd probably pay only $15. In addition, the Gervolinos pay all of their bills for prescription drugs, eye exams, and dental care. How much does this type of stripped-down coverage cost? A stiff $390 a month, or $4,680 a year.

Like other self-employed folks, the Gervolinos get a tax break for buying health insurance on their own. However, they can deduct only a portion of the premium they pay. The percentage is 60% in 1999 and it will rise until it reaches 100% in 2003.

The Gervolinos have been on their own for seven years, and they've learned that they must shop for a new policy every year or two. "Insurance companies always raise the premium at least fifty to a hundred dollars a month after you've been with them for a while," explains Barbara.

How can you find out how much your family would have to pay for individual coverage? Assume you'll have to shoulder a large deductible, like the Gervolinos have. It's the only way to keep premiums down. You'll probably have to pay at least 20% of covered expenses after you meet your deductible. So, try to find a policy that places a cap on your annual expenditures.

Two other points are very important to keep in mind. First, ask how long your premium will remain stable. It's reasonable to expect your rate to remain unchanged for at least one year. Second, look for a policy that's *noncancellable* or *guaranteed renewable* as long as you pay your premiums. That said, try these sources for price quotes:

- **Call two or three agents who sell individual health insurance.** Check your local Yellow Pages for agents in your area. Insurance expert James Hunt thinks you should also call USAA Life (800-531-7015). Best known for its low-cost life insurance, USAA doesn't underwrite health policies. However, it operates an insurance agency that may be able to find an affordable policy for you.

- **Use Internet quote services.** This business is still in its infancy and you may not be able to get quotes online for policies sold in your state. It's worth checking out www.insweb.com and www.quotesmith.com, however.

- **Call your state insurance department for a list of health insurers that do business in your state.** If the insurance agents you're working with haven't mentioned some of the insurers on the list, ask why not. While you're at it, ask if your state's insurance watchdogs keep records of consumer complaints against health insurers. Avoid companies that log lots of complaints.

- **Call associations you belong to and ask if they offer health insurance.** Don't assume that this type of group plan is a better deal than individual coverage, however.

- **Look for health insurance purchasing groups in your area.** In some areas, small businesses have set up *consumer-choice health purchasing groups*. These CHPGs bargain with health insurers like big companies do. Owners and employees of firms in the CHPG can choose among health plans that contract with it. Some CHPGs permit self-employed sole proprietors to join them as well. To find out if there's a CHPG in your state, log on to the Institute for Health Policy Solutions' Web site (www.ihps.org). Also, call local chambers of commerce and trade associations for your industry to see if they've established buying groups you can join.

Once you get your price quotes, you may feel relieved. Congratulations—but don't quit your job just yet. Instead, skip ahead to page 170. Starting there, I tell you how to keep your family from suffering gaps in its health care coverage. If you go without coverage for a while, you may give up important rights under a federal law that makes it easier to get coverage if you or a member of your family has had health problems.

What if you're not so fortunate and the price quotes you get are too high for you to handle—especially if you stop working or switch to a part-time job? No, you don't have to resign yourself to keeping your full-time job. But you will have to make major changes in your lifestyle if spending more time with your kids means you must give up a job that gives your family group health insurance. The one option you don't have is going without health insurance. One short hospital stay could put you in a financial hole that'll take years to dig yourself out of.

Don't expect the government to pay for your kids' health care if you can't. You have no hope of getting Medicaid unless you're very poor or disabled. The Children's Health Insurance Program that Congress passed in 1997 probably isn't the answer to your prayers, either. Under this program, states provide free or low-cost health insurance for children under eighteen whose families can't afford to buy private coverage. The states don't care if you've got a big mortgage or other burdensome bills; they care how high your income is. In New York, a family of three can qualify if it earns less than $31,890 a year. But in Texas, the cutoff is only $13,650. Still want more information? Log on to www.healthfinder.gov. Or, call 877-543-7669 toll-free to reach your state's health department.

What *can* you do?

- **Look for ways to cut your spending so you'll have more money available for health insurance.** Go back to Chapter 1 and examine the worksheet you filled out. Can you drop your cable TV subscription, eat out less often, give homemade gifts to relatives and friends, or take a vacation every other year instead of annually? If your budget is already uncomfortably tight, read on.

- **Tap your savings.** Turn back to the worksheet you filled out in Chapter 3 to see how much savings you could spend on insurance, and for how long. Obviously, this is just a temporary solution to your problem, and it works only if you're lucky enough to have substantial savings. Decide in advance that you'll use this strategy for a set period, say one year or eighteen months. If your spouse's business isn't generating enough cash to pay for health insurance by then, consider using the next two strategies to get group health insurance. Or, assuming your husband feels as strongly as you do about raising a family on less than two incomes, convince him that he must look for a job that comes with health benefits.

- **Get group health insurance by working part time.** You could shift to part-time work for your old employer or go someplace new. (For advice on switching from full-time to part-time work, see Chapter 17.) How many companies give health insurance to part-time employees? More than you might think. Hewitt Associates, a benefits consulting firm, reports that 80% of large companies cover part-timers who work at least thirty hours a week. The fewer hours you work, the less likely you are to get health benefits. Hewitt found that the percentage of companies that provide health insurance to part-timers fell to 58% for employees who work twenty to twenty-nine hours a week, and to 19% for people employed less than twenty hours a week.

If this strategy works for you, you may have to pay a higher monthly premium for health insurance than you did when you worked full time. But paying even 100% of the cost of group coverage is cheaper than buying insurance on your own.

■ **Moonlight to get health benefits.** I never gave much thought to this idea until our favorite mature baby-sitter mentioned that she once worked twelve hours a week at a grocery store's deli counter so she could get group health insurance. Grocery store workers in our area belong to a strong union. The situation may not be the same in your area. However, your husband might be able to get health insurance by moonlighting at a discount store or fast-food restaurant.

Whatever you do, please don't ditch your current health insurance until you have written proof of new coverage. That's because your new insurer may not cover medical conditions that you've already had diagnosed or treated. If you're in this fix, you have some rights under the Health Insurance Portability and Accountability Act. This federal law gives you the opportunity to buy health insurance no matter how sick you are. However, there's no guarantee that you'll be able to afford the policies that you qualify for. In addition, the rules are tricky, and you must follow them precisely.

Let's say you work full time and get group health insurance. You then quit your job to take a part-time position at another company that also provides health benefits. Under the law, your new group plan must cover preexisting conditions as soon as you join it if you've had health insurance for the previous twelve months. If you let your insurance coverage lapse, however, your new plan can make you wait before it covers you for preexisting medical conditions. It can only make you wait up to twelve months, however.

If you lose group health insurance and must purchase individual coverage, watch your step. Under federal law, you've got the right to buy insurance that covers preexisting conditions without any waiting period, but only if:

- **You've had eighteen months of continuous health care coverage.** In addition, you must have had group insurance coverage for at least the last day of that eighteen-month period.
- **You've used up your coverage under COBRA.** You can keep your group coverage under this federal law if the company you worked for employed twenty or more people. You may generally keep your old insurance for up to eighteen months. However, you must pay the whole premium, plus a

2% administrative fee. For details, ask your former employer or log on to the federal Department of Labor's Web site (www.dol.gov/dol/pwba/public/pubs/COBRA/cobra95.htm).

If you meet those conditions, there's one more thing to remember. You must apply for insurance within sixty-three days of losing your prior coverage.

What happens next depends upon where you live. In some states, you will not have the right to buy insurance from private companies. Instead, you'll be able to buy only from your state's high-risk insurance pool. For your rights in your state, log on to the Web site of Georgetown University's Institute for Health Care Research and Policy (www.georgetown.edu/research/ihcrp/hipaa). Or, call your state insurance department.

Getting and keeping individual health insurance isn't easy. In fact, if you pull it off and want to reenter the workforce after your kids are grown, I think you deserve to brag about your accomplishment on your résumé. The skill and persistence you showed qualify you for any job.

CHAPTER 11

Eat on the Cheap

You knew it, and Uncle Sam confirms it: Feeding a growing brood costs a bundle. Of the money that parents spend on their kids, 15% to 20% goes for food, says the U.S. Department of Agriculture. The average four-person household lays out $6,693 a year for groceries and meals out, or nearly 13% of its income. Affluent folks (household income: $70,000 and up) spend considerably more on average—$8,874 a year. You don't need college-level math to figure out that trimming your food bill by just 5% to 10% can save you hundreds of dollars a year.

There's only one foolproof way to cut food bills: Cook.

Relying heavily on restaurant chefs and deli countermen to prepare your meals means you pay for labor as well as ingredients. So, if you hate to cook—or don't know how to cook and don't want to learn—forget about saving big bucks on food. In fact, skip this chapter and read about other ways to cut your expenses. Before you jump ahead, however, let me make it clear that when I say *cook,* I don't mean *cook everything from scratch every night.* In my book, hamburgers made from scratch on store-baked buns served with fresh green beans and frozen French fries counts as a home-cooked meal.

Remember too, if you quit or cut back on work, you'll have more time to cook. Just think: No more dashing out of your office promptly at five o'clock each day to pick up your already-hungry kids at the day care center or baby-sitter's house. No more waiting impatiently for water to boil while your kids cling to your legs and scream for spaghetti. No more grabbing fast food or Chinese takeout two or three nights a week so you can avoid cooking under pressure.

Instead, you and your kids are usually home together in the late afternoon. At four-thirty or five o'clock, you tell them they can watch TV while you cook dinner. (If you're purer than me and never use TV as a baby-sitter, put *Peter and the Wolf* or something similarly highbrow on the CD player.) If the meal you decide to prepare doesn't require much chopping or tending, you can make a few phone calls, skim the newspaper, or sort the mail while keeping one eye on the stove. You'll have dinner on the table before your kids start whining, and you'll probably give them a meal that would make a nutritionist smile. Of course, you'll also save money.

How Little Can You Spend at the Supermarket and Still Eat Right?

Government economists and nutritionists put their heads together to figure this out. It's useful to compare your actual spending against their hypothetical budgets to see how much you could possibly save on food. Flip back to Chapter 1 to get the annual amounts you spend on groceries (line 11) and meals out (line 22). Subtract the approximate amount you spend at the supermarket on household supplies like laundry detergent and paper towels from line 11. (If you don't know how much you spend on such items, use $639, which is the national average for families with children.)

Compare your spending on groceries only to the U.S. Department of Agriculture's cheapskate estimates for feeding a family of four shown in the table below. (I'll deal with eating out later in this chapter.) The USDA assumes that you buy all meals and snacks at stores and prepare them at home. Its estimates date from January 1999. For updated information, or to customize the data to reflect your family's size and your children's ages, log onto www.usda.gov and click on the Center for Nutrition Policy and Promotion.

Grocery Bills of the Truly Thrifty

Family of four with kids ages 1 to 2 and 3 to 5 . . .	*Thrifty budget*	*Low-cost budget*
	$86.40 a week/ $4,492.80 a year	$108.40 a week/ $5,636.80 a year

Family of four with kids ages 6 to 8 and 9 to 11 . . .	*Thrifty budget*	*Low-cost budget*
	$99.60 a week/ $5,179.20 a year	$127.70 a week/ $6,640.40 a year

Source: U.S. Department of Agriculture

If the USDA's budgets seem miserly to you, you probably eat more like an average American than a government nutritionist. You'd spend less if you ate more fruits, vegetables, grains (like pasta and rice), and beans, and fewer cheeses, eggs, fats, oils, soft drinks, and sweets. Is it any wonder that Uncle Sam also says that fewer than one in eight Americans eats a healthy diet?

Does this mean you must eat legumes on lettuce for lunch and give your kids green pepper slices with water for an afternoon snack? (I'm not making that Scrooge-like snack suggestion up. I read it years ago in a women's magazine.) Not at all. While researching this book, I tracked my food expenditures for an entire year. I spent an average $103 a week on groceries for two adults, a seven-year-old and a two-year-old. The amount I spend falls between the USDA's thrifty ($90.40) and low-cost ($115.30) budgets for a family like mine. Yet I don't skimp on portions, buy day-old bread, or gravitate to store-brand products. We eat a variety of foods, and don't feel the least bit deprived. Here's the proof—a list of my grocery store purchases (italicized items are store brands) for two typical months:

Fresh Fruits and Vegetables
Apples
Asparagus
Avocados
Bananas
Broccoli
Brussels sprouts
Carrots

Corn
Cucumbers
Grapes
Green beans
Green peppers
Herbs
Kiwi fruit
Lemons
Lettuce
Melons
Mushrooms
Nectarines
Onions
Oranges
Peaches
Pears
Plums
Potatoes
Raspberries
Red peppers
Snow peas
Strawberries
Sugar snap peas
Summer squash
Tomatoes
Winter squash

Bread, Cereal, Pasta, and Grains
Bakery bagels
Bakery breads

Breakfast cereals
Dry pasta
Granola
Lentils
Rolls
Whole wheat bread
Whole wheat crackers

Meat and Fish
Beef franks
Beef sausage
Chicken breasts
Crabmeat
Ground beef
Porterhouse steak
Rib-eye steak
Salami
Salmon fillets
Shell steak

Dairy Products and Eggs
American cheese
Cream cheese
Eggs
Heavy cream
Margarine
Milk
Parmesan cheese
Swiss cheese
Unsalted butter
Yogurt

Juice
Apple
Orange
Pineapple
Various all-fruit

Canned and Frozen Fruits and Vegetables
Canned peaches
Canned refried beans
Plain frozen vegetables
Tomato sauce
Unsweetened applesauce

Condiments
Baking powder
Honey
Jelly
Mustard
Pancake syrup
Pickles
Sugar
Worcestershire sauce

Soft Drinks
Cola
Tonic water

Snacks and Sweets
Bakery doughnuts
Bakery muffins
Candy

Cheez Doodles
Cookies
Graham crackers
Granola bars
Ice cream
Ice pops
Marshmallows
Pretzels

Convenience Foods

Biscuit mix
Brownie mix
Canned soup
Macaroni and cheese mix
Peanut butter
Rice mixes
Spaghetti sauce
Taco dinner kits

Frozen Convenience Foods

Burritos
Chicken nuggets
Pirogies
Pizza
Ravioli
TV dinners
Waffles

Store-Prepared Foods

Quiche
Tuna salad

Nine Ways to Save on Food

How do I spend so little on so many goodies? I try very hard to follow these simple rules:

- **Don't buy takeout food at the supermarket.** Today 20% of shoppers buy whole meals at the supermarket, not just ingredients to cook at home. Supermarket takeout is a $100 billion a year business, says the Food Marketing Institute. Busy families with kids are more likely than other shoppers to buy sushi and cut and cleaned salad greens at the grocery store.

  This trend is a bonanza for grocers and a budget-buster for consumers. *Business Week* reports that supermarkets specializing in prepared foods boast profits of 12% to 15%. That's much higher than the 2% to 3% profits that most traditional grocery stores earn.

  The only store-prepared food I regularly buy at the supermarket is tuna salad. I know I could make tuna salad for much less than the $5.99 a pound I usually pay, but I buy it at the deli counter to indulge my husband. He swears that this particular tuna salad is the quintessence of tuna salad. I think he's nuts, but I don't complain because he saves us at least $1,200 a year by brown-bagging the same lunch virtually every day: tuna salad and a slice of American cheese on whole wheat bread, with a piece of fresh fruit. If he bought a cheeseburger and fries daily in Manhattan, he'd spend much more—and probably increase his cholesterol counts.

- **Avoid convenience foods.** Only 38% of all meals we eat today include at least one item made from scratch, down from 43% a decade ago. This trend is also costing us a small fortune. With a few exceptions, like cake mixes, convenience foods cost more than ingredients that you combine and cook yourself.

Sure, it's unrealistic to expect even full-time stay-at-home parents to shun convenience foods completely. Everyone needs a few prepackaged meals on hand to serve when he or she is too busy to cook because of ballet lessons, soccer practice, or PTA meetings. Savvy shoppers choose the convenience foods that feed the most mouths for the least money. Take macaroni and cheese. Don't buy the $2.00 frozen version that takes six minutes to microwave and feeds just one. Grab an eighty-nine-cent (fifty-nine cents on sale) box of macaroni and cheese mix instead. It takes only 10 minutes to prepare on the stove and feeds at least three.

Whatever you do, don't fall for convenience versions of meals that don't require cooking in the first place. Consider those single-serving "breakfast kits" that your kids beg for after seeing them advertised on TV. Each kit includes an ounce of cereal, a four-ounce carton of shelf-stable milk, and a plastic spoon. (What's with the spoon? Is throwing a plastic spoon into the wastebasket easier than throwing a stainless steel spoon into the dishwasher?) The kits cost a whopping $1.29 apiece, so you'd spend $6.45 a week on them if your kid ate one before rushing off to school every day. For $6.08, you could buy a gallon of milk ($2.79) and a 15-ounce box of cereal ($3.29 if it's not on sale) instead. You'd have enough cereal for three weeks and enough milk for lunches, dinners, and snacks as well.

- **Serve main courses when they're on sale.** We eat boneless chicken breasts when they're $1.99 a pound, not $5.99. When chicken breasts are on sale, I stock up and freeze dinner-size portions for future use. I deviate from this strategy only for birthdays, dinner parties, and holidays. Then I buy whatever meat or fish my heart desires from a top-flight butcher or fishmonger, damn the cost.
- **Buy fresh fruits and vegetables in season and on sale.** Why buy blueberries in February when they cost five times as much as they do in July? Besides, fresh produce usually tastes best when it's locally grown.

Ann Butcher does even better. Ann, a former dental assistant, is a stay-at-home mom to two boys, ages fourteen and eleven. She grows her own beans, beets, carrots, corn, cucumbers, garlic, onions, peas, Swiss chard, and tomatoes on three quarters of an acre. She also cans and freezes vegetables, makes jams, and bakes her own bread. No, Ann and her husband Joe aren't full-time farmers. He runs his own business installing and repairing garage doors. She's taking courses at a community college so she can start a home-based business preparing income tax returns. The Butchers just like to eat well without spending a lot of money.

- **Purchase plain varieties of frozen and canned vegetables.** Fancy blends swimming in fatty, artificially flavored sauces cost more than bags of unadorned peas and carrots.

It takes only a minute to toss the peas and carrots together with some butter or margarine and a moderate amount of salt.

- **Eliminate impulse purchases.** I treat my kids to expensive snacks like Cheez Doodles, potato chips, and rocket ship–shaped ice pops. But I buy that stuff when it's on sale, not whenever it catches my eye, or more likely, my kids' eyes. No one feels deprived because some sort of salty or sweet snack is on sale every week. Truly, it's no strain to forgo full-price ice pops for a week or two and eat sale-priced premium ice cream instead.

- **Plan for leftovers.** The USDA reports that only 4% of households with kids plan to use leftovers in meals. What do the other 96% use their microwaves for? I always plan for leftovers because it saves precious time as well as money. If you keep a cache of leftovers in the refrigerator, you won't have to reach for a pricey TV dinner or pick up takeout when your kids complain of starvation on busy weeknights. Pop a pork roast in the oven on a lazy Sunday, when you have time to embellish it with homemade potatoes and a fresh vegetable. On a crazy weeknight, serve leftover pork with instant mashed potatoes and frozen veggies. Having leftovers around also eliminates or reduces the need to buy expensive luncheon meats.

- **Clip coupons.** Coupon clipping has gotten a bum rap as a fool's pastime. Market researchers report that coupon redemptions have decreased over each of the last five years. It isn't a good idea to clip coupons for expensive convenience foods you otherwise wouldn't purchase. But clipping coupons for products you regularly buy is. So is checking your favorite grocery store's weekly advertising flyer for so-called clipless coupons or bonus club savings. To get the sale price, you present your bonus club card to the cashier. In a typical week, I use five manufacturer's coupons and take advantage of five bonus club specials to cut my grocery bill by at least 10%.

- **Always check unit prices.** The price of a product per pound, fluid ounce, or some other unit of measure appears on the shelf beneath it. If you always compare unit prices—and take into account coupons and store specials—you'll find that bigger packages and store brands aren't always cheaper than smaller boxes and national brands.

To Pull It Off, You Need a Plan

You've probably guessed that you can't effectively use most of these money-saving strategies unless you shop from a list. To do that, of course, you also need a menu plan. I swear by my weekly plan, but I know I don't have much company. Seven in ten Americans don't decide what they'll eat until evening sneaks up on them, reports *Restaurants and Institutions* magazine. If you're in the majority, you probably have a couple of concerns about advance planning, namely:

- **It sounds too rigid.** Believe me, it's not. You map out your week, but you can flip-flop Wednesday's menu with Monday's if circumstances change. Here's how things typically go at my house: I plan to cook pasta on Monday, serve leftover pork roast on Tuesday and make chicken breast on Wednesday. Monday goes as planned, but on Monday night my husband says he'll be home late on Tuesday. So, instead of serving just some of the leftover roast, I make macaroni and cheese for my kids. When my husband gets home, we make plenty of chicken breast with rosemary and lemon sauce. Over dinner, he says he doubts he'll be home for dinner on Wednesday, so I plan to finish the chicken breast with the kids, along with a box of Spanish rice and fresh green beans. We finally finish the pork roast on Thursday.

- **It takes too much time.** It takes me no more than one hour a week. Best of all, my up-front investment of one hour means I usually make only one trip to the grocery store each week. The average shopper makes 2.2, and I know mothers who go once or twice a day! Sure, I occasionally have to run out and buy more milk or bread because the kids drink or eat more than usual. Once in a while, I also make a special trip to our local gourmet supermarket to pick up something special that's on sale, like filet mignon or fresh tuna. But I normally do all of my grocery shopping in one weekly trip.

Here's my eight-step game plan:

1. I find the advertising flyer for my favorite grocery store in my Sunday newspaper. Sale prices are good Sunday through Saturday. I also check the newspaper for advertising inserts filled with manufacturer's coupons. I slip all of the ads into a file folder marked "Groceries," which also contains last week's shopping list and menu.

2. On Sunday night, I check my family's calendar for the coming week to figure out when I'll have time to go grocery shopping. If I decide to do it on Friday, for example, I'll

make a note on my calendar to compile my shopping list on Thursday.

3. On Thursday, I get out my "Groceries" file folder and a box of coupons I've previously filed by type of product (i.e., cereal, juice, yogurt). I've labeled each of the seventy file cards, starting with bags and ending with yogurt. I copy all of the items from last week's list that I need again, like milk, bread, and bananas, on to my new list. (If I typed my list on my computer, of course, I wouldn't have to bother recopying items by hand.)

4. I quickly check my cupboards, refrigerators, freezers, basement, and linen closet for items I need to buy now or within a week or two. I try to buy products when they're on sale or when I have a coupon for them. If I have a coupon for a sale item, I feel like I've hit the lottery. So, if I can make it through the week without buying an item that's frequently on sale, I note that on my list.

5. I skim through my favorite grocery store's flyer, looking for sale items that I buy. I don't necessarily add them all to my list, however. First, I always ask myself: "Do I really need it now?" If I already have four pounds of ground beef in the freezer, I don't buy more even if it is on sale. I know from planning menus weekly that ground beef will be on sale again before we're likely to use up what's on hand. And I'd rather have more cash in our checking account than beef in my freezer.

6. When I get to the section of the flyer that lists specials on meats and fish, I plan my menu for the coming week. I rarely buy meat or fish for more than two or three dinners, however. That's because my freezers are usually well stocked with meats that I bought when they were on sale.

7. When I've finished my list, I clip coupons from the advertising inserts I've collected. I clip coupons only for products I usually buy, or for new products I want to try. I keep my coupons in a plastic box divided with file cards.

8. The last thing I do is check for coupons for items on my list. If we need cookies, cereal, or some other product for which we enjoy any number of brands, I take the most valuable coupons from two or three manufacturers. If I have coupons of equal value for the same product, I take the one that will expire soonest.

What About All That Other Stuff We Buy at the Supermarket?

If you're like me, you probably purchase most of your household cleaning and laundry supplies at the supermarket too. (I occasionally buy laundry detergent, paper towels, and toilet paper on sale at the discount store closest to my home.) When I buy household supplies at the supermarket, I also try to buy items I like when they're on sale or I have a coupon for them. I frequently succeed, but I could do better. For instance, I bought eighty rolls of national-brand toilet paper last year, spending forty-one cents a roll on average. The lowest price I paid was thirty cents a roll, so I could have saved $9.00 over the year had I managed to buy all eighty rolls at the lowest possible price.

Joy Carlson, a former teacher who now tutors part time, cuts the cost of cleaning supplies and paper goods by buying large quantities twice a year at a warehouse club. She also bought diapers for her daughter, who's now a second grader, at the warehouse club. She paid $33.79 for a box of 144 large-size name brand diapers at the club, or twenty-three cents a diaper. Supermarkets in her area charge about thirty-one cents a diaper.

Only very careful shoppers save money at warehouse clubs, however. That's because warehouse stores actually charge more for some items than grocery stores do. And, like all types of stores, warehouse clubs showcase plenty of high mark-up temptations—like fresh flowers and heat-and-eat meals— alongside the dirt-cheap diapers.

I found this out for myself by conducting a little experiment. While writing this book, I visited the warehouse club closest to my home. I paid $40 for a refundable annual membership fee. Then I spent a morning searching the club for products that I usually buy at the supermarket. Some items— like bananas for thirty-six cents a pound—were great buys, but not for a family of four. In our house, much of the minimum five-pound purchase would rot. I did find twenty products that I could buy without worrying about spoilage, however. Here's my scorecard:

Warehouse club prices were lower for eight items, including bath soap, milk, paper towels, and toilet bowl cleaner.

Supermarket prices were lower for six items, including dishwasher detergent, laundry detergent, and toilet paper.

Six products were a toss-up, including ketchup and apple juice.

Total savings if I bought a year's worth of the eight cheaper items at the warehouse club: $72.

Total savings if I bought a year's worth of the items that were cheaper at the club, leaving out milk because I don't have time to visit the warehouse weekly: $37. (I know I could freeze the milk, but I don't usually have enough room in my freezers for gallons of milk.)

Annual loss after accounting for $40 membership fee: $3.

Needless to say, I asked for a refund of my membership fee.

How to Save on Meals Out

I realized my family's eating habits were unusual when a doctor's appointment ran longer than expected. I stopped at a fast-food restaurant on the way home because my kids were starving. Feeling guilty about giving my daughters a dinner that comes with a toy but no vegetables, I zipped into the restaurant's parking lot and almost bumped the car in front of me. There were sedans and SUVs stretched from the takeout window to the street, and the parking lot was almost full too. Once inside, we met some friends and dined with them!

Until then, I had no idea that families flocked to my local burger joint for dinner. My family usually eats fast food only when we're traveling on an interstate highway. I did some research and figured out why I was out of the loop. I calculated that we spend 23% of the money we use for food on meals away from home. That percentage is 37% for the typical four-person household and 43% for affluent foursomes.

The portion of meals that Americans eat away from home has nearly doubled over the past two decades, from 16% to 29%. Families with kids are leading the charge out of the kitchen. Nearly 40% of families with kids seventeen and younger eat out once a week, compared to 30% of families without children. If you eat out a lot, your bank account will shrink while your body bloats. Government nutritionists point out that meals we eat outside our homes contain more fat, fewer nutrients, and less fiber than food we cook at home.

If you quit or cut back on work, circumstances will rarely force you to eat out. Most nights, you'll have time to cook. So you can go retro, and eat out mostly on special occasions, as most of us did when we were kids. My husband and I eat out together or with friends about once a month. We usually go to inexpensive ethnic restaurants. Our typical tab for sushi and sake runs $35. We eat at truly outstanding restaurants in Manhattan two or three times a year. (One meal we had last year set us back $285.73, but we don't regret a penny of it.) We also take our kids out to lunch or dinner about once a month at kid-friendly chain restaurants or old-fashioned department store tearooms. (I have a soft spot in my heart for those disappearing dinosaurs because that's where I learned a few social graces in my youth.) It typically costs half as much to take the kids to lunch instead of dinner. They usually order pasta or hot dogs from the children's menu whether we eat early or late. My husband and I are the ones who can cut costs at lunch, because entrees are usually cheaper then and we never order wine or dessert at midday.

Do we feel deprived because we don't eat out more often? Hardly ever. We enjoy eating at home because I enjoy cooking and my daughters love to set the table with panache. Most evenings, they clamor for candlelight!

CHAPTER 12

Spend Less
on More Fun

When I asked part-time nurse Beth Auletta how she and her husband Brian save money on entertainment, she quipped: "Four kids provide plenty of entertainment!" There's a germ of truth in her joke. When you've got more time to spend with your kids, you can savor the kind of spontaneous fun that costs little or nothing. There will be plenty of days when just turning on your lawn sprinkler will make everyone in your family forget about going to the movies.

Of course, staying home to save money is nothing new. Now that we baby boomers are doing it, however, it's called cocooning. You can cocoon without feeling cooped up if you do things at home that you used to do elsewhere.

For instance, many of the families I surveyed rarely go to the movies anymore. They rent videos instead. Hugh Norman, a former stock analyst who stays home with his two children while his wife Alice works on Wall Street, goes one step farther and frequently borrows tapes from the library. There he can get many of his choices free.

Plenty of parents also drop their gym memberships. Tara Silber quit her gym, saving a few hundred dollars a year. She does aerobics at home and goes bicycling with her infant son.

Much as I enjoy cocooning, I'm the first to admit that staying home with small children can get claustrophobic. That's especially true if you're used to going to work, as I was. I used to work in Manhattan, at Rockefeller Center. The world-famous Museum of Modern Art was just three blocks away; Saks Fifth Avenue's flagship store was also within walking distance. From my window, I could see tourists from around the globe, street vendors selling everything from books to knishes, and all sorts of Manhattan eccentrics. Nowadays, it's an exciting day if I see a lost soccer mom make a U-turn in my cul-de-sac. Is it any wonder that I occasionally get the strong urge to break out of my cocoon, if only to go for a walk around someone else's cul-de-sac? If you've just had a baby or quit your job to stay home, you may think I'm nuts. But believe me, the nesting instinct will eventually wear off.

What can you do with your kids when you don't want to spend another dime at the mall or on yet another baby gymnastics class? The first section of this chapter features parents' tips for cost-conscious weekday and weekend activities. Part two covers how to *really* get away—vacations that you and your kids will love but that won't bust your budget.

Activities That Don't Require a Wallet

- **Take a walk.** Explore all of the parks and nature preserves near your home, or spend an hour window-shopping in the nearest town with a real downtown. If your children are very young, a walk around your block may be enough to amuse them and yourself. Wear an outfit with pockets so you have someplace to put all of the pebble and pine cone souvenirs your toddler wants to take home.

- **Hang around playgrounds.** Call me cheap, but I swear I'll never buy playground equipment for our backyard. (Our house is one of the few in our area that lacks one of those elaborate wooden structures that cost $1,200 and up.) I don't see why we need a personal playground when there are plenty of clean, safe, and downright exciting public playgrounds nearby. We've got playgrounds with tires for climbing, mazes for hiding, and seesaws for riding. A trip to the playground gets us out of the house, and gives us an opportunity to socialize with other kids and adults.

- **Go out on the town.** I'm not talking about going nightclubbing with your spouse. Take advantage of the free events for families that your town or its merchants sponsor. We never miss the (very short) parade that brings Santa to our suburb on the day after Thanksgiving. Our kids also enjoy the Easter event our local Chamber of Commerce sponsors, where they have their faces painted and join an Easter egg roll. If you live in a suburb of cul-de-sacs and strip shopping centers, check your local newspapers to see what's going on in neighboring communities.

- **Transform an errand into an outing.** If life has been dull and I'm low on fruits or vegetables, I haul the kids to one of our local farm stands. One features goats and sheep to pet and a hatchery full of chicks. Another makes a Halloween maze out of haystacks and is home to a friendly old dog. I just hope that the farm stands stay in business until my kids are grown; one has already been replaced by a huge grocery store, another is now being bulldozed to make way for an upscale shopping mall. I don't think these places will exist when my children have children.

When we need to buy a birthday present for a friend, we've got a good excuse to spend an hour or so browsing in the type of toy store that lets kids play with the merchandise. Of course, this strategy works only if your kids know that *they're* not going to get a present every time they visit a toy store.

So far, all of my suggestions assume that the weather is decent. What can you do if it's raining, snowing, or five degrees below zero? Read on.

- **Turn your kids into library rats.** I take my kids every week, even if we can't fit story time or an arts and crafts program into our schedule. They still have plenty of fun. They choose books, videos, and software to borrow, put together puzzles, watch the fish swim around their tank, and greet friends.
- **Make a targeted trip to the mall.** Wander around your local mall without a game plan and you're bound to spend more than you want to. Your kids will get hungry and whine for lunch, or you'll see something you don't really need but buy because it's on sale.

Try this instead: Eat breakfast or lunch at home, and pack a snack of juice and cookies or fruit to take with you. At the mall, give your kids and yourself a low-cost treat, like a carousel ride for $1.00 apiece. Take a break on a bench to eat your snack and watch the passing crowds. My kids like to comment on what the teenagers are wearing. ("Yuck! I will never pierce my nose!" my seven-year-old frequently declares.) Browse in a store that sells stuff that your kids find amusing though they know they cannot buy. My girls love to admire the porcelain figurines of Cinderella and Elvis at the Franklin Mint store. Give your kids a couple of pennies to toss into a fountain on your way out, and you've killed a couple of hours and spent just $3.02.

- **Maintain a file of fun stuff to do on miserable days.** Amanda Pinder, who has four kids under age five, scans local newspapers for free or low-cost events like story times at bookstores. Then she enters the pertinent information on the computer in her kitchen. On days when the weather is awful and her kids can't play outside, she scrolls through her listings to see what's doing when. If you're not as computer-literate as Amanda is, keep a clipping file that you can thumb through when you can't think of anything else to do.

How can you spend some time alone with your husband without spending a lot of money? Women's magazines are always urging us to schedule "date nights" with our spouses. Only a couple of the mothers I surveyed hire baby-sitters and go out with their husbands once a week. Most folks I talked to go out on "dates" twice a month at most. My husband and I try very hard to go out alone or with another couple at least once a month. However, we schedule quiet dinners together at home after the girls are in bed just about every week. Tell your kids that you're cooking crab, calf's liver, or some other delicacy that they think is gross, and they won't even complain if you skip a meal with them.

Get Away Without Going Broke

When it comes to travel, you can save a few bucks by following the usual advice. Here it is, with a few caveats:

- **Tag along on your spouse's business trips.** Your husband's company pays for his plane ticket and for your hotel room, at least for the days when he's on duty. It's a nice deal, if you can get it. Since your spouse's employer chooses when you'll vacation, it helps if your children haven't yet started grade school. And need I mention that you'll have more fun if your spouse does business in Boston instead of Birmingham? Unfortunately, my husband's typical itinerary doesn't include tourist spots. On the rare occasion when he's sent to a luxurious resort, he's there to bond with colleagues, not his wife and kids.

    Other families are luckier, however. Lucy and Jim Breton and their four children, who range in age from eight to three, recently enjoyed a trip to the luxurious Breakers resort in Palm Beach, Florida. Jim, a banker, was there for a conference. His employer paid for the hotel room as well as airfare for Jim and Lucy. The Bretons found discount airfares for the kids, and called on an old family friend who lives near the resort to baby-sit the kids when they went out together in the evenings. They didn't even spend much feeding the kids. "I fed them from the free buffet on the concierge floor," laughs Lucy.

- **Pay for airfare with your spouse's frequent flyer miles.** It may be a pain to have a spouse who's often away on business, but there is a pay-off. Ted Andersen, a business consultant, frequently flies to Europe and Mexico to meet clients. He uses his frequent flyer miles to vacation with his wife Nina, a stay-at-home mom, and two kids. They spent last spring break on the beach in Miami.

■ **Go off season.** High-season prices at some summer re-sorts don't take effect until July 1. If your kids get out of school in late May or early June, hit the road shortly after school lets out.

Don't assume you'll save serious money, however. When I examined package tours to Walt Disney World, one "value sea-son" deal beat regular rates by just $8.40 a day. Would you pull your kids out of school for a week so you can save $42? I hope not.

Plus, rates are often lower during the off-season for a very good reason. You'll spend less to visit the Caribbean dur-ing hurricane season, for example. You should also do some research to make sure that there's enough going on during the off-season to amuse you. We took our most disappointing family vacation to a ski resort during the summer. Sure, we paid $116 less per night for our condo than we would have in December. At $180 a night, however, it still wasn't cheap. The weather was so lousy we only got to use the pool once, and there wasn't much else to do.

■ **Surf the Web for last-minute specials.** You can track down deals on airfares, hotels, rental cars, and package tours on www.travelocity.com, www.expedia.com, www.preview travel.com, www.priceline.com, and www.itn.com. The Inter-net truly is a wonderful resource, but it works best for folks who don't much care where or when they travel. What good is a last-minute deal if your husband can't get away from the office, or you can't find a kennel for your dog?

That's it for the standard advice. Now let's think out-of-the-box.

Don't just rack your brain trying to cut the cost of an expensive trip. Plan a vacation to a destination that's a bargain to begin with. My husband and I figure we'll take simple vacations while our kids still get thrills from water slides and pony rides. Splurges we'll save for later. Before we had kids, we frequently visited Europe. Now we can't imagine going back to Paris until our youngest is old enough to appreciate the difference between Big Macs and haute cuisine. Call us stingy, but we also don't see the point of spending more than $2,000 for a week at Disney World until our baby is tall enough to get on all of the rides.

- **Pick a destination you can drive to.** The savings are obvious and substantial. No airfares, airport parking fees, or taxi fares, and no car rental costs once you reach your destination. You pay only for gas and maybe tolls. Another advantage: You can take lots more stuff with you, including your kids' car seats. Yes, you have to put up with some whining from the backseat. But it's not pleasant being stuck on a runway in Kansas City while your plane awaits a part that has to be flown in from Miami, either. Our first daughter logged plenty of airtime, much of it stressful, until it once took us ten awful hours to fly from my in-laws' house in Ohio to ours in New Jersey. We figured we could drive to Ohio in the same amount of time, and we've done so ever since. If spending the better part of a vacation day cooped up in a car with small children seems a bit much for you, search for vacation spots within a five- or six-hour drive of your home.

- **Get back to nature.** Families on a budget camped when we were kids, and many still do today. A number of parents I surveyed, including Audrey and Roger Van Heest, pitch tents when they travel. Last year, the Van Heests and their three teenagers traveled to Glacier National Park from their home in the state of Washington. If you're just getting started with camping, don't spend more than you have to on gear. The Van Heests bought their first tent at a garage sale for $10 and typically pay only $5.00 to $10 a night at campgrounds that feature rest rooms and hot showers. "We don't bring a TV with us, and we keep it very simple, which is part of the joy," says Audrey. "We roast sausages on sticks and make s'mores—yum-yum!"

- **Choose no-name lodgings.** If you prefer to have a roof over your head, book a hotel, motel, or guest house that doesn't have to charge for corporate advertising and overhead. I'm not suggesting you stay at fleabag motels. I'm thinking of clean but old-fashioned places. They may have outdoor pools and playgrounds, but they don't boast indoor pools or health clubs. Such gems rarely or never advertise. Travel agents don't recommend them either, because they don't pay commissions. How do you find them then? Read as many travel articles and guidebooks as possible, and note which low-cost lodgings the authors mention repeatedly. The Mulherns once spent a week on a pig farm on Canada's Prince Edward Island that they read about in a guidebook. The two-room cottage cost them less than $400 a week.

- **Choose a rustic resort.** If you want to play tennis with your husband while your kids frolic at a day camp, a resort vacation is for you. Problem is, you'll pay $300 a night—and up—at a big-name resort that boasts lavishly decorated dining rooms and nonstop fun for your kids. You can find places that cost about a third less, however. Their facilities aren't as fancy, and your kids will have to entertain themselves for part of the day. And your husband won't have to wear a tie to dinner. (He'll be disappointed, I'm sure.)

The trick is finding a moderately priced resort that hasn't seen better days. Some places charge less than the best resorts because they haven't resurfaced their tennis courts or painted their rooms in fifteen years. Again, read as much as possible about a place before you book. You can trade information with other travelers on www.familytravelforum.com.

- **Consider a different type of theme park.** When you hear the words theme park, what comes to mind? A mouse with big ears? A CEO with a big salary? A corporation that posts big profits? To American families, Disney World is nirvana. Everyone I know who's been there says it's a spectacular experience. It's not cheap, however. Adults pay $274 for a seven-day pass to all of the amusement and water parks.

You'll pay much less to visit a theme park devoted to our nation's history. One such place is Colonial Williamsburg, the former capital of Virginia that the Rockefellers restored. Adults pay just $35 for a pass that's good for a year. Sure, Williamsburg is much smaller than Disney World. But it's no less spectacular, in its own way. You can watch a woodworker craft a highboy, march with a fife and drum corps, and pose for pictures with George and Martha instead of Mickey and Minnie. Best of all, you can do it all without waiting in line.

- **Eat smart on the road.** Get a room or suite with a kitchenette so you can eat breakfast in. Take supermarket snacks like juice boxes, crackers, pretzels, cookies, and fruit with you instead of buying overpriced morning and afternoon snacks at tourist attractions. We almost always pack lunches to eat on the way to our vacation destination instead of stopping for fast food. Since drinks at fast-food places are enormous and priced accordingly, don't order drinks for everyone. Instead, bring paper cups with you and share. If your kids are light eaters and you can usually read their appetites, don't hesitate to ask waiters if they can share a meal. You may save money even if the restaurant charges for an extra plate.
- **Vacation at Grandma's house.** Some mothers I surveyed said it was tough to find enough money to take a *real* vacation because they had to travel great distances to see their parents and in-laws at least once a year. Why not solve the problem by vacationing *while* you visit Grandma and Grandpa? You'll spend nothing on lodging and very little on food.

Yes, you can have fun even if your parents don't live in Boca Raton or Palm Springs. We spend about two thirds of our vacation time each year visiting my parents near Cleveland and my in-laws in central Ohio. Tourism is *not* a major industry in Ohio. Yet we find plenty of fun things to do there. In Cleveland, we're still working our way through all of the wonderful museums, and we've yet to dip our toes in Lake Erie. Near my husband's hometown, we've hiked a trail that he helped cut during his Boy Scout days. We've also toured an ice cream museum and an office building that looks like a gigantic picnic basket. (No kidding. The company headquartered there sells handcrafted baskets at house parties.)

Of course, vacationing with relatives isn't always cheap. It depends how far apart you live. The Normans can't drive from their home in New Jersey to Hugh's mother's place in California. Airfare for their family of four costs a small fortune. So, Hugh and Alice buy Grandma a roundtrip plane ticket instead. Now she vacations with them at their house every summer.

- **Spend part of your vacation at home.** If you simply can't afford even a week's worth of hotel bills, spend a portion of your vacation sleeping in your own beds. Make your time together a real vacation, however. Plan to go sightseeing somewhere every day. Visit the zoo, take a hike, or go to that house museum you drive by daily. Eat breakfast at home, pack a picnic lunch, and eat dinner out. Don't do any of the mundane things you usually do. Pay bills that'll come due while you're "vacationing" before you begin your break. Mow the lawn, too. Let your answering machine take all of your calls. After you tuck your kids in each night, have a glass of wine with your husband, watch a movie together, or just sit on the deck. Don't sort through the mail, read business publications, or check your e-mail. You'll have a great time, and you won't even have to unpack when your vacation's over.

Part
Three

CHAPTER 13

Create a Cash Reserve

Yes, you can live on less than two incomes and still survive life's occasional financial disasters without sinking into debt. And no, it doesn't take two incomes to send your kids to college or retire comfortably. In this chapter, the first of three on saving money, I'll explain how to stash away cash you can use if your roof leaks or your husband loses his job.

I'm not going to kid you: Most of the families I surveyed save less now than they did when both spouses worked full time. It's not that they don't save *anything*. Most still put plenty away for retirement. They also manage to save something for their kids' college costs, though usually not as much as they want to. When it comes to saving for other purposes, however, they struggle.

A few exceptional families save *more* money now than they used to. Don't be shocked. The same may be true for you in a few years *if:* You develop good shopping and saving habits *and* your husband continues to receive raises. Take the Silvestris, for instance. Regina, a former international banker, stays home with Eugenia, 4, and Peter, 2. Dennis is a financial executive for a pharmaceutical company. When Regina and Dennis had two incomes and no children, they didn't have much time to shop for bargains. They also didn't think much about investing for the future. "If you don't have a family you don't tend to think about finances much," says Regina. "It's a different story now that we have dependents." They learned about mutual funds and started investing. Regina shops for clothes when they're on sale at the end of a season. If she has to hire a repairman, she takes the time to get estimates from several. Someday you may be able to save more than ever, just like the Silvestris. Until then, saving even a little bit for a rainy day is a great feat.

   In this chapter, I'll discuss how much you should try to set aside for emergencies, and tell you where to find the money to save. I'll also tell you where to keep your cash reserve so it's easily accessible yet earns more than it would in a savings account. Finally, I'll sort out your options if something awful occurs that your emergency cache doesn't cover.

How Much Do You Really Need?

Most financial experts say you should keep three to six months' income in a place where your principal is safe, like a savings account or money-market fund. This sum shouldn't include your retirement savings or investments earmarked for your children's college costs. It also shouldn't include investments in stocks, bonds, mutual funds, or rental real estate that put your principal at risk.

I think most people could stash away three months' salary and still sleep at night. To me, sticking six months' salary in a super-safe but low-yielding savings account or money fund is like insuring yourself against a flood, not a rainy day. Check out the chart below and see if you agree:

Rainy Day Fund vs. Flood Insurance

Gross annual income	3-month cash reserve	6-month cash reserve
$30,000	$7,500	$15,000
40,000	10,000	20,000
50,000	12,500	25,000
60,000	15,000	30,000
70,000	17,500	35,000
80,000	20,000	40,000
90,000	22,500	45,000
100,000	25,000	50,000

If you're earning $40,000 a year, what's the chance that you'll ever need to shake $20,000 from your piggy bank? The odds are in your favor, if you have decent insurance. That's true even if downsizing steals your husband's job and he can't find a new one for months. You could squeak by on unemployment compensation and severance pay if you slash expenditures. Moreover, you, your husband, or both of you could take temporary jobs to earn extra income.

Don't get me wrong. You *should* try to save $20,000. Just don't keep that much cash in a low-interest savings account or money fund. Let's say you stash $20,000 in a money-market fund yielding 4%. In a year, you'll have $20,800. Better yet, put just $10,000 in a money fund and invest the rest in a stock mutual fund. If the money fund earns 4% and the stock fund returns 8%, you'll have $21,200 in a year.

Where to Find Money to Save

Here's what you need to know if you don't have at least a quarter of your annual income sitting in a safe place. If your cash cushion is already well stuffed, don't stop reading. Someday you may have to replenish your savings after tapping it. Whatever your situation, here's what to do:

- **Pay yourself first.** This idea isn't original, but it's sure effective. Why do you think that most of the families I surveyed still save like crazy for retirement? A portion of their breadwinner's paycheck goes directly to a 401(k). Says former teacher Yvonne Lowry: "My friends who have two incomes are always amazed that my husband and I save on one income, but our savings habits carried over from our two-income days. My husband never decreased the percentage of salary that he contributes to his 401(k). It's money I never see—and never miss."

Why's it so tough for families already saving 5% or 6% of their income for retirement to put away even 1% or 2% more for a rainy day? Easy. Their employers don't let them use a payroll deduction plan to save for that purpose. (You can have money deducted from your paycheck to purchase U.S. savings bonds at some companies, however. For details, see page 220.) So create your own payroll deduction plan. Here's how:

1. **Make regular investments in a money-market fund.**
   Most mutual fund companies offer automatic investment
   plans. You specify how much and how often you want
   money to flow from your bank account to your money fund.
   You could, for instance, transfer $50 from your checking ac-
   count to your money fund each month.

2. **Squirrel away a couple of bucks each day.** Most people
   withdraw a certain sum from their bank's ATM each week
   for incidentals like parking, coffee, and snacks. Withdraw
   your usual amount, but give up one daily treat, like a cup of
   designer Java or a megamuffin. Put the money you would
   have spent on that item in a jar each evening. At the end of
   each week, deposit the money you've saved in your bank. If
   a family earning $40,000 a year puts just $1.10 in a jar each
   day, they'll save a little more than 1% of their income. To
   save about 4% of their salary, they must drop $4.38 into
   their jar each day.

3. **Write a check to your money-market fund when you
   pay your other monthly bills.**

4. **Save your windfalls.** This is my favorite way to save,
   probably because it requires hardly any effort. Whenever a
   fat check lands in your mailbox, ship it directly to savings.
   Money *never* magically appears in *your* mailbox you say?
   Come now, what about your tax refund or that $100 check
   you got from your parents for your birthday?

5. **Save what you used to spend on an old debt.** Let's say
   you write the last $350 check for your car loan in July.
   Come August, write a check for $350 to your money-market
   account. Then do it again, month after month. Lucy and
   Jim Breton save their former *mortgage payment* every
   month. Lucy and Jim bought Lucy's grandmother's house in

1997. They used an inheritance from Lucy's father to make a 75% down payment, then borrowed the rest from Jim's dad. They finished paying off the loan in 1999 and have since saved their old mortgage payment.

6. **Live beneath your increasing means.** When sales manager Mike Schuler gets a raise or earns a bigger bonus than he did the previous year, he and his wife Holly invest the extra cash. Says Holly, a former financial analyst who's home with the couple's two children: "As our savings grow, we have peace of mind that we'll have something to fall back on in case something should happen to Mike's job."

7. **If your family's breadwinner receives stock options, save them for important stuff.** Watch them grow and be glad you don't have to skimp as much as others do to build an emergency fund. Says Susan Heinsohn, a stay-at-home mother of two whose husband Clark develops software for Microsoft: "Because we've been blessed with stock options, we're always saving for the future without really trying." The Heinsohns have used Clark's options to pay off their college loans and make down payments on houses. Clark and Susan wisely save on their own too, since options can decline in value. Clark invests his 401(k) contributions in a variety of mutual funds. For more about how to handle stock options, see Chapter 16.

Where to Keep Your Cash

There's no one answer because we're talking about three types of cash: your ready cash, your liquid hoard, and your cash investment stash. Here's where to put all three types of savings:

- **Keep your ready cash in a checking account.** This is the money you know you're going to spend on groceries, utility bills, and your mortgage during a typical month. It's money you can get your hands on immediately if you need to.

Don't worry about earning interest on the cash you use to pay your monthly bills. Why keep a lot of cash in a checking account that yields only 1.50% or so? Bundled bank accounts that combine a checking account and a money fund paid only about a half of a percentage point more when I wrote this chapter. Just keep enough money in your checking account to avoid the pesky fees that banks charge if you slip below a minimum balance or bounce a check. Take the rest of your cash reserve and invest it elsewhere.

Granted, that's easier said than done, since most banks nowadays nibble you to death with fees if you don't keep $2,500 or more in their money fund. Examine your bank statements for the last six months or so to see if your bank is nickel-and-diming you. If it's not, congratulations. However, if you've got more money in your account than you need to pay your ordinary bills, call your bank and ask how low your balance can go before you incur fees. Then shift your excess cash to a money-market fund run by a mutual fund company or to the income-producing investments that I describe below.

If your bank is gouging you, shop for a new one. Or shift your business to a thrift or credit union. (Thrifts are savings banks and savings and loan associations that compete with commercial banks for consumers' deposits.) To see what banks and thrifts in your area have to offer, log on to www.bank rate.com, and click on "Checking/ATM." You can compare

minimum initial deposits as well as minimum balances required to avoid fees. You can also check out service charges,
fees for bounced checks, and the availability of online banking.
Of course, you'll also have to make some phone calls to make
sure that the deals are still available and that you qualify for
them.

A credit union may be your best bet, if you can get into one.
Credit unions charge lower fees than banks, and typically pay
nearly one and a half percentage points more on money-
market accounts. To hunt for a credit union you can join,
check www.bankrate.com. Alternatively, you can call or write
to the Credit Union National Association (800-358-5710;
P.O. Box 431, Madison, WI 53701).

- **Keep your liquid hoard in a money-market mutual
  fund.** This is cash you want to be able to get your hands on
  within a day or two. It's the money you use for big but expected expenses, like your annual life insurance premium.
  It's also what you tap to pay major bills that crop up unex-
  pectedly, like auto repairs.

Why bother moving to a mutual fund company when you
can get a money-market account at your bank? Yield. When I
wrote this chapter, you could earn 2.10% from a bank money-
market account vs. 4.30% from a money fund, both before
taxes.

Still, plenty of people keep their liquid hoard in the bank.
The two main reasons why: Inertia and fear.

The first reason needs little explanation. You open a checking account at a bank, and sign up for a money-market account
at the same time. You keep shoveling cash into the money fund

even though it pays only pennies in interest because you're too busy to shop for a sweeter deal.

The second reason takes lots of explaining. The Federal Deposit Insurance Corporation insures cash you stash in a bank money-market account but not in a money-market mutual fund. The FDIC insures your deposits of up to $100,000 per bank. So, if you want to deposit more than $100,000, split your hoard among two or more banks. However, do you really need a life vest to wade in the shallow end of a swimming pool? Money-market funds invest in high-quality, short-term securities like certificates of deposit, high-grade corporate bonds, and U.S. Treasuries. No investor in a money fund has ever lost money.

If that's not enough to calm your nerves, consider *government* money funds. These funds buy only direct obligations of the U.S. government, like Treasury bills and securities issued by federal agencies. Of course, you give up some yield for extra safety. When you take into account that thirty-nine states exempt such funds from their income taxes, however, you may actually earn more with such a fund than with a taxable money fund. Don't get too excited, however. You still have to pay taxes to Uncle Sam on your earnings.

Don't confuse *government* money funds with *tax-exempt* money funds. You don't pay *federal* income tax on earnings from tax-exempt funds. Tax-exempt money funds typically yield at least one and a half percentage points less than taxable money funds.

Investors in fifteen states (Arizona, California, Connecticut, Florida, Maryland, Massachusetts, Michigan, Minnesota, New Jersey, New York, North Carolina, Ohio, Pennsylvania, Texas, and Virginia) can choose funds that escape federal, state, and local income taxes. Which is best for you, a taxable or a tax-free fund? You'll have to do some math, which I explained on pages 55–56.

Once you decide between taxable and tax-exempt, which money fund should you choose? After all, there are more than 1,300 of them. A good place to start shopping is IBC's Money Fund Report's Web site, www.ibcdata.com. Also follow these steps:

1. **Zero in on a mutual fund family you want to join.** Let's say you save so religiously that your cash reserve becomes bloated. Then it's time to start investing in stock and bond funds. It would be convenient to simply phone your money fund and transfer some of your dough to one of its sister funds.

2. **Don't just pick the fund with the highest yield.** Many money funds that rise to the top of lists of high-yielding funds published in newspapers and financial magazines do so because they've temporarily waived management fees. Once fees kick back in, their yield will look average, or worse.

3. **Look for low fees instead.** Annual expense ratios of .60% to .70% of a fund's assets are typical. Read fund prospectuses to find one that charges less, like Vanguard's Prime Money Market Fund, which was recently a low .33%.

4. **Check for minimum investments you can live with.** Most money funds want you to invest at least $1,000 to start, but some have lower initial minimums. Find out how big your subsequent deposits must be too.

5. **Ask if the fund offers an automatic investment plan.**

If it does, you can have money whisked from your bank checking account to the fund each month.

6. **Check the check writing rules.** Some money funds let you write as many checks as you want each month; others set limits. You can't really substitute a money fund for a bank checking account, however, because money funds typically force you to write checks for a minimum amount, often $500.

7. **Ask if you can redeem shares by telephone.** This is an extremely convenient feature. Let's say it's Thursday and your son's preschool tuition is due the following Monday. You call your money fund today and wire cash to your bank checking account. The cash is in your account on Friday, when you can write a check to the preschool. While you're at it, however, check with the money fund and your bank to find out if they charge a fee for this service.

■ **Keep your cash investment stash in certificates of deposit, U.S. Treasury securities, or U.S. savings bonds.** This is the portion of your cash reserve that you can tie up for a few months or even a few years in order to earn more interest than liquid money funds pay. Take a closer look at these super-safe investments:

1. **Certificates of deposit** feature FDIC insurance. Banks, savings and loan associations, and credit unions issue CDs. You invest a specific sum—typically at least $500—and your money earns interest for a specified period. When the CD matures, you get your investment back plus interest. You can buy CDs that mature in three or six months, or in one, two,

two and half, three, four, five, or seven years. The longer the term, the higher the interest rate.

Some people shy away from CDs because they worry that they'll need their money before maturity. It's unlikely that you will, if you invest the portion of your cash reserve earmarked for emergencies or a long-term goal, like a new car. And even if you do, you'll lose only interest; your principal is safe. Also, you could purchase CDs with staggered maturities. That way you'll always have some ready cash at hand.

Check financial magazines or your local newspaper's business section for lists of high-yielding CDs, or log on to www.bankrate.com. That Web site lets you compare rates, yields, minimum deposits, and the way interest compounds. You thought all banks used the same method to compound interest? Nope, and that fact complicates shopping for CDs. Some banks pay simple interest, which means they don't pay interest on the interest your CD earns. Others compound interest daily. That's the best deal, if all else is equal. To make sure you're comparing apples to apples, look at annual percentage yields. That number tells you the percentage increase you'll earn if you hold a CD until maturity. Alternatively, ask bankers one simple question: How much money will I get back when my CD matures?

2. U.S. Treasury securities pay interest that's exempt from state and local income taxes. The federal government issues and backs Treasury bills, notes, and bonds that mature in thirteen weeks to thirty years. The longer you tie up your money, the higher the interest rate you get. You need at least $1,000 to buy Treasuries, which sell at auction. To invest more, you must bid in multiples of $1,000.

Don't stash your cash reserve in Treasury bonds, which mature in more than ten years. Instead, consider Treasury bills or notes. T-bills mature in one year or less. Treasury notes mature in more than one year but in no more than 10 years.

You can purchase T-bills or notes from the government without paying a commission. Place your order on the Internet (www.treasurydirect.gov), over the phone (800-943-6864), or at the Federal Reserve Bank in your area. If you're willing to pay a commission, you can also buy through banks and brokerage houses.

T-bills and notes work differently. Let's say you want to invest $1,000 in a ninety-one-day Treasury bill. If the bill fetches $980 at auction, you immediately get back $20. When your bill matures, you get $1,000 back, so you've earned $20 on a $980 investment. In other words, the interest you earn is the difference between your purchase price and the amount you receive when your bill matures.

Treasury notes, on the other hand, work like Treasury bonds. You buy them at a stated interest rate and collect interest payments twice a year.

To maximize the income you earn from Treasuries or CDs, use an investment strategy called *laddering*. Here's how it works: You invest $1,000 in a five-year Treasury note this year, then buy another one next year and so on for five years. When the first note you bought matures, reinvest the proceeds for another five years by buying a new note. That way you'll be able to spend some cash each year if you need to. If you can afford to leave your cash reserve alone, however, you can keep reinvesting in five-year notes so you earn interest at a higher rate than you would with a one-year Treasury bill.

3. U.S. savings bonds are tailor-made for small investors. Savings bonds sell for 50% off their face value, and you can purchase the least expensive one for only $25. They're also easy to buy. Many ordinary banks and savings and loan associations sell them. You can buy them on line at www.treasury direct.gov. You or your husband may even be able to buy them through a payroll deduction plan at work. Call your employer's payroll department to find out.

To me, the downside of savings bonds is their complexity. Indeed, if you hate to keep financial records, save up a larger sum and invest in a CD or Treasury security instead. Here are the basics, but you can find out more—lots more—by logging on to www.treasurydirect.gov:

The Series EE bonds that you can buy today don't have a guaranteed rate of return. Instead, they earn 90% of the average yield on five-year Treasury securities for the preceding six months. (Yes, small investors earn less than folks who can scrape up $1,000 to buy a five-year Treasury note.) Series EE bonds increase in value each month. Twice a year, on May 1 and November 1, the government announces the interest rate that they'll earn for the following six months. When I wrote this chapter, Series EE bonds were paying 5.19%. For current rates, call 800-US-BONDS or log on to www.treasurydirect. gov. Your earnings compound twice a year, but you don't receive any income until you redeem your bond.

Series EE bonds reach their face value seventeen years after their issue dates. You can then redeem them or leave them alone. If you cash in your chips, you get back the bond's face amount plus the interest you've earned. You pay federal income tax on your earnings, but dodge state and local taxes.

If you do nothing, your bond enters one or more *extension*

periods. It stops earning interest only when it reaches its *final maturity,* thirty years after its issue. You can then redeem your bond, or exchange it for a Series HH bond.

What if you need your money back before your children start having children? You can get your hands on it without penalty after five years. If you redeem a savings bond before it's five years old, however, you surrender the last three months' worth of interest it would have earned. For example, if you cash in a bond after holding it twenty-two months, you'll get back your original investment plus nineteen months' worth of interest payments.

Some families can get a tax break by buying savings bonds for their children's college funds. For details, see Chapter 15.

Where to Turn When Disaster Depletes Your Cash Reserve

It happens. You're slowly building up a rainy day fund when the rains come pouring down. You've accumulated some cash, but not enough to cover the damages. I'm not talking about spending more money than you should on a discretionary purchase, like a Caribbean cruise or a new kitchen. I'm talking about unavoidable financial disasters. Your aging mother suddenly needs your help, so you fly cross-country four times in six months. Your dentist tells your husband that he needs a ton of periodontal work, and you don't have dental insurance. How can you pay off surprise debts without spending lots of money on interest? If you don't have any compassionate relatives willing to give you an interest-free loan, consider these options:

- **Negotiate with your creditor.** Your husband's dentist may let you pay him in installments, at a nominal rate of interest. On the other hand, he may want all of his money right away, and remind you that he takes Visa and MasterCard. It doesn't hurt to ask, however.
- **Borrow against cash value life insurance.** If you or your husband has this type of coverage, call your insurer to find out how much you can borrow from your policy's investment account.

> **Typical cost:** You pay an interest rate pegged to the return on long-term corporate bonds. When I wrote this chapter, the rate was around 7%. If you have a policy issued before 1980, however, you'll pay just 5% or 6%.
>
> **Pros:** It's tough to find lower interest rates.
>
> **Cons:** If you die before you repay your loan, your insurer will subtract your unpaid balance from the death benefit your survivors receive. Also, if your policy pays dividends, the real cost of borrowing is higher than the stated interest rate. Ask your insurance agent to figure out your true cost.

- **Crack open your 401(k).** Most employers let you borrow as much as half of your vested account balance up to $50,000.

> **Typical cost:** The prime rate plus one percentage point.
>
> **Pros:** You can usually get your hands on the cash within days, and your credit history has no bearing on the interest rate you pay.
>
> **Cons:** You're in trouble if you lose or quit your job because

most employers give borrowers just a few months to repay their loans. If you can't, and you're under 59½, you'll likely owe income tax plus a 10% early withdrawal penalty on your outstanding balance. There are other negatives too. See Chapter 14 for details.

- **Get a home equity loan.** You can typically borrow up to 80% of your home's value, minus your mortgage balance. Although you can take fifteen or twenty years to repay a HEL, you'll save interest expenses if you pay it off in five years. A good place to start shopping for a low-rate HEL is www.bankrate.com.

  Typical cost: The prime rate plus one to three percentage points. When I wrote this chapter, you could get a HEL for 8.73%, a bargain compared to getting a 14.44% personal loan from a bank.

  Pros: In most cases, you can take a tax deduction for interest you pay on a HEL up to $100,000.

  Cons: You can lose your home if you default on your loan. Also, you may have to pay hundreds or even thousands of dollars in points, appraisal fees, and other charges to get a HEL.

- **Borrow against your investment portfolio.** If you own stocks, bonds, or mutual fund shares, you can use them as collateral for a margin loan from your stockbroker.

  Typical cost: Rates hover around the prime, and often vary with the amount you borrow.

  Pros: The price is right.

Cons: This strategy can unravel if interest rates rise or the securities that serve as your collateral plunge in value. If that happens, you'll get a margin call—a warning to put up more stocks, bonds, or mutual fund shares as collateral, or else. If you don't cough up additional securities, your broker will sell some of your shares to repay a portion of your loan balance.

As you can see, borrowing to supplement a rainy day fund isn't the worst thing that could happen. Still, I hope that the heaviest rain you'll ever have to deal with is merely drizzle.

CHAPTER 14

Retire on Less Than Two Incomes

C an you really?

Nowadays we hear and read that even highly paid two-career couples aren't saving enough for retirement. If that's true, what about us? Will we have to mooch off our kids when we're geezers? Are we sacrificing our future financial security if we quit or cut back on work today?

Don't let the Chicken Littles get to you.

If you learn to live comfortably on less than two incomes today, you'll be in better shape when you retire than two-income couples who always feel pinched.

Contrary to popular belief, our parents and grandparents were never guaranteed a cushy retirement. If your parents or grandparents are enjoying their golden years, chances are they did *something* right. But I'll bet they didn't do anything Herculean, like eat rice and beans six days a week so they could save 25% of their income for old age.

You, too, will have to make an effort to secure your retirement. But your odds of success are better than ever. Why am I optimistic when so many others are gloomy? Simply because much of what you hear about retirement today is just plain hooey. Let's look at some fashionable notions:

- **You'll need a million bucks to retire.** To grasp just how absurd this notion is, ask yourself how many of our parents and grandparents have that kind of money. Very few indeed, yet we believe that today's retirees are living it up. Truth is, households headed by folks sixty-five and older have a median net worth of $20,642, excluding their home equity. The figure shoots up when you factor in home values, but only to $86,324. Most of today's retirees didn't get rich during their working lives, and aren't rich now. The same will be true for us, so don't lose sleep worrying about stashing away a cool million.

- **But we're saving even less than our parents did.** Wrong. Back in 1993, the Congressional Budget Office published a very interesting study. The study said that baby boomers weren't blowing all of their money on BMWs and trips to the Bahamas. To the contrary, middle-aged boomers were nearly twice as wealthy as their parents had been at the same age. (Yes, the researchers did take inflation into account.)

- **Okay, but we won't get Social Security.** In poll after poll, baby boomers say they'll never collect those monthly checks. Do the people who answer these polls vote? *I* wouldn't vote for a politician who promised to dismantle the safety net I've financed since I earned my first paycheck. Would you? Even if you can imagine the politically powerfully baby boom generation permitting Congress to kill Social Security, look at the bright side: You'll get to keep—and invest—the nearly 8% of your salary that Uncle Sam now skims off the top.

- **Well, we won't get private pensions.** Alarmists imply that today's retirees all receive pensions while none of us will. (A pension pays you a set amount per month after you retire. Your employer typically funds your pension.) Truth is, most retirees today *don't* get pensions. Moreover, the lucky ones who do collect, on average, less than $750 a month. As was true in the past, you're more likely to get a pension if you work for a big company. Unlike in the past, most large employers today also offer 401(k) retirement savings plans. *You* must fund a 401(k). Most companies match employees' contributions, however. Smaller employers are more likely to offer only 401(k) plans.

- **You'll need 70% to 80% of your old salary to retire comfortably.** Well, maybe—if you plan to call it quits tomorrow. But probably not if you're twenty to thirty-five years away from retirement. If my husband and I suddenly turned sixty-five tomorrow, we could live quite nicely on about 40% of our current income. How could we swing it? Easy. By age sixty-five, we'll have paid off our mortgage and dropped our life insurance policies. Our kids will be much too old for preschool or summer camp. (In fact, they'll be finished with college.) Moreover, we won't have to pay Social Security taxes anymore, or save for retirement.

So, put all of those retirement planning myths out of your mind. Don't you believe that you won't be able to retire in style unless you and your spouse spend the next thirty years working for big corporations with gold-plated retirement plans. Few retirees ever had it so easy. Employers' fortunes wax and wane, and when they wane, generous retirement plans are often scaled back. It's legal as long as workers get to keep benefits they've already earned. Things change. So, don't be afraid to make the changes *you* want to. Go ahead and quit or cut back on work. A comfortable retirement is still within your grasp. You've just got to make the most of the savings plans available to you *whenever* they're available to you. Here's how to wring the most from Social Security, employer-sponsored retirement plans, and your own savings.

Get as Much as You Can From Uncle Sam

You can't live well on Social Security alone. Yet, few us can afford to live without it, especially if we're not big earners. Thankfully, the less you earn, the more help you'll get from Social Security. If you make $20,000 a year and retire today at sixty-five, you'll collect 56% of your old income. If you earn $40,000, you'll get 42%. And if you make $60,000, you'll get 27%. You stop paying the 6.2% Social Security portion of FICA tax once you earn more than a maximum amount that rises with inflation. The cut off is $80,400 in 2001. Of course, you also stop earning credits that will increase your Social Security benefit. (By the way, you pay the 1.45% Medicare portion of FICA tax on all income you earn.)

To get the most out of Social Security, married couples must work as a team. That's especially true if you stop working or work only part time for a number of years. If you earn less than your spouse does, you've got two options. You can collect the benefit you've earned. Alternatively, you can get a benefit based on your husband's work history, whichever is greater.

To get your own check, you must work and earn enough to qualify for Social Security credits. Most people need to earn forty credits over their lifetime to collect benefits. You can earn up to four credits in each year that you work. In 2001, for example, you get one credit for each $830 that you earn. That amount rises with the average wage. Actuaries at the Social Security Administration calculate your benefit based on your average earnings that you paid Social Security tax on over thirty-five years. If you work more than thirty-five years, the SSA counts the thirty-five years in which you earned the most money. If you work fewer than thirty-five years, years in which you didn't work will pull down your average annual earnings *and* your benefit.

You can find out how much you'll get from Social Security by checking your Social Security Statement. Your statement, which the SSA prepares, shows how much you've earned over your career. It also gives you the estimated monthly benefit you'll receive at retirement. (Remember, your benefit will increase with the cost of living. Most private pensions do not.) The SSA has sent statements each year to all workers twenty-five and older since October of 1999. If you haven't gotten your free copy, call the agency toll-free (800-772-1213) and ask for Form SSA-7004. Or, log onto the SSA's Web site (www.ssa.gov).

To prepare its estimate, the SSA assumes you'll continue to work until retirement and earn about the same amount—adjusted for inflation—that you did over the last two years. Of course, that means the SSA's estimate will be incorrect if you're working now but plan to quit your job or switch to part-time work soon. Fortunately, the agency will redo its estimate using assumptions you provide. It'll take at least four weeks to get an answer, however. If you're in a hurry, you can do it yourself by downloading a computer file from the SSA's Web site.

How You Can Boost Your Social Security Benefits

- **Draw benefits on your spouse's work record instead of your own.** Our Social Security system dates from the days when men were supposed to be breadwinners and women were supposed to be housewives. Consequently, it's quite kind to stay-at-home spouses and those who earn much less than their partners. You can collect the bigger of two benefits: the one you earned, or half of your retired spouse's benefit if you retire at 65. (You get less if you're between sixty-two and sixty-five when your partner calls it quits.) Let's say your husband will get $1,000 a month while you stand to collect just $250. If you take the benefit you earned, you'll together receive $1,250 a month. You can collect $1,500 a month, however, if you choose to take half of your husband's benefit instead.

- **Consider working part time instead of leaving the workforce.** If you're a big earner, your own Social Security benefit will probably be greater than a portion of your husband's benefit. So it makes sense to do all you can to increase your benefit. By working part time while your children are young instead of not working at all, you can augment your average earnings and boost your benefit.

- **Start saving to make up for the lower Social Security benefits you'll receive.** It's not hard to do, thanks to the miracle of compound interest. Let's say you and your husband are on track to receive $1,000 a month at sixty-five. You take some years off starting at thirty, however, so your monthly benefit shrinks to $750. (On average, women's Social Security checks are 25% smaller than men's because they earn less and interrupt their careers more often.) You can more than make up the $250 a month you sacrificed to stay home with your kids, however. Here's how: Starting at age thirty, invest $2,000 a year in a tax-deferred IRA. If your account earns 6% a year, you'll have $236,242 at sixty-five. Even if you and your husband live to a hundred, you'll be able to draw roughly $563 a month from your IRA before taxes. (To learn more about IRAs, see the last section of this chapter.)

What Your Spouse Can Do

- **Take a second job or start a part-time business.** Does your husband earn less than the maximum amount subject to Social Security tax? (The cut off is $80,400 in 2001.) If so, he should consider moonlighting. Any additional income he earns up to that limit will boost his Social Security benefit. Hold on a minute before you hand him the want ads, however. If his salary is close to the cutoff, any extra income he earns will have a small effect on his future benefit. That's because the system rewards workers with low incomes more than it rewards those with high salaries.

Make the Most of Employer-Sponsored Plans

Building a retirement fund is much easier if your employers kick in some of the cash. How much you'll get from your bosses depends on who you work for, how many years you hold a job, exactly when you quit a job, and how well you manage your investments.

How much control you have over your retirement plans at work depends on the types of plans that your employers offer. Companies have two basic types. There are *defined benefit* plans, which most people call pensions. And there are *defined contribution* plans like 401(k)s. Let's tackle old-fashioned pensions first.

How Pensions Work and Why You May Get at Least One

A pension plan promises to pay you a fixed, or defined, monthly benefit for life. The size of your pension usually depends on your final salary, the number of years you worked for your employer, and your age at retirement. If you retire early, you'll typically get a smaller pension than had you worked until age sixty-five.

If you or your husband ever work for a company that has a pension plan, your odds of collecting benefits are fairly good. That's because you can earn the right to collect benefits at most companies after only five to seven years of work. The more years you sweat, of course, the bigger the benefit you'll get. If you quit a job years before retirement, you probably won't get your pension right away. Say you've earned a $500-a-month pension when you leave your job at thirty-five. You'll collect that amount when you reach age sixty-five.

If your company has a pension plan, you probably don't have to contribute money to it. Employers contribute the cash and make sure it grows. All you need to do is show up for work.

Employers use various formulas to figure out how big your pension will be. Many multiply your years of service by 1% to 2% of your average annual pay over your last three to five years of work. Say you worked twenty years and earned an average of $55,000 during your final three years of service. You retire at sixty-five. If your employer multiplies twenty by 1% of $55,000, you'll get $11,000 a year. That works out to 20% of your average earnings over your last three years of work. If you work for the same company for just five years, you'll collect only $2,750 a year, or 5% of your average earnings over your last three years of work.

How You Can Boost Your Pension Benefits

- **If you haven't already quit your job, try to stick around until you've earned a pension.** At most companies, you win the right to benefits, or become vested, after five years of service. Some plans vest you gradually, meaning you earn the right to a small portion of your pension after three years. The percentage you're entitled to then gradually increases until it hits 100% after seven years.

You accumulate credits toward a pension while you're on paid leave or vacation, but usually not while you're on unpaid maternity or parental leave.

Don't try to figure out your vesting date on your own. You

may miscalculate because employers have different ways of determining which years count toward a pension. In general, you'll get credit for a year if you work a specified number of hours during that year. To be sure, talk to a pension expert in your company's benefits department. Also, ask them for the following documents so you can double-check their answer:

1. **Your pension plan's document.** It's tough to make sense of this tome unless you're an actuary or a pension lawyer. Don't worry; you'll find the important stuff—explained in English—in . . .

2. **Your pension's summary plan description, or SPD.** By law, your employer had to give you one within ninety days after you joined your pension plan. Don't tear your house apart trying to find it. Ask for a new one, since the law also requires employers to update their SPDs if they've changed their pension plans significantly.

3. **Your annual benefits statement.** This is the easiest document to understand. It tells you if you've earned a pension, and if so, how large a monthly benefit you'll receive at retirement age if you stop working now. Some employers automatically distribute these statements annually. If your firm doesn't, you have the legal right to ask for a copy once a year. You'll get a similar statement after you quit your job if you've earned a pension.

- **If you decide to work part time, consider putting in enough hours to qualify for pension coverage.** You generally must work at least 1,000 hours a year, or about 20 hours a week, to be covered. Check with your employer to be sure.

- **Go back to your old job at the right time.** If you quit your job but hope to return to it when your child starts grade school, watch your calendar carefully. Here's why: If you aren't vested in your old employer's pension plan, leaving for five or more years can cause you to lose all the credits you've earned toward a pension. However, you won't lose a year in which you left because of pregnancy or to care for a new-born or adopted child. So if your employer is amenable, you could take a year-long maternity leave—plus up to five more years off—before returning to work without losing any pre-viously earned pension credits.

- **If you decide to return to work when your kids (and you) are older, try to snag a job that comes with a generous pension plan.** Retiring from a company with a rich pension plan is usually better than working for the same firm early in your career. Why? Because many employ-ers sweeten pension payments for early retirees to shoo them out the door. Consequently, your monthly benefit rises precipitously once you qualify for early retirement. At most companies, you can get out at fifty-five if you have at least ten years of service.

What Your Spouse Can Do

- **Job hop judiciously.** The grass always looks greener on the other side, but it's got to be as verdant as AstroTurf to make jumping worthwhile. Let's assume that two workers earn equal salaries over their careers. One stays at the same company for forty years, while the other changes jobs four times. The stable employee will get almost twice as big a pension as the job hopper. Job hoppers get hurt because pension credits accumulate more rapidly as you get closer to retirement. So urge your husband to consider if the extra income he'll earn at a new company is enough to make up for pension benefits he'll lose if he leaves his job shortly before he begins piling up pension credits.

The Retirement Plan That You Command

Unless you own your own business, you and your husband will probably have 401(k)s at some point. These plans are the most popular type of defined contribution retirement savings plan. Unlike pensions, defined contribution plans don't pay you a fixed amount each month for life. The amount of money you end up with depends on three things. First, how much you and your employer contribute to your account. Second, how well you manage your money. It's your job to make the money grow by putting it in investment funds offered by your employer. Finally, the more years your money grows, the better off you'll be.

Also unlike pensions, defined contribution plans are portable; meaning you can take your account balance with you when you leave a job. If you reinvest your savings in a new employer's savings plan or an IRA, your stash will grow tax-deferred until you tap it at retirement.

One of the best things about a 401(k) is that your contributions come out of your *pretax* income. You can contribute a portion of your pay to your 401(k) up to a limit set by your employer. However, you can't contribute more than $10,500 on a pretax basis each year. That amount rises with the cost of living. (For more about the tax benefits of stashing cash in a

401(k), see Chapter 4.) Another rule applies if you're highly paid compared to your coworkers. The law prohibits employers from having tax-deferred retirement plans that favor highly paid employees. Consequently, your employer may place a lower limit on the portion of your pay you may contribute to your plan.

Your employer will probably help you to fund your 401(k). Nine out of ten employers with 401(k)s do. They typically kick in fifty cents for every dollar you invest up to 6% of your salary.

In this section, I'll talk mostly about 401(k) plans. For one thing, 401(k)s are very popular. For another, you have a lot of control over your 401(k). There are other types of defined contribution plans, of course. Public schools, churches, and other tax-exempt organizations offer 403(b) plans. As with a 401(k), you contribute pretax dollars to your account. However, you may not be able to choose your own investments.

Companies with no more than 100 employees can set up SIMPLE plans. (SIMPLE is short for Savings Incentive Match Plan for Employees.) You can save up to $6,000 a year in a SIMPLE, an amount that increases with inflation. Your employer also helps fill your account.

How You Can Boost Your 401(k) Balance

- **If you haven't already quit your job, try to stick around until you've earned the right to your employer's contributions.** You can take all of the contributions you made to your account—plus their earnings—with you whenever you leave your job. Some employers also let you take their contributions to your account, plus their earnings. But many won't let you touch that money until you've participated in your 401(k) for a certain amount of time. Some employers fully vest you after five years of service; others practice gradual vesting, starting after your third year. Find out when your magic day arrives by calling your employee benefits department. Days you spend on unpaid maternity leave might not count toward vesting requirements.

■ **Don't blow your 401(k) when you quit your job.** Please, please, please, find the money elsewhere to make a down payment on a house, buy an SUV, or take your kids to Disney World. You'll not only lose the nest egg you worked long and hard for, you'll also get slapped with income tax on your withdrawal, plus a 10% tax penalty—assuming you're under fifty-five. Instead, keep your savings growing tax-deferred by performing one of two tricks:

1. Roll over. You can roll over your 401(k) balance into an IRA (but not a Roth IRA) tax-free. The mechanics are simple, but you can mess up if you don't know the rules. First, open an IRA at a brokerage house or mutual fund company. What if you already have an IRA? Open a new one. Here's why: If you keep your 401(k) rollover separate from your other investments, you may someday be able to roll it over into a new employer's 401(k). Next, ask your former employer to make the check for your account balance payable to your new IRA, not to you.

If the check's made out to you, your old boss must withhold 20% of it for taxes. Then you've got sixty days to deposit the check in an IRA. If you want to roll over the 20% that your former employer withheld, you'll have to come up with the equivalent amount of money yourself and deposit it in your IRA. Finally, you'll have to settle with the IRS when you file your tax return.

If you're planning to quit your full-time job to take a part-time position at a new company, here's another tidbit. Your new employer may let you transfer your 401(k) balance to its plan tax-free. Ask.

2. Sit. You can choose to keep your 401(k) at your old company if it's worth more than $5,000. Why not, if you're pleased with your old plan's investment choices and performance? If things change, you can roll your balance over into an IRA in the future.

What Your Spouse Can Do

- **Make the maximum contribution.** If your husband can't swing the max, he should contribute at least as large a percentage of his income as his employer will match. If he doesn't, he's passing up extra pay.

If he's not saving a cent in his 401(k), he should start socking away 2% or even 1% of his pay as soon as his plan's administrator will take the cash. After a few weeks, neither of you will miss the money much, since it disappears into the land of compound interest before you ever see it. Whenever your husband gets a raise, increase his contribution by a percentage point. For many families living on less than two incomes, 401(k)s have been a godsend because they make saving easy. "We now save more than ever because my husband's employer established a 401(k)," says Tara Silber.

■ **Manage his stash like a pro.** It's hard to go wrong over the long haul if you heed three basic rules:

1. **Go for growth.** Buy stocks. The more years until retirement, the more risk you can take. Most people do buy stocks for retirement. Stock funds or employers' shares account for about three quarters of all 401(k) assets.

2. **Diversify.** You reduce investment risk by spreading your bets around. Stocks periodically tumble, so you should balance that risk by also holding fixed-income investments like bonds. Also, diversify within broad categories. For example, don't put all of the money you want to invest in stocks in a mutual fund that buys the shares of large companies. Instead, you could put 50% of your hoard in it, 25% in a fund that buys small companies' stocks, and 25% in a foreign stock fund.

    Two more things to bear in mind: First, don't load up on your employer's stock with your own 401(k) contributions. Some employers that match employees' contributions do it with their own shares, which they may not allow you to sell until you're 55. If your company's stock plunges in value, you'll be sorry you had so many eggs in one basket.

    Second, if you have investments outside of your 401(k), don't put the same picks in both portfolios. Let's say that you like to buy risky, high-tech stocks for your own portfolio, for example. To reduce your overall risk, you might invest your 401(k) money in a less volatile fund that buys big companies' stocks.

3. **Don't try to outsmart the market.** Chasing the hottest funds is a loser's game. By the time you hear that health care stocks or some other sector is sizzling, prices will have

climbed and you'll buy near the top of the market. Another common mistake is selling a fund immediately after it falls in value. Do that and you'll lock in your losses. Hang on and buy more shares while their price is depressed and you'll prosper when the sector recovers.

- **Keep his 401(k) intact when he leaves his job.** Go back to page 238 if you need a refresher on how to preserve your retirement fund.

- **Don't break into his account until he retires.** Most employers let you make hardship withdrawals from your 401(k). You can use the money you withdraw to buy a home, pay certain medical expenses, and cope with a few other emergencies. However, you'll have to pay income tax on your withdrawal. In most cases, you'll also pay a 10% early withdrawal penalty if you're under age 59½. (The IRS waives the 10% penalty if you withdraw money to pay medical bills that exceed 7½% of your adjusted gross income.) Plus, your employer may prohibit you from investing in your 401(k) for a year after you make a hardship withdrawal. So, don't even consider cracking open your retirement piggy bank unless you've tried to raise cash other ways.

- **Don't even *borrow* from his 401(k).** It's awfully tempting to borrow from yourself so you can remodel your ancient kitchen, furnish your family room, or take a cruise. Plus, it seems everyone is doing it; nearly a quarter of 401(k) participants have outstanding loans. The terms seem enticing—at first glance. Most employers let you borrow as much as 50% of your vested account balance up to $50,000. You typically pay the prime rate plus one percentage point. There are three big problems with borrowing retirement savings, however:

1. **You can't take a tax deduction for the interest you pay.** As a result, you may be better off with a tax-deductible home equity loan.
2. **Your savings may shrink.** If your 401(k) is earning 10% and you take out an 8% loan, you'll lose 2%. Stop contributing to your account while you repay your loan and you'll do even more damage.
3. **You may have to repay your loan in a hurry.** If your husband quits or loses his job, his former employer may give him only sixty days to pay off his loan. If he can't cough up the cash and he's under 59½, he'll likely owe income tax on his outstanding balance plus a 10% early withdrawal penalty.

The Best Ways to Save on Your Own

Not all of us can depend on pensions and 401(k) plans. Many of us must also save for retirement on our own. An online cottage industry has sprung up to help you figure out *exactly* how much you should save. I tried out more than a dozen online retirement calculators. I found all but one to be tedious, misleading, or both. Most calculators ask you to answer questions that you simply can't answer. For instance, one calculator asks you how Congress will change Social Security. What if your guesses are way off the mark? The retirement saving goal that the calculator tells you to shoot for will be too. Other calculators assume that no one will get a pension or Social Security.

I did find one calculator that spits out realistic answers—hurrah!—and is a snap to use. It's called the Ballpark Estimate. It's quick and easy to use because it makes some assumptions for you. It figures you'll earn 3% after inflation on your investments. It also assumes you'll need 70% of your current gross income when you retire. Yes, those assumptions are conservative and may prove wrong. But any guesses you might make could also bomb. So why spend a lot of time speculating? To fill out a Ballpark Estimate online, visit the American Savings Education Council's Web site (www.asec.org). Or, you can call the Securities and Exchange Commission toll-free (800-732-0330) for free copies by mail. To answer all of the questions, you and your husband will need the last annual benefits statements you got from your current and previous employers. You'll also find it helpful to have filled out the worksheet in Chapter 3.

You'll probably feel relieved after you fill out a copy of the Ballpark Estimate. Let's say you stay home full time while your husband earns $40,000 a year. You're both thirty-five and want to retire in thirty years. Your husband's company offers a 401(k) but not a pension plan. So far, he has $21,000 in his 401(k) plan. (I didn't pick that number out of the air. That's the median value of retirement accounts held by families headed by thirty-five- to forty-four-year-olds.) When you retire, you'll both collect Social Security. (Yes, you will!) If you assume you'll need 70% of your husband's current salary to live comfortably in retirement, the Ballpark Estimate says you'll need to accumulate $113,600 in additional savings. You can reach that sum if your husband puts $2,272 a year in his 401(k). That works out to about 5½% of his current salary. If your husband's employer kicks in 50 cents for every dollar he contributes to his 401(k), he needs to save $1,515 a year, or a bit more than 3½% of his salary.

If you need to save more than you can in a 401(k) or don't have such a plan, where should you stash extra cash? It depends if you're self-employed or saving to supplement employer-sponsored retirement plans. Here's the scoop:

How to Supplement Employer-Sponsored Retirement Plans

Nowadays there are enough different types of IRAs to make your head spin. It helps to remember two basic things:

1. **You can contribute up to $2,000 a year to IRAs, whether you have one or several. The same goes for your spouse.**
2. **There are two main types of IRAs, traditional accounts and Roths.**

In a traditional IRA, you don't pay taxes on your contributions or their earnings until you withdraw them. You may even be able to take a tax deduction for contributions you make to your account. If you take money out of your account before age 59½, you'll generally pay income tax plus a 10% early withdrawal penalty. There are some exceptions to that rule, however. You can withdraw up to $10,000 to buy your first home without paying the 10% penalty. (The same is true if you help buy a first home for your kids, grandchildren, or ancestors. Yes, you could buy a first house for your in-laws or grandparents.) You can also dodge the 10% penalty if you withdraw money from your account to pay medical bills that exceed 7½% of your adjusted gross income. Finally, you can avoid the 10%

penalty on withdrawals used to pay higher education expenses for yourself, your spouse, your kids, and your grandchildren.

Money you put in a Roth IRA is never tax-deductible, though it does grow tax-free. All withdrawals from Roths are also tax-free—if you make them after 59½ and after you've held your account at least five years. Plus, you can withdraw up to $10,000 from your account tax-free no matter how old you are if you meet two conditions. You must have held your account at least five years. In addition, you must use the money to purchase a first home for yourself, your kids, grand-children, or ancestors. If you take money out of your account before age 59½ to cover educational or medical costs, you'll pay income tax on the earnings you withdraw. However, you will not have to pay a 10% early withdrawal penalty. Roths have a couple of other features that may matter to you when you're older. After you reach 70½, you can keep contributing to a Roth but not to a traditional IRA. Also, you don't have to make withdrawals from a Roth during your lifetime. You must start to take withdrawals from a traditional IRA at age 70½, however.

Got all that? Then check out these saving strategies:

- **Fund a traditional tax-deductible IRA.** You and your husband can do this if you don't have retirement plans at work. You qualify even if you have retirement plans at work if your adjusted gross income falls below certain limits. For the details, see Chapter 4.
- **Open a tax-deductible spousal IRA.** This account's per-fect for parents who've quit or cut back on work but earn too much to fund a traditional tax-deductible IRA. (Again, see Chapter 4 to find out if you can fund a traditional tax-deductible IRA.) A spousal IRA may work for you if you

earn less than $2,000 a year and don't have an employer-sponsored retirement plan while your spouse does. The two of you can contribute a total of $4,000 to IRAs. You can allocate your combined contribution between your two accounts in any proportion as long as you don't put more than $2,000 in one account. Naturally, the IRS limits the deductibility of your contribution based on your AGI. For all of the details, turn back to Chapter 4.

- **Fund a Roth.** Do this if you earn too much to contribute to a traditional tax-deductible IRA. You can put up to $2,000 a year in a Roth if you're married and have an AGI below $150,000. The amount you may contribute phases out if your AGI falls between $150,000 and $160,000.

What You Can Do If You're Self-Employed

When it's up to just you and Uncle Sam to provide for retirement, putting only $2,000 a year in an IRA won't do. You should set up and fund a tax-deferred savings plan that permits larger contributions. If you or your husband employ others, talk to an accountant about starting a retirement plan for your firm. Corporate retirement plans are beyond the scope of this book. If you or your spouse run a one-person shop, however, consider these options:

- **Set up a SEP or a Keogh.** What's a SEP? The letters stand for Simplified Employee Pension. As for Keogh plans, there are different types. If you're starting a business, the best for you is a profit-sharing defined contribution Keogh. That's also true if your earnings fluctuate from year to year.

You can make big contributions during boom years, and small contributions or none at all during bad years. SEPs work much like this type of Keogh, but require less paperwork.

You can open a SEP or a Keogh at a bank, brokerage house, or mutual fund. The rules for withdrawals before 59½ are the same as for traditional IRAs. The big difference is how much more you can contribute and deduct each year. You can contribute the lesser of two amounts: $22,168 or 13.04% of your net self-employment income up to $170,000. (The $170,000 limit will rise with inflation.) What's net self-employment income? It's the money you earned from your business after expenses, minus your SEP or Keogh contribution and half of the self-employment tax you paid. Don't go nuts trying to do the math yourself. Use tax preparation software, or get help from an accountant.

You can establish or contribute to a SEP up to the due date of your tax return, including extensions, and still take a tax deduction for the previous year. By contrast, you must open a Keogh before the end of the tax year for which you want to take a deduction. You have until you file your tax return to contribute to your account, however.

- **Move up to another type of Keogh when you start making big bucks.** The Keogh family also includes money-purchase and defined benefit plans. You can contribute much more money to them than to a profit-sharing Keogh. However, you have to sock away a set percentage of your earnings each year. Neither of these plans is a do-it-yourself project. You'll need the assistance of an accountant *and* an actuary. Of course, if you're making enough money to save a bundle of it, paying their fees won't be a problem.

Keep one thing in mind, whether you're self-employed, work for someone else, or don't work at all right now. If you save something for retirement year after year, you'll be all right in the end.

CHAPTER 15

Save for Your
Kids' College Costs

R ead any article on the cost of sending your kids to college and you're bound to get depressed. If the cost of college climbs 6% a year, it'll cost you a whopping $281,361 to send a baby born this year to a private college for a BA. To have that pot of gold in place eighteen years from now, you'll have to start saving $888.57 a month *right now* and earn 4% on your investments. Can't swing that kind of savings on two incomes, let alone one? You've got plenty of company. In fact, lots of families spend less than $888.57 a month on their mortgage payment!

No wonder almost every parent I surveyed feels they're saving too little for college. Amanda Pinder, who's at home with four kids under age five, jokes that her husband, an ex-Marine, has come up with a way to educate their brood for free. "Neil is hoping for four Annapolis appointments," she says. Annapolis, of course, is the home of the U.S. Naval Academy, which doesn't charge tuition.

My advice: Chill out. If you still have money left to save for college after salting away enough for your own retirement, fine. But don't fret if you can't even come close to socking away the huge sums that some financial experts insist you must save. Here's why I think we should all relax:

- **You'll pay some college costs with money you earn while your kids are in college.** Let's say college costs do rise 6% a year. You'll pay about $70,000 a year to send a baby born this year to a private college. That number seems astonishing if you're earning, say, $50,000 a year today. But don't forget that your income will rise along with college costs. If your earnings also increase 6% a year, you'll be making $142,716.96 a year when junior is ready for college. Surely, you could pay a third, or perhaps even half, of that $70,000 tuition bill out of current income.

I know what you're thinking. What if our income doesn't rise nearly as fast as the cost of college? It may not; but then again, tuition may not increase 6% a year for eighteen years straight, either. The projected cost of college I calculated for the year 2018 seems awfully precise, down to the last dollar. Change a few assumptions, however, and you'll get a number that's nowhere near $281,361. Let's say, for example, that college costs rise 4% a year instead of 6%, and that you earn 8% a year on your investments instead of 4%. (That return isn't far-fetched if you invest in stocks.) You'd need to scrape up $193,841 and could do it by saving $401.09 a month.

- **Your kids may not choose expensive private colleges.** Eight in ten students attend state schools. Today it costs an average $10,458 a year to send a kid to a public college in his home state vs. $22,533 for a private school.

■ **You may not have to pay a college's full "sticker price."** Colleges give discounts, which they politely call financial aid. In general, the pricier the school, the more likely it is to distribute aid. Most private colleges can't enroll enough students whose families can pay full price, so they discount. A handful of prestigious colleges could fill their freshman classes with rich kids. But top colleges prefer to enroll a diverse mix of bright students, so they also discount.

Don't get *too* excited by the prospect of financial aid, however. Loans now comprise 60% of financial aid awards. Moreover, you or your child will have to repay loans—with interest. So, save as much as you can for college. The more you save now, the less you'll have to pay out-of-pocket or borrow later.

In this chapter, I'll tell you how to set a realistic savings goal. I'll cover the pros and cons of using various types of investment plans to accumulate cash for college. I'll also discuss your options if it turns out you didn't save enough.

Let's Get Real

Okay, you know you can't afford to put away nearly $900 a month to send just *one* of your kids to college. You also know, in your heart, that if you promise to save whatever you can, you'll put away little or nothing. You need a goal, something to shoot for.

To come up with a goal you can reasonably hope to achieve, you've got to give up two widely held notions. First, forget about saving enough to cover every cent of your kids' college costs. After all, how many people pay cash for their houses? Aim to save about *half* the projected cost of college. Be happy if you can put away *one third* of the cost.

Second, give up the idea that you can grow a substantial college stash without taking any investment risk. You *must* invest some of your college savings in stocks. Indeed, you should put *most* of your money in stocks while your children are young, and there's time to recover if the market takes a tumble. If you've got the gumption to invest in stocks, you can reasonably expect your savings to grow 10% a year or so, given the historical performance of the stock market.

That said, let's set some savings goals. On the high end, shoot for saving one half or one third of the cost of sending a newborn to a private college. On the low side, aim to save one half or one third of the cost of sending a newborn to a state university. In all cases, assume you'll earn 8% a year on your investments. Also, figure that the cost of college rises 6% a year.

To raise half the cost of sending a newborn to a private college, save $291 a month. To cover one third of the cost, save $192 a month.

To raise half the cost of sending a newborn to a public college, save $135 a month. To cover one third of the cost, save $89 a month.

Granted, it's tough to save even $89 a month. So, don't place the entire burden on yourself. If your kids get checks for birthdays and holidays from their grandparents, deposit them in their college funds.

If you want to plug in your own assumptions, log on to www.finaid.org, a Web site created by college planning expert Mark Kantrowitz. You can use its calculators to project college costs and calculate how much you should save.

Where to Invest the Money You Save

When it comes to college savings, *everyone* wants your money. Your state government wants you to contribute to its college savings plan. Your stockbroker or mutual fund company wants you to open an Education IRA or a custodial account. Your insurance agent wants to sell you a life insurance policy that'll cover college costs. My advice: Read the fine print before you invest in anything. Don't hand over your hard-earned dollars if you don't understand how a savings plan is supposed to work. And watch out for sales commissions and fees that can take a big bite out of your investment earnings. Here's a look at the major types of savings plans you can choose:

- **State plans.** All 50 states and the District of Columbia have them. You can get the details of any plan by logging on to www.collegesavings.org. The College Savings Plans Network sponsors this site, which connects you to your state's Web site. To reach the appropriate state agency by phone, call 877-277-6496 toll-free.

There are two basic types of state college savings plans:

1. Prepaid tuition plans let you pay college costs in advance, at today's prices.

The details: You make lump sum or installment payments in return for course credits. When your child starts college, she can use the credits at any school that participates in the plan. Most plans include only in-state public colleges, but a few feature in-state private schools as well.

Your contributions grow tax-deferred until your child starts college. At that time, your kid pays taxes on the gains at her rate, which will presumably be lower than yours. Some states exempt your gains from state income taxes.

What happens if your child skips college, or goes to a school that's not part of the prepaid plan? You don't lose the money you've invested. Rules vary by state, but you generally get back your principal, plus a modest amount of interest.

Be warned that you can't contribute to a prepaid tuition plan *and* an Education IRA for the same child in the same year. Of course, you may not be able to contribute to an Education IRA anyway, if your income exceeds legal limits. (For more about Education IRAs, read on.)

The upside: You won't have a worry in the world if you invest enough to prepay tuition in full at a college your child eventually attends.

The downside: If your child doesn't attend a college that's part of the prepaid plan you invested in, you'll probably wish you'd put your savings elsewhere. That's because prepaid plans usually invest conservatively. If you had invested more aggressively on your own, odds are you would have earned bigger returns.

The bottom line: Prepaid plans are perfect if you're sure that your kids will want to attend a participating college. Trouble is, there's no way to know when they're babies where they'll eventually go to school—and that's when you should start saving for college. Consequently, most parents are better off with a more flexible college savings plan.

2. College savings or 529 plans differ from prepaid tuition plans in two major ways. First, 529 plans (named for a section of the tax code) don't guarantee that your contributions will earn a specific rate of return. Second, you can use the tax-deferred college fund you build up in a 529 plan at any school, public or private.

The details: You usually contribute to the plan sponsored by your home state. Plans in many states are also open to nonresidents. The state invests all of the contributions it collects, or hires an investment adviser to do the job.

You don't pay tax on your investment gains until your baby starts college. At that time, your kid pays taxes on gains at her tax rate. Many states exempt gains from state income tax if you're a resident and your child attends an in-state public college. Some states even let you deduct contributions to their 529 plans on your state income tax return. Again, you can get the details on any plan by calling the College Savings Plan Network or checking its Web site.

If your kid decides to skip college, you can transfer her 529 plan to a sibling. If you withdraw money from the plan for other purposes, however, you must pay a penalty of at least 10% on your earnings.

As with prepaid tuition plans, you can't contribute to a 529 plan and an Education IRA in the same year.

The upside: You'll enjoy tax breaks.

The downside: You give up control over your investments. Consequently, you've got to study a savings plan before you invest in it to make sure that its investment philosophy jibes with your own. New Jersey's initial plan invested no more than 40% of its assets in stocks. That was too conservative for my taste, so my family hasn't yet used it. Some states invest aggressively when your child is young, then gradually shift to more conservative choices as your child gets older.

You've also got to watch out for expenses. Some states charge modest fees to invest your money, but others hit you hard. For example, Iowa charges only 29 cents for every $100 you invest, while Indiana charges 50 cents a year for every $100 you have in your account, plus mutual fund management fees.

The bottom line: Use a 529 plan if you agree with its investment philosophy and can stomach its fees.

■ **Education IRAs.** These accounts escape federal income tax if you use them to pay college bills. You can contribute up to $500 a year for a child under age eighteen. Your right to fund an Education IRA begins to phase out once your adjusted gross income hits $150,000; it ends when your AGI reaches $160,000. You can get around those limits, however, by giving your kids cash to fund their own accounts.

You can't take tax deductions for your contributions, but they do grow tax-free. Your child won't pay tax on withdrawals if he uses them by age thirty to pay higher education expenses. If he doesn't attend college or doesn't use all of the money in his account, you can transfer the remaining cash to a brother or sister. If your kid withdraws money from an Education IRA and spends it on something other than college costs, however, he'll have to pay tax on his gains, plus a 10% penalty.

You can't contribute to an Education IRA and a state 529 or prepaid tuition plan for the same child in a single year. If you do, you'll have to pay a 6% excise tax on your Education IRA contribution.

Education IRAs carry other restrictions as well. Remember the HOPE scholarships and lifetime learning credits I covered in Chapter 4? Well, you can't claim either of them in the same year that you take a tax-free withdrawal from an Education IRA for a child. Of course, who knows if you'll qualify to take one of those credits years from now? My advice: Don't let this potential problem stop you from funding an Education IRA. If you determine that taking one of the tax credits is a better deal when your kid is in college, you can always pay taxes on the money you withdraw from his Education IRA. You'll still have enjoyed years of tax-deferred investment growth.

The upside: You can save for college tax-free.

The downside: You can't save much. If you invest $500 annually in an Education IRA that earns 8%, you'll have $20,223.13 after eighteen years. That's better than nothing, of course, but it'll cover less than a year at a public college if costs rise 6% a year.

High fees are another problem. Some brokerage houses and mutual funds impose annual maintenance fees that take a big bite out of your account's earnings. If a $500

Education IRA earns 8%, or $40 a year, for example, a $15 fee will devour nearly 38% of its return.

The bottom line: If you can open an Education IRA without paying fat fees, there's no harm in doing so.

- **IRAs.** There are lots of different types of IRAs, but they all have one thing in common. If you withdraw money from an IRA before age 59½ and use the cash for higher education expenses, you won't have to pay a 10% early withdrawal penalty. (By the way, this rule applies whether your kids, you, your spouse, or your grandchildren incur those educational expenses.) You must pay income tax on withdrawals, however.

  I covered tax-deductible IRAs in Chapter 4. For information on nondeductible IRAs, including Roths, see Chapter 14. If you're an older parent, take a close look at Roths. Withdrawals from Roths are tax-free if you make them after age 59½ and after you've held your account at least five years.

  The upside: Your savings grow tax-deferred. Plus, you control your investments.

  The downside: Raiding your retirement savings to pay for college isn't a good idea. You can't get a scholarship or a loan to pay for your retirement.

  The bottom line: If you're saving enough for retirement, consider using an IRA to save for college. How much should you save for retirement? See Chapter 14.

- **U.S. savings bonds.** If you're looking for a super-safe, tax-deferred investment for college costs, consider Series EE savings bonds. You buy bonds for 50% of their face value, and the least expensive ones cost only $25. You can also use Series I bonds, which sell for face value. (For more details about how savings bonds work, turn back to Chapter 13.)

You don't have to pay taxes on the interest your bonds earn until you redeem them. At that time, you pay federal tax, but not state or local levies. However, your earnings may also escape at least some *federal* tax under certain circumstances. Here's the deal. You redeem bonds and use the money to pay tuition and fees in the same year. The tax-free proceeds you collect can't exceed the tuition and fees you pay, however. In addition, you can't use tax-free money to pay for room and board or books. Alternatively, you can redeem bonds and put the money in a state savings plan or an Education IRA for your child. (That's assuming you qualify to fund an Education IRA, of course.) You must also meet an income test in the year in which you cash in your bonds. The income limits increase with inflation. In 1999, savings bond interest is fully tax-free for married couples filing jointly with adjusted gross incomes below $79,650. It's partly tax-free if your AGI falls between $79,650 and $109,649. If your AGI is $109,650 or more, forget about tax breaks. By the way, you must count the interest you earned on the savings bonds you redeemed when you tote up your income.

Got all that? Well, there are more rules to remember—lots more. Only bonds issued after 1989 qualify for tax breaks. You must hold the bonds in your name, not your child's name. Moreover, you must have been at least twenty-four years old when you bought the bonds or received them as gifts. Finally, you can't use tax-free proceeds from savings bonds to cover the same college costs that you used to claim a HOPE scholarship or lifetime learning tax credit for the same child.

> **The upside:** Everyone can buy bonds to save for college on a tax-deferred basis. If you meet the income test, you get away tax-free.
>
> **The downside:** The modest returns you'll earn probably won't keep pace with college costs. And given the paltry pay off, there are way too many restrictions to keep straight.
>
> **The bottom line:** If you're investing for the long haul, don't put all, or even most, of your money in savings bonds. Invest in stocks for higher returns. When your child is four or five years away from college, however, savings bonds can serve as a safe haven, and provide tax benefits too.

- **Life insurance.** You can build up cash values tax-deferred in a universal life policy. If you want to shoot for higher returns, get a variable universal policy whose cash value you can invest in stocks. When your child enrolls in college, you can withdraw an amount equal to the premiums you've paid tax-free. You can also borrow against the policy's cash value.

> **The upside:** This is yet another tax-deferred way to save for college.
>
> **The downside:** The returns you'll earn won't wow you. How come? Mainly because some of the premiums you pay cover the agent's commission and pay for insurance coverage.
>
> **The bottom line:** Don't buy life insurance to pay for

college. You can accumulate more cash with other investments.

- **Mutual funds.** You call the investment shots, but you don't get the nifty tax benefits that other college saving vehicles promise. If you're going to take this route, invest most of your money in stocks when your child is young. When she's four or five years away from college, you can gradually shift assets and invest new savings in less risky investments like U.S. savings bonds or certificates of deposit.

Always buy no-load funds, so you don't have to pay sales commissions. Also, reduce your risk by investing in three to five funds with different goals.

The upside: You make your own investment decisions. Moreover, your child can use the money at any college.

The downside: You make your own investment decisions. Yes, this can be bad news if you're not comfortable investing money. Get too aggressive, and you risk blowing your kids' college savings. Invest too wimpishly, and you'll rack up meager returns.

In addition, your savings won't grow tax-deferred, or better still, tax-free. Depending upon how much money your savings earn, you or your child will owe taxes each year. To minimize your tax bill, you must make yet another decision: Should you save in your child's name or in your own?

If you invest in your name, you pay taxes on your gains at your tax rate. If you invest in your child's name, however, she pays tax at her presumably lower rate—to a point.

Here's how it works. You open a custodial account for your child at a brokerage house or mutual fund family under the Uniform Gifts to Minors Act or the Uniform Transfers to Minors Act. (Whether you open an UGMA or an UTMA depends upon which state you live in.) You or your husband serve as custodian of the account. That means you make deposits and investment decisions.

If your kid is under age fourteen, the first $700 of her investment income escapes taxation in 1999. The next $700 is taxed at her rate. (Those limits increase annually with inflation.) *Your* top marginal tax rate applies to your kid's unearned income above $1,400.

The "kiddie tax" goes away once your offspring turns fourteen, however. Then she pays taxes on all of her unearned income above $700 at her rate.

The "kiddie tax" is a pain, but investing in your kid's name instead of your own still saves on taxes. Besides, you can minimize its impact by choosing investments that don't generate a lot of income. (For some suggestions, flip back to Chapter 4.)

So, what's not to like about custodial accounts? Mainly, they can hurt your chances of getting financial aid. Here's why: When college financial aid officers figure out how much of their sticker price you can afford to cough up, they expect students to contribute up to 25% of their own assets each year to the cause. Parents, by contrast, must deplete only 3% to 5% of their assets annually.

I don't see this as a major problem, but some people do. In the first place, the requirement that you spend college savings on college costs doesn't strike me as unfair. After all, you were saving this money for college, right? So why get upset if you have to spend the money on college bills?

Second, it's not a given that you'll even qualify for financial aid ten, fifteen or eighteen years from now. Or, you may qualify for aid only in the form of loans. Why give up a certain tax break today to gamble on what may or may not happen in the future?

There's also a middle path you can take. Start saving for college in a custodial account. When the account's fat enough to throw off $1,400 in annual income, switch to saving in your own name. When your child turns fourteen, you'll have a better idea if you're likely to qualify for financial aid. If you think you might qualify, continue saving in your name. If you don't think you'll get aid, go back to saving in your child's name.

There's one other problem with custodial accounts. Gifts you make to them are irrevocable, meaning you can't take them back. When your precious one turns eighteen or twenty-one, depending upon your state's regulations, she's legally entitled to the assets in her account. Moreover, she can spend them on anything she wants, like a convertible instead of college. You don't have this potential problem if you save for college in your name. The money is yours. Of course, parents sometimes give into temptation too. Your husband could suffer a mid-life crisis and use your kids' college cash to buy a sports car. Or, you could decide you really need an in-ground pool because . . . well, because your sister-in-law has one. My point is that saving for something that's important to your family must be a team effort. If you don't trust your children or your spouse to stick to the plan, why even make one?

The bottom line: Investing in mutual funds is your best hope for big gains unless your state's savings plan invests younger kids' contributions aggressively. If that's the case, the state plan may have the edge because of its tax advantages.

Is your head spinning yet? There are so many college saving strategies to choose from nowadays that it can paralyze you. Don't drive yourself nuts trying to figure out which strategy will give you the biggest payoff years from now. There's no way to know for sure. Also, you don't have to limit yourself to one strategy. For example, my husband and I have opened custodial accounts for our daughters. We've also funded Roth IRAs earmarked for college. We haven't invested in our state's savings plan yet because its initial investment mix was too conservative. But we may put money in it now that it invests more aggressively in stocks.

The other thing to keep in mind when you're wondering how you'll ever save for college on less than two incomes is this: You probably won't stay home or work only part time forever. Take the Van Heest family. Roger Van Heest is a Presbyterian minister. His wife Audrey stayed home with their three children, who are now nineteen, seventeen, and thirteen, until the youngest was five. At that time, she felt she had to go back to work part time because they had relocated to an area where housing is expensive. Roger had an office in their home, so he was home for the kids when Audrey couldn't be.

Audrey worked part time for a church and a school district for nearly seven years, then switched to a full-time schedule at school. Last year she went back to college to earn a teaching certificate. "If I teach full time, my salary will pay for our seventeen-year-old daughter to attend a private college," Audrey explains. "Since our youngest is thirteen, I'll still be on her schedule. In fact, she has many after-school activities that make her day longer than mine!"

Your children can also help reduce college costs, as the Van Heests' kids have done. Their nineteen-year-old son surprised them by enlisting in the Navy. By the time his four-year hitch is up, he'll have about $30,000 for college in the Navy's scholarship fund. The Van Heests' seventeen-year-old daughter took college courses while she was in high school at the state government's expense. She also took Advanced Placement classes to earn college credits. She'll save thousands of dollars because she won't have to take many introductory-level courses in college.

So you see, praying for financial aid isn't the only option even for a family like the Van Heests, who lived on one income for a dozen years.

Part
Four

CHAPTER 16

Give Up Paid
Work Gracefully

Now that you've read fifteen chapters on managing money, I hope you're confident that you and your spouse can raise your family on less than two incomes. I take up a completely different topic in the final chapters of this book. All three are about managing the *career* that you've chosen to put on hold for a while. That's right, you can't stop thinking about what you used to do for money, not even when you're up to your eyeballs in unpaid work.

When you're home most or all of the time, you can easily get so caught up in domestic duties that you neglect your own need to keep learning. You can't get a baby-sitter in the middle of the day, so you turn down lunch invitations from your former coworkers. You have to help your son with his homework, so you don't have time to even read the newspaper anymore. Listen to Abby Zolnoski, a former city planner who quit her job after the birth of her daughter eight years ago. Abby stayed home until her daughter Ariel was in second grade. She didn't keep in touch with old colleagues, read trade publications, or maintain the computer skills that were so essential in her old job. She didn't even do volunteer work that might enhance her résumé. Not keeping up her professional skills "was a major mistake" says Abby. Meanwhile, her husband Ron, a bill collector, came to expect her to handle all of the housework. Abby wanted to go back to work at least part time while Ariel was in school all day. She was nervous about looking for a job, however. Then she got lucky. Her sister-in-law told her of a part-time position in the research department of the medical center where she worked. Abby got the job and enjoys her new line of work. But the transition at home hasn't been quite as smooth. "Slipping into traditional sex roles while I was at home was a major problem," Abby explains. "Getting back out is *very* difficult for me."

The moral of Abby's story is that it's much easier to return to work if you stay prepared for that possibility. Maintain your skills, keep up with changes in your field, and get some help around the house from your spouse. (You should also expect your kids to pitch in once they're old enough.) What's the point if you think you never want to work for pay again? Just this: You never know what the future holds. Someday you may need— or just want—a paycheck again. You may think you never want another job *now,* but who knows how you'll feel once your babies are in high school or go off to college?

The first thing you need to do to prepare for eventually returning to work is to quit your current job with class. That's what this chapter is about, in part. It also covers how to get all of the benefits you deserve before you resign, like disability pay after you give birth. If you've already quit your job, skip ahead to the final section of this chapter, which discusses the fine art of staying home happily.

Chapter 17 is about how to switch from full-time to part-time work right now. Read it if you feel you can't live comfortably on only one income, or if you just don't want to drop out of the work world completely. My final chapter is about how to go back to a full-time job whenever you're ready.

How to Quit Without Making Anyone Mad at You

Much as you may want to, you shouldn't burst into your boss's office and shout "Take this job and shove it!" What does it matter if you offend someone? Word will get around your office and everyone will remember you as a jerk. Meet up with your old boss or a former colleague five, ten, or even fifteen years from now when you're looking to go back to work, and don't be surprised if he or she doesn't hire you.

Think it's unlikely that you'll ever cross paths with your old coworkers again? Ha! Remember Eileen Mulhern, whom we first met in Chapter 6? When the first of her two children was born nearly ten years ago, Eileen quit her time-consuming job as an editor at a news service to freelance part time from home. With her second child about to enter third grade, she decided to look for a full-time job. I'll tell you more about how she managed to snag a plum position at a company that designs Web sites in Chapter 18. Let me just tell you now that Eileen got the job, in part, because the design director at her new company had also once worked for the wire service that she'd left. He vouched for the quality of her work to his boss, who hired her.

Debbie Edelberg actually ended up working for her old boss

again. After she had her first baby nine years ago, Debbie quit her job as an assistant controller for a chain of clothing stores to stay home full time. (Her husband David works in advertising.) After just a few months, Debbie's old boss called. He had moved to a new company and asked her if she'd like to work for him just a half day a week. She did for about a year, then quit when her husband took a job in a new city. She's now home full time with her nine-year-old daughter and four-year-old son.

So just how do you say good-bye with style?

- **Ideally, give more than two weeks' notice.** If you were the boss, wouldn't you appreciate having more than two weeks to choose your successor or figure out how to split your workload among other employees? Of course, giving more than two weeks' notice makes the most sense if you're working when you announce your resignation. If you're on maternity leave, you presumably discussed who would take over your duties with your boss before you had your baby.

  If you really can't stand to work a minute more than eighty hours, give two weeks' notice but offer to stick around a week or two longer if your boss really wants you to. With any luck, he won't ask you to.

- **Don't explain why you're quitting in great detail.** Just tell your boss the unembellished truth: You want to spend more time with your kids. Don't tell her that the day care centers you visited all smelled bad. Don't describe the fights your family gets into most evenings when dinner still isn't on the table at 7 P.M. and your second grader hasn't finished his homework. Why spare your soon-to-be former boss these gory details of the two-income lifestyle? Bosses hate to hear underlings complain. That's why corporations put up suggestion boxes—*not complaint boxes*—in their cafeterias. And as I said earlier, you never know when you'll meet your old boss again.

- **Don't blame your employer for your decision.** Why not, if it's the company's insistence that you work sixty hours a week that's driven you to resign? Again, my advice is purely pragmatic. The corporate culture isn't going to change just because you leave in disgust, and that's true even if you're a star performer. The executives at the top got there partly because they log long hours without complaint. They'll find someone to replace you, perhaps someone young, childless, and willing to work punishing hours—as you once were.

Okay, so what do you have to lose by telling your boss off? Your reputation as a gracious person. Criticizing your boss's commitment to the company is just plain tactless. Just imagine how you'd feel if she told you that you were doing the wrong thing by putting family before work. Rosemary O'Brien, whom we first met in Chapter 10, remembers being "scolded" by her principal when she quit her part-time job as a school speech pathologist. Rosemary had switched to part-time work after the birth of her first child. She decided to stay home full time when her second baby was about a year old. "My building principal told me I was unwise to abandon a part-time job which provided excellent pay and *full* benefits," Rosemary recalls. "He also tried to convince me that my students needed me and I could not be replaced. I disagreed. If anyone needed me, it was my own children. Speech pathologists are a dime a dozen, but devoted mothers are priceless!" Rosemary and her supervisor thought differently. You and your boss probably do too. You know it, and so does she. So leave it unsaid and don't create any hard feelings.

- **Pass the torch.** Tie up loose ends, finish up all of the projects that you can before you leave, and willingly train the person hired to replace you, if he or she arrives before you leave. Also, offer to answer any questions by telephone that crop up after you leave.

The Smart Way to Cash in Your Chips

Sometimes it pays to stick with your job as long as you can, although you're 99.9% sure you want to quit. Here are five reasons why that may be the case:

1. **You need a little more time on the payroll to qualify for pension benefits.**
2. **You'd like to keep your group health insurance as long as possible because your spouse isn't covered.**
3. **You hold stock options, but don't yet have the right to cash in on them.**
4. **You'd like to earn as much money as possible before you quit your job.**
5. **Your employer wants to cut staff.** Rather than firing people, he plans to coax workers to resign with severance offers. You could volunteer to resign and walk away with thousands of dollars to fatten your savings account.

So, if you're not planning your exit to coincide with the birth or adoption of a child, go ahead and work as long as it takes you to earn pension benefits or vest your stock options. If you're planning to stop working after you give birth to a child or adopt one, however, there are other benefits you should look into before you pick a quit date. You must find out about your employer's short-term disability and maternity leave policies. Then you'll know how much paid and unpaid leave you can take before you officially resign. Here's what to do:

- **Find out if you can take short-term disability leave.** Some employers call this benefit sick leave. Whatever you call it, it's insurance that pays you if you can't work because of an illness or injury. About two thirds of large employers offer this coverage. Under federal law, companies with fifteen or more workers must not discriminate against pregnant workers. So, if an employer offers disability leave, it must do so for all workers, including those who are pregnant. To take disability leave, your doctor must say that you can't work due to pregnancy or childbirth. Generally, he or she will have to write a letter to your employer.

Benefits vary, so get the details about your plan from your employer. Some firms provide plans that meet requirements mandated by state law. (Some states have no such regulations, however.) Other employers offer more than what they are required to. My old employer was very generous. I got my full salary and benefits for twelve weeks after I gave birth to my kids. If I hadn't had cesarean sections, I probably would have gotten eight weeks off with pay. By contrast, Sally Corrado's employer pays workers on short-term disability leave two thirds of their regular salary up to a maximum amount. Sally, an accountant, got the maximum, which didn't amount to two thirds of her salary. She had to stop working about a month before her due date. One major reason: She no longer fit behind the steering wheel of her compact car, which she needed to drive to work.

- **Find out if you can take unpaid leave.** Why bother if you plan to quit your job? Here are three good reasons:

1. **You may get to keep group health and disability coverage while you're on leave.**
2. **You may get to keep your group life insurance and other benefits while you're on leave.**
3. **You can take time to try out what it's like to live on less than two incomes before you quit your job.**

You may or may not get unpaid leave, despite the much-ballyhooed federal Family and Medical Leave Act. In general, the FMLA requires companies that employ fifty or more workers within a seventy-five-mile radius to give up to twelve weeks of unpaid leave during any twelve months to employees for the birth or adoption of a child. (The law does the same for employees who want time off to deal with a serious medical problem, or to care for a child, spouse, or parent with a serious health condition. It also protects you if you decide to return to work after your leave is over. In most cases, the law guarantees that you'll get the same or an equivalent job when you return.) To be eligible for benefits, you must have worked for your firm at least twelve months and for at least 1,250 hours during the previous twelve months. (That works out to roughly twenty-four hours a week.) Under most circumstances, you have to give your employer thirty days' notice that you plan to take a leave. Given all of the fine print, it's no wonder that the FMLA doesn't do a thing for about half of all American working women.

On the bright side, however, you do get to keep group health and disability coverage under the FMLA. That's a very important benefit if your spouse doesn't get health insurance at work and you need time to shop for an individual policy. Your employer may also let you keep your group life insurance or other benefits while you're on leave, although the law doesn't require him to do so.

In most cases, your employer can require you to substitute any paid leave you have coming for a portion of the time off you're entitled to under the FMLA. Paid leave might include personal, sick, or vacation days. In addition, you don't build up credits toward pension benefits while you're on leave.

If the FMLA applies in your case, your company can't do less for you than the law requires. It could do more, however. I was lucky to work for a corporation that gave up to twelve *months* of maternity leave. (Most of it was unpaid, of course. And yes, I took it all.)

If the FMLA doesn't apply in your case, you may still have some rights under state law. At least fifteen states and the District of Columbia have their own family leave laws. If your firm falls under the purview of the FMLA as well as a state law, it must comply with whichever law's provisions are most beneficial to you.

■ **Make the most of your stock options.** About 8% of people employed by private companies now have stock options. If you're one of the lucky ones, please remember to cash your options in before they expire. When you quit a job, you typically have sixty to ninety days to do so. Get the details from your employer.

An option gives you the right to buy your employer's stock at a predetermined price after a certain date. When that magic day arrives, you hold vested options. It typically takes three to five years for options to vest. When you buy your company's stock at the preset price, you exercise your options. Of course, exercising your options is only worth doing if your company's stock is trading *above* the preset price that you can buy it at. If the stock's current price is below that preset price, your options are "under water," or worthless.

Let's happily assume that you quit your job and take with you options that are worth something. You can exercise them immediately or wait until the last possible moment, if you think your company's share price will climb higher. Unless you're a top executive, you probably have so-called nonqualified options. Let's say your company's stock is trading at $100 a share and you have an option to purchase 1,000 shares at $50 each. You have to cough up $50,000 ($50 × 1,000 shares), plus income taxes on your $50-a-share gain. Don't have that kind of money to lay out? Relax, most people don't. That's why most employers will let you use their stockbrokers to pull off what's called a cashless exercise. The broker buys the stock for you and immediately sells it. You get a check for your profit, minus taxes and any fees the broker charges for lending you the money to buy the stock or for selling the shares. If your employer doesn't offer you the chance to do a cashless exercise, call three to five brokerage houses and compare their fees for the same service. You'll probably pay more than you would have had your company's broker done it for you, but at least you'll be able to cash in on your options.

Now that you're out of your office door, it's time to think about how to be happy at home. Is domestic bliss really something you have to work at? It all depends on the individual. Sandy Provost, who stopped working when her son was a baby, remembers how she felt when she was thinking about quitting. "When I was at work, I was constantly thinking about what my son was doing," she recalls. "When I was home with my son, however, I never thought about work." Five years later, she says, "I don't *ever* sit around wondering what the people back at my office are doing." Switching gears may not go as smoothly for you, so read on.

How to Be Happy at Home

I think one of the greatest rewards of being home with kids is the time you gain to reconnect with family members, friends, and neighbors. No, it's not quite like the old days, when families whiled away most summer evenings visiting with each other on their front porches. Even stay-at-home moms don't have that much unstructured time on their hands nowadays. They're busy shuttling between baby gym classes, tennis lessons, and PTA meetings. Still, we have *more* time to become part of our communities than do parents who juggle full-time jobs.

Some of the things I feel that my daughters and I have gained since I've been home may sound silly to some people, but they are truly meaningful to us. We can take a walk and chat with neighbors old and young. If the girls feel like playing with other kids, they can knock on neighbors' doors and ask their kids to come out to play. We don't have to use the phone to schedule a play date for next week. I can attend activities at my daughters' schools whenever I want to, without worrying about using up my vacation days. I can go outside on weekdays and enjoy my gardens. I can even get a tan—which is something I hadn't been able to do since I got my first summer job as a college student.

Most of the parents I surveyed for my book also loved staying home. There were a few, however, who complained that the stay-at-home life was a drag. They said they couldn't find other stay-at-home parents to socialize with. Or, they found other stay-at-home parents to socialize with, but had nothing in common with them. They joined PTAs and women's clubs and ran up against cliques tighter than those that had excluded them back in high school. They were convinced that parents with full-time jobs thought they were dull, dumb, or lazy. They were sick to death of talking to other mothers about temper tantrums, toilet training, and soccer scores.

To them, I say if you'd rather work, please do. You're not doing your kids or yourself a favor by staying home and hating every minute of it. If you've been at home for a while, however, I would add only this: Beware of romanticizing the work world. When I worked full time for a large publishing company, I had one thing in common with the vast majority of the colleagues I socialized with: We worked in the same business. When we chatted over lunch or at business conferences, we talked about business. Much like stay-at-home parents who talk about their business . . . kids. I was fortunate to make some close friends while on the job. But I certainly didn't form deep bonds with most or even many of the people I worked with. Think about your closest friends—the people you'd invite to your kids' weddings. You probably didn't meet them all in one place. You may have met some in high school, some in college, some at work, some at your church or synagogue, and others at your kids' preschool. Keep up with old friends as you add some new ones. Just because your main identity is now MOM, you don't have to hang out only with others in the same situation. Go out to dinner occasionally with a friend who doesn't have children. You're sure to talk less about kids and more about other things than you do with other parents.

Indeed, I think the key to being happy at home is knowing when the standard advice on that subject doesn't work for you. You recognize it, you shrug, and you do something else that pleases you. Here's what I mean.

Everybody tells new mothers that they'll go crazy unless they get out of the house. When I tried to follow that advice when my firstborn was a colicky infant, I felt more miserable than I would have had I stayed home with her. I vividly remember going to the YWCA for an exercise class to which new mothers brought their babies. The babies were supposed to coo contentedly on the floor or snooze. Most, including mine, didn't. They cried. And screamed. And fussed. I dropped the class after one session, and resigned myself to staying home a lot until my daughter was older and more settled. In a few months, she was mobile, and we were both happy to go to baby gym classes together.

As for those clubs that you're supposed to join so you can

converse with other adults, go ahead and try them out. But don't think twice about quitting if you don't have a good time. Do something else to get out among adults. Volunteer at the local library or hospital. Take an inexpensive class. Make an effort to go out to dinner or the movies with old friends. If you can't afford to hire a baby-sitter so you can go out during the day, schedule events for evenings or weekends when you can count on your spouse being home. When you're out, make an effort to talk about things in addition to your kids.

Do what feels right for you and your children, not what you think you *should* be doing.

One more tip: Don't become a stay-at-home snob. Says Nora McElrath, the former advertising executive who stays home with her three children, "When you stay home, it's easy to get a little holier than thou about everything. When I first quit my job, I thought *everyone* should stay home with their kids. I now realize that it's not so black and white." Indeed, who among us doesn't know a stay-at-home mom who lets her kids eat too much candy, watch too much TV, and stay up much too late?

Trade Full-Time
for Part-Time Work

S ome of the mothers I surveyed for this book worked part
time for pay, or had done so for a while after having kids.
Some continued to work primarily for the money. They
figured they couldn't shift to living on just one income without
drastically altering their lifestyle. Many had other reasons for
working part time, too. Some wanted to maintain their skills
and professional connections in fields they planned to reenter
when their children were in grade school or even later. Others
wanted to try out new careers.

If you're thinking about doing some work for pay, I've got
good news. This is a great time to work part time. Many employers are willing to let valued full-time workers switch to
part-time work because they want to keep them. Companies
are also hiring plenty of independent consultants to tackle
temporary projects. Moreover, the World Wide Web makes it
easier than ever to work from home.

Still, the mothers I talked to who were very happy with their
part-time jobs had carefully laid the groundwork for success.

Step one is to figure out what you want to get out of part-time work and how much time you can devote to it. The first section of this chapter will help you focus your goals. The three subsequent sections cover shifting from full-time to part-time work for your current employer, self-employment, and switching careers.

How to Know What You Want Out of Part-Time Work

Grab a sheet of paper and a pen and jot down your answers to the following questions:

- **What motivates you to consider part-time work?** Everyone wants money, of course. Do you have other goals as well, such as keeping in touch with colleagues or developments in your field? Or would you consider doing work that doesn't require much training just to earn some extra bucks? I love writing, and I didn't want to give it up completely.
- **Do you want to stay in the same field or change careers?** I obviously stuck with the tried-and-true.
- **If you now work full time, can you trade your current job for a part-time position?** I wasn't interested in doing this, and I don't think my old employer would have been, either.
- **Do you prefer to work for one employer or a number of different clients?** I like to juggle assignments and employers.
- **How many hours a week are you willing to work?** My

self-imposed limit was fifteen hours a week while my kids were awake. If I needed more time to complete a project (and I certainly did to write this book!), I worked nights after tucking my daughters into bed.

- **Do you want to choose your own hours or can you work within an employer's schedule?** I wanted to set my own schedule because I wanted to vacation when my kids were off from school. I also planned to work while my daughters were at school or half-day summer camp.
- **Are you willing to work nights or weekends?** When necessary, but I never want to make a steady habit of it. A few mothers I surveyed worked *only* nights and weekends because they wanted their husbands to care for the kids while they were out.
- **Will you need child care?** I needed a part-time baby-sitter who came to my house until my younger child was old enough for nursery school.
- **How much will it cost?** Turn back to Chapter 6 to refresh your memory.
- **What's the minimum income you need to earn to make part-time work worthwhile?** Remember to consider the cost of child care, if you'll need it. Don't forget about taxes, either.

The right choice for me was part-time freelance work, given my desire to choose my own hours, do without child care, and maintain my skills and contacts. Read on to learn what other mothers decided to do and how you can do it too.

Turn Your Current Job
into a Part-Time Gig

You may be surprised by your boss's willingness to let you switch from full-time to part-time work. Hewitt Associates reports that half of all major companies offer part-time positions. Sure, some bosses think they're letting you work part time if you cut back from sixty to forty hours a week. However, other employers offer schedules that are a mother's dream.

Get a load of Beth Auletta's situation. Beth, a registered nurse, started working in a hospital's recovery room back in 1985. Four years later, she gave birth to twin boys and switched to the hospital's select-a-shift schedule. Supervisors from the hospital's various departments post the twelve-hour shifts they need to fill, then Beth and other part-time RNs pick the shifts they want to work. In her ten years of part-time work, Beth has never moved from the recovery room. Beth's twins are now ten; she and her husband Brian also have a nine-year-old daughter and a seven-year-old son. Beth typically works only one or two days a week, usually while her children are in school. When I spoke to her late last summer, she had worked just two days during the entire summer. She hadn't even taken evening shifts because she wanted to attend her kids' Little League games. Come fall, she planned to go back to working one or two days a week. As you'd suspect, Beth doesn't get any benefits from her job. But that's not a problem because her husband, who's an engineer, does. "I work in an ideal place," says Beth. "God had me in the right place at the right time."

Of course, nursing is a field that has traditionally offered part-time work. That's one of the reasons that women flock to it. The same is true of teaching, which offers the opportunity to work part time as a substitute or tutor. But what about corporate America? It all depends on your industry, your company, and your boss's attitude. A few women told me that their supervisors had turned them down flat when they asked to switch to a part-time schedule. By contrast, other moms told me that their bosses asked them if they wanted to work part time. As you'll learn if you read on, some bosses are astonishingly flexible.

> **Best for which parents:** Working part time for your present employer makes sense if you love what you're doing and plan to return to full-time work when your kids are older. (See Chapter 18 for more about that strategy.) It's also ideal if you need a steady paycheck. (You may even get to keep your benefits, but probably only if you work at least twenty hours a week. If your boss doesn't want to give you benefits, ask if he'll reconsider if you pay part of their cost.) If you freelance or start your own business, on the other hand, paydays won't be predictable.
>
> **Upside:** I've already mentioned the weekly or biweekly paychecks. Since your boss already knows and admires you, you may also gain the privilege of working at home, bringing your baby to work, or adjusting your schedule when your needs change. (And your needs *will* change, as you have more children and as your children grow.)
>
> Jessie Yallum, a graphic designer who once worked full time, then part time, at a law firm, now works only from her home. Jessie works around her three-year-old daughter's schedule, and typically puts in about ten

hours a week. "Thank God for the Internet!" says Jessie, who sends her designs to her boss electronically. Jessie, whose husband Stu raises funds for a university, doesn't have definite plans for returning to work full time, but says, "I know there is a job waiting there for me if I ever want it and that's a good feeling."

Lucy Breton, whom we met in Chapter 12, was able to work at home *and* bring her baby to the office whenever she had to come in. Before she had the first of her four children, Lucy worked as payroll and insurance administrator for a billboard company. After the birth of her first child, Lucy proposed to her boss that she give up some bookkeeping duties, cut her hours to twenty a week, and work mostly at home four days a week. Her employer upgraded her home computer, gave her a FAX machine, and said she could bring her daughter to the office with her. Lucy did most of her work at home while her daughter slept, and didn't need child care. In fact, she estimates she typically worked only ten or fifteen hours a week. (Are you shocked? I wasn't. Just think about how much time meetings, lunches with colleagues, and watercooler conversations waste.) Alas, like all babies, Lucy's daughter grew into an active toddler. "Working part time was great while it lasted," Lucy recalls. "But I gave it up when my daughter was seventeen months old and my second baby was on the way."

Hope Longo, on the other hand, has never worked at home, but still enjoys incredible flexibility. Before she had her son Jared two years ago, Hope worked for three years as a client service manager for a company that markets the coupons you get at the checkout counter in your grocery store. When her four-month maternity leave was up, she told her boss that she wanted to come back to work part time or not at all. Her boss welcomed her back part time. She switched from being a salaried to an hourly employee, but still gets annual raises. Since then, Hope and her husband Mark, a computer technician, have had a daughter Natalie, who's now six months old. And Hope has experimented with different schedules to accommodate her children's needs. First, she worked five mornings a week, which worked well while she was breast-feeding Jared. Then she worked three days a week. Now she puts in two days a week as an office manager. Her sister and sister-in-law, who both have children of their own, care for her kids while she's at work. (Although I don't like the idea of relying on relatives for child care, Hope doesn't see it as a problem. "I'm the youngest of six kids," she explains. "I've done a lot of baby-sitting for my older siblings over the years. Now it's payback time!")

Downside: You may work more hours than you bargained for—without pay. What are you going to do if you're about to leave when your boss declares that the sky will fall unless the entire staff assembles for an emergency meeting? Will you have the nerve to say sayonara? Maybe not every time it happens. So spell out your rate for overtime work when you cut your deal with your boss.

Also, let's be realistic: Your chances of winning big promotions or raises will diminish if you switch from full- to part-time work.

How to pull it off: First, it helps immensely if you're an outstanding performer. If your boss isn't crazy about your work, she won't find it hard to deny your request.

Second, present a detailed plan that addresses objections your boss might have. For example, you could explain in writing how you'll pass assignments on to colleagues who'll cover for you on your days off.

Finally, try to get a high-ranking colleague to support your proposal to work part time. Lucy Breton got help from a woman who ranked third in her firm's hierarchy. She helped Lucy talk to the boss and even agreed to back her up in case of an emergency.

Start Working for Yourself

For many of us, self-employment is a big part of the American Dream. I took this route because I wanted to choose my own hours and work for a number of different clients. Like most of the other mothers I surveyed who started their own businesses, mine doesn't require me to lease a shop or purchase inventory. Almost all of the self-employed moms I met sell their ideas and their knowledge. They work part time as calligraphers, editors, graphic artists, producers, teachers, and writers. One mother does sell a product: Candy Strickland, a former chef and mother of two, bottles her own Worcestershire sauce and sells it to shops in her area.

Best for which parents: You've got an edge if you work in a field that uses lots of freelance talent. It's also helpful if you're experienced and have a Rolodex filled with people who can give you assignments. If you plan to work only ten or fifteen hours a week, it's tough to find time to market yourself.

Upside: You call the shots, deciding which jobs to take. By working for different employers, you'll make new contacts, which will be useful if you eventually decide to go back to work full time. You may even make more money per hour than you did when you worked full time. The key is charging enough for your time. Explains Nancy Krzywicki, the former magazine editor turned freelancer we met in Chapter 1, "I don't hesitate to demand top dollar and I only accept jobs that pay me a certain rate."

Downside: If you don't have much of a track record, you may not get much work. Consider Rochelle Tomporowski's situation, for example. Rochelle attended art school, but wound up working in accounting after graduation. When she had her son Kyle three years ago, she dreamed of staying home with him and building a freelance graphic design business. But she didn't get much business because she hadn't done much work in her field. When she did get work, she found it difficult to concentrate while Kyle was in the house and she didn't want to send him to day care. Now Rochelle takes on design projects only occasionally, and spends most of her time caring for Kyle and her thirteen-month-old daughter Eliza. Her husband Dean, who's a manager at a security company, works part time as a firefighter to supplement their income. Though things didn't work out as she'd planned, Rochelle doesn't regret staying home with her kids. She figures she'll try to find full-time work as a graphic designer once both kids are in school all day.

Instead of getting too little work, some mothers who start their own businesses run into problems because they take on too much work. If you never turn down assignments, you'll be the mom who always has a cell phone glued to her ear at her kids' soccer games, ballet recitals, and swim lessons. Take a deep breath and remember this: You have only yourself to please. You quit a full-time job so you could spend more time with your kids, and you can work as little as *you* want to. None of your clients need to know exactly how many hours a week you work. So relax and enjoy yourself and your kids.

How to pull it off: Call everyone you know who might be able to give you work and tell them that you're looking for freelance or consulting jobs. Take only the assignments that interest you and pay well enough to be worth your time. Get an answering machine so you won't feel compelled to pick up the phone when your baby is crying or your seven-year-old twins start wrestling. If you have clients who insist on pestering you after business hours, get a separate telephone line for work, and don't take calls after 3 P.M. or 5 P.M. or whenever *you* decide that your business is closed.

Do a Different Type of Work

To me, this is the toughest way to earn some extra money. You're not only switching from being at work to being at home, you're also learning how to do a new job. Some moms manage to do it, however. Remember Kathy Shannon, the full-time bank teller who became a part-time fitness instructor after she had her two daughters? Well, in her "spare time," she also earned a bachelor's degree in business to prepare for reentering the workforce full time.

The mothers I surveyed who had changed jobs made the switch three different ways. Some made a change that meant they needed to acquire new credentials, like a graduate degree. Others became part-time salespeople, usually for direct-sales companies like Avon Products, Discovery Toys, or the Pampered Chef. Still others took on two types of jobs that are plentiful and require no special training. You guessed it: They baby-sit other people's kids in their homes or clean other people's houses. Here's a look at the pluses and minuses of each strategy:

Switch Professions

Best for which parents: If you dislike your current work, or feel that you can't comfortably combine it with motherhood, you're ripe for a new challenge. Take Nicole Donner, who was a catering manager before she had her first baby four years ago. Nicole didn't want to work full time, but wished she could supplement her husband Andy's income as a restaurant manager. Since she "loved the childbirth education class" she took, she looked into becoming a certified childbirth education instructor and labor support assistant. She had to read textbooks, go to seminars, attend births, and take an exam, which she passed last year. Now that she has three kids who range from four years to eight months old, she teaches childbirth classes and attends births only occasionally. "I plan to work more when my kids are older," she says.

Upside: Freed from the grind of working full time, you may discover your true calling.

Downside: If you need a college degree or some other credential to get a job in your new field, you'll spend time and money on classes.

How to pull it off: Know exactly what you're getting into before you invest a lot of time or money in a new pursuit. Ask people working in the field that interests you what kind of training they needed and what their jobs are really like. Also, find out about the opportunities for part-time work.

Next, identify nearby colleges or vocational schools that offer the courses you'll need. Find out how many classes you'll need to take, when they're offered, and how much they cost.

Finally, figure out if you'll be able to get to classes and complete your homework without running yourself ragged. If your husband doesn't get home in time for you to attend nighttime classes and your kids aren't in grade school yet, you'll need to find child care.

Make the Most of Work-at-Home Opportunities

Entrepreneurs have long known that many stay-at-home moms would like to earn money and do some socializing at the same time. Thus, the invention of the Avon lady and the Tupperware party.

Not every work-at-home opportunity is legitimate, however. You'll find fraudulent schemes advertised in newspapers, magazines, and on the Internet. Take those tiny classified ads you see in the back of some magazines that say "Moms! Earn extra cash at home!" You have to send money or charge a toll call to your credit card to get the details, of course. And what do you get? Usually instructions for running your own fraudulent ads designed to rip off other unsuspecting mothers. In other cases, you must buy a box of trinkets that you'll supposedly earn a fee for assembling. When you try to get paid, however, you'll discover that the company has disappeared.

Please don't fall for these scams. To learn more about how to spot them, log on to the Federal Trade Commission's Web site (www.ftc.gov). Click on "Consumer Protection," then click on "Franchise & Business Opportunities." You can also call the nonprofit National Fraud Information Center (800-876-7060) or check out its Web site (www.fraud.org). Click on "Internet Fraud Watch," then click on "Internet Tips."

That said, read on to find out how to make the most of a legitimate work-at-home job.

Best for which parents: Consider direct sales if you want to choose your own hours and do without childcare. It helps if you're genuinely enthusiastic about the products you'll have to sell. Unless you work long hours scouting for prospects, you'll sell mostly to family members, friends, and neighbors.

Upside: You work as much or as little as you like, and you can set your own hours. Rosemary O'Brien, a former speech pathologist with four children who range in age from nine to four months, sells kitchen utensils at house parties. She schedules parties for evenings when her husband, a banker, can be home to care for the kids. Tori Simon, a mother of three, works for the same company and holds two to four parties a month. She typically earns $200 to $600 a month, which is enough to satisfy her. "I do it more to take a mom's night out than for money," she explains.

Downside: You may have to work harder than you thought you would to earn as much as you'd hoped to. It's tough to make a killing in sales working only part time, even if you sell big-ticket items, like real estate or investments.

How to pull it off: Check out a company's reputation before you spend money on sales manuals or inventory. Find out if the firm belongs to the Direct Selling Association (202-347-8866, www.dsa.org), a trade group with more than 140 members. Call your state attorney general's office and your local Better Business Bureau.

Ask the company for copies of its annual report and audited financial statement. Also, get a written description of the firm's compensation system. Many companies use the multilevel marketing approach. That means you earn commissions for your sales *and* for sales made by other salespeople you recruit. Don't be shy about asking sales reps you know how much they work *and* how much they earn.

Don't join a company that promises to pay you solely for recruiting new salespeople. You've come across a pyramid scheme, which most states outlaw. When the supply of fresh salespeople inevitably dries up, the pyramid will collapse.

Fill an Obvious Need

We've become so fixated on money as a symbol of success that we've forgotten that all work is noble. (Don't credit me with that thought; the nineteenth-century essayist Thomas Carlyle said it first.) Even women denigrate child care and housekeeping, which have traditionally been women's work. Well, some mothers I surveyed *don't* have a low opinion of baby-sitting or housekeeping. They know that part-time sitters and cleaners are in great demand, and that they can earn good money filling that demand. Take Lindsey Warren, for instance. Lindsey worked her way through college by cleaning houses. After graduating, she worked in accounting for a large business. When she had her first daughter nine years ago, she spent her eighteen-week maternity leave thinking about what kind of part-time work she could do to supplement her husband Bob's income as a parts manager for a car dealership. For her, the best answer was to go back to cleaning houses. "It was a good, quick way to earn some extra money," Lindsey explains. "At first, I worked around my daughter's feeding times." At most, she cleaned ten hours a week. Today Lindsey has five children ranging in age from nine years to nine months, and spends just two hours a week cleaning one house. "The money I make is my extra spending money," she says.

Best for which parents: Consider caring for kids or cleaning houses if you don't want to expend a lot of effort finding a part-time job. Yes, baby-sitting and housecleaning are hard work. But you probably won't have to look hard for a part-time job. And you surely won't have to spend time or money earning new credentials.

Upside: You can work as little or as much as you want. Housekeepers can usually choose their own hours.

Downside: You won't use the skills or credentials you worked long and hard to earn.

How to pull it off: The easiest way to find work is through family members, friends, and neighbors. If you need to advertise, you can do it without spending money. For example, the bulletin board in my local children's shoe store usually features at least one ad from a stay-at-home mom looking for baby-sitting jobs.

If you find the right part-time work, I guarantee you're going to love it. In fact, many of the mothers I surveyed enjoy working part time so much that they swear they'll never go back to a full-time job!

CHAPTER 18

Go Back to a Good Job When You're Ready

W hen I was outlining this book, it seemed sensible that the last chapter be about going back to work full time. After all, many mothers who put their careers on pause while their children are very young eventually return to the nine-to-five routine. Only 32% of married American moms with children under age six work full time, year round. But 46% of married mothers with kids six to seventeen do so.

After I began writing, something struck me. If 46% of moms with kids six to seventeen work full time, that means that the *majority* stay home full time or work only part time. What's going on? I got some answers when I started to survey parents who had quit or cut back on work. They explained to me why more moms (and dads) didn't rush back to work full time as soon as their children were old enough to go to school all day. Here are some of the comments I heard.

- Sondra Esposito used to travel all over the world searching for household products that the department store she worked for could sell. She stopped working when her daughter, now three, was born. She also has a ten-month-old son. "I'll never go back to my old job again," she told me. "I never want to devote ten or more hours a day to anything other than my family."

- Bonnie Kelly, who was once a CPA at one of the nation's biggest accounting firms, stays home with her three children, who range in age from seven to four. She also told me she has no plans to return to her old job. Right now, she "listens for opportunities that I think would fulfill me personally."

- Amanda Pinder, the former sales manager who has four kids under age five, somehow manages to stay abreast of changes in her profession. She reads trade publications, keeps in touch with old colleagues, and does volunteer work that will enhance her résumé. Yet, she says, "I'm not anxious to go back to work!"

- Regina Silvestri loved her old job in international banking and hated to leave it. "But I always knew that quitting was the right thing for me to do for my children," she says. Now that she's been home for a while with her daughter Eugenia, four, and son Peter, two, she adds, "If I were to go back to work, I'd probably choose a totally different type of job." Right now, party planning interests her as a profession she might pursue someday.

- Judy Harris was one of many moms who had decided to take up teaching as a new full-time career. Many said they had become interested in teaching because they got such pleasure from watching their own children grow and develop.

Not surprisingly, many also mentioned that teaching was the perfect profession for mothers who want to share their kids' schedules. You don't have to worry about who's going to watch your kids after school or during summer vacations! Before she had children, Judy worked in marketing and advertising. Now that her daughter Stephanie is eleven and her son Taylor is seven, Judy has gone back to college to get her elementary school teaching certificate. She also works part time as a librarian at the preschool that her children attended. "Although I'd considered teaching as a career when I first went to college, the catalyst for my career change was working in the school library, which is something I first did as an unpaid volunteer," says Judy.

You may be wondering if this lack of enthusiasm for returning to the rat race is a girl thing. I don't think so. Hugh Norman, the stock analyst-turned-stay-at-home-dad, told me that he has "no intention of reentering the workforce at this time." And both of his kids are in grade school.

What's with these people? Had staying home made them soft? Were they afraid to swim with the sharks again after years of playing Go Fish? Had they gotten lazy?

None of the above. These folks aren't the type to sit around in their pajamas and watch soaps all day. They're active parents and busy volunteers. They had *good* reasons for postponing their return to full-time work, or for thinking about changing careers. Here are some of the things they mentioned to me.

- **Their kids still need a lot of their time.** These parents want to be there when their kids come home from school. They want to help with homework, play chauffeur, or just take time to chat over cookies and milk. They don't want to patch together child care for summer or school vacations. Says Amanda Pinder, "I think it's important to be available to my kids when they get home from school even when they're teenagers. I also want to be there to make sure they don't get into any trouble."

- **They live well on less than two incomes and don't feel they need to go back to earning a big salary.** They feel free to stay home as long as they want. They also feel they can choose work they love. They don't have to go back to a job that they had merely tolerated just because it pays a lot. They had been there, done that, and don't feel the need to do it again. They are the kind of people who get the greatest pleasure from doing a job well. They don't base their self-esteem on prestigious titles or fat salaries.

- **They had discovered new skills that they want to put to work.** Judy found out that she enjoys sharing literature with young children. Regina discovered that she likes to plan parties.

If you're thinking, "Well, good for them. But *I* want to get back on the fast track and make big bucks again. Am I going to be able to get a decent job?" listen to Eileen Mulhern, who worked part time from home as a freelance writer and editor for nearly ten years after the birth of her children Emma, nine, and Robert, seven. Previously, Eileen had been an editor at a news service. Although she'd had a varied and successful freelance career, Eileen told me she was "haunted" by worries about going back to work full time. "Could I even get a job?" she wondered. "Had I been rendered obsolete?"

She had the usual reasons for feeling that the time was right for her to find a full-time job. "Once both of my kids were in school full time, I had a lot of time on my hands. I could have taken on more freelance work, but I was kind of tired of working alone. I missed getting up and going to an office in the morning. I missed being part of a team and sharing the creative process with other people."

She took stock of her skills and of opportunities in her area. She didn't want to go back to her old employer because she knew she'd never move up there unless she moved around the country. Moving didn't make sense for her husband, who's a columnist for the local newspaper. She wasn't very enthusiastic about doing public relations work for a big company. Nor was she willing to start at the bottom to get into the television news business. The Internet, however, beckoned. The field was new, and it was booming.

Eileen posted her résumé on job search Web sites. She also looked for openings the old-fashioned way, by asking friends and colleagues for leads. A friend who works as the sales director for an Internet consulting company told her that her firm needed someone to write sales proposals and produce content for Web sites it designs for its clients. Eileen sent her résumé to the company's president, but he told her he wanted to hire someone with marketing experience.

A few months passed. Apparently, the president couldn't find exactly the person he was looking for. Meanwhile, he needed someone to do some projects, so he hired Eileen on a freelance basis. (The design director, who had worked with Eileen at another company, recommended her.) You can guess the rest. She shone, and he offered her a full-time position. Why she stopped working full time nearly ten years ago never even came up during their interviews. Says Eileen: "The economy has changed so much that employers are looking to hire people they can retrain. They know they're not going to find someone with *exactly* the skills they need."

Now, granted Eileen had acquired a very impressive résumé during the almost ten years that she worked from home. What happens when full-time, stay-at-home moms decide it's time to go back to work? They get back on track, though often not at the salary level they would have reached had they not taken time off from work. How much of a wage penalty they pay, however, rests to some extent with them.

Marguerite Cermak's story is an interesting one. Marguerite interrupted a banking career to spend four and a half years at home with her three daughters, who now range in age from fourteen to nine. Marguerite didn't work for pay while she was at home. She didn't read trade publications or keep up with changes in the banking industry in any other way. "How could I have when I was taking care of three kids?" she asked me.

When she decided to return to work, she thought she'd switch industries so she wouldn't have to spend three hours a day commuting between her New Jersey home and a New York City bank. Her husband Scott, an attorney, also commutes to Manhattan. Since she had honed her sales skills as a banker, she tried to find a sales job. The only jobs she turned up, however, required her to start at the bottom for $30,000 a year. (I should note that she was looking during the recession of the early 1990s. If you have a choice, go job hunting during an economic boom, as Eileen did.)

Marguerite decided she'd rather put up with commuting than take a big pay cut, so she started looking for a banking job. She found one quickly, and her new employer just happened to offer her the same salary she had earned in her old job. She thought the offer was fair, considering that her new title was lower, and she no longer had to supervise a staff.

Getting back into the groove wasn't a problem. "I had an easy transition back," says Marguerite. "I called on some of the same customers I'd called on in my previous job." Don't ask about her commute or experiences with baby-sitters, however. She's been back at work for six years and was looking for her fifth sitter when I talked to her. Then there's the problem of bringing work home. "Now that my kids are older, I don't have a lot of time to work at home," says Marguerite. "They don't go to bed at seven o'clock anymore, and we're all very busy going to their swim meets and band competitions on evenings and weekends." Ten years have passed since Marguerite left her job, and it hasn't gotten any easier for her to balance the demands of family and work. "When I see friends who are considering going back to work," she concludes, "I tell them not to do it under the circumstances that I have, with a long commute."

How to Remain Ready for Your Return to Work

What will you choose? A quick commute to a small company near your home that can't afford to pay you much? Or a longer commute to a huge corporation where you can earn more money? A strictly nine-to-five job that offers little opportunity for promotion? Or big bucks to be on call twenty-four hours a day? You may not be ready to decide anytime soon. You'll be in a better position to get the kind of job that you want when you want it, however, if you lay the groundwork starting now. Here's what to do.

- **Polish your old skills and get some new ones.** If you need a license or permit to do your old job, don't let yours lapse. Irene Ryerson, the dental hygienist who quit her job when she was pregnant with her daughter, now five, takes continuing education courses to keep her license valid.

If you feel you need to strengthen your computer skills, experiment with the Internet or new software at home. Nowadays, thanks to technology, you can learn a lot without leaving home. And you can do it at night, after your kids go to bed. Holly Schuler, the former financial analyst who's home with a three-year-old and a six-month-old, volunteered to publish a newsletter for her local Newcomer's Club. "I wanted to learn how to use Microsoft Publisher and this forced me to do so," she explains. "I also try to keep our home computer upgraded, and I use the Internet frequently. I haven't taken any computer courses yet, but I may when my children are older." If you don't have a computer at home, take a course at your local library or community school. Library courses are often free.

If you plan to change careers when you return to work, you'll probably need some new credentials, like a graduate degree. Don't forget to take any tax breaks you may be entitled to, like the lifetime learning credit or a HOPE scholarship. For more about those programs, turn back to Chapter 4. I also covered tax write-offs for student loan interest payments in that chapter.

It's now easier than ever for parents to fit college courses into their busy schedules. Thanks to the Internet, you can now take classes, submit homework, and communicate with professors and fellow students from your own home. It doesn't necessarily cost less to take a course over the Internet than it does to sit in a classroom, but it sure is more convenient.

Before you take a course on the Internet, figure out if it will impress future employers. Find out exactly what credentials you'll need to get the job you want. Make sure that the courses you take will lead to the degree or certificate that you need. Also, stick with programs that one of the six regional educational accrediting associations have given their stamp of approval to. You can search for accredited courses in your field on www.lifelonglearning.com.

- **Keep up with what's going on in the work world.** In theory, you should have lunch with old colleagues, read trade journals, and attend business conventions. In reality, you wouldn't have much time for your kids if you did all that. Plus you'd spend a ton of money on baby-sitters, business lunches, conference fees, and $500-a-year subscriptions to trade publications.

I can't imagine doing all that, although I freely admit that I'm a Type A personality. (I read *Business Week* magazine while waiting in the pickup line at my daughter's preschool, for example.) My motto is everything in moderation. So call up or have lunch with former colleagues *occasionally*. Pick a cheap restaurant. Go to the library once or twice a year and skim trade publications. If your local library doesn't subscribe to the obscure journal that covers your field, ask a former co-worker who gets a subscription at work to save old issues for you. Who cares if you read last month's news three months from now?

- **Never say that your brain is dead.** I'm serious. A lot of stay-at-home moms say it. I've said it myself, usually after I forget to do something routine, like give my kids their vitamins. Our brains are certainly not dead. To the contrary, they're probably busier than ever. Think about how much brainpower it must take to referee a fight between your kids, chat on the phone about the next PTA fund-raiser, shift a load of laundry from the washer to the dryer, and watch to make sure the pasta on the stove doesn't boil over—all at the same time.

I firmly believe that if you keep telling yourself that staying home is making you dumb, you'll start to believe it, on some level. And it might hold you back from trying hard to get the job you really want when you're ready to return to work.

You're still using many of the skills you used when you worked. You still juggle more than one project at a time. You manage people. (Give yourself extra points for this one, since the people you manage are young and immature.) You make schedules and stick to them. You plan gatherings. You cut costs.

Nowadays stay-at-home parents also worry a lot about technology passing them by. I don't think it's as big a problem as many people fear it is. Yes, you will have to retool if you once designed software and you haven't touched a computer in five years. But most of us don't create technology. We just use it, and it's getting easier and easier to use. Rochelle Tomporowski, the graphic designer who's home with two children, was worried because she last worked with the 3.0 version of a popular design software program. Now many offices use the 6.0 version. Does this mean she's unemployable? I don't think so. She'll master the latest version, either on her own or by taking a quickie course at a community college or art school. I've used three different word processing programs since I quit my job, and haven't missed a beat.

Marguerite Cermak backs me up on this. When she left her job in 1989, the bank where she worked had yet to put a personal computer on every desk. When she went back to work nearly five years later, everyone had a PC and a network linked all of the machines together. Although she hadn't kept up with the computer revolution while she was at home, she quickly picked up the knowledge she needed on the job. What struck her as a more cataclysmic change was the fact that banks had virtually eliminated secretaries. "Now I have to do all of my own typing!" she laments.

If these anecdotes don't help you feel more confident, listen to this. I also searched for academic studies that addressed this issue and found one that did. The bottom line: Yes, your work skills erode to some extent when you're out of the labor force. But the researchers also found that work skills are "restored rather quickly and fairly extensively once women reenter the labor force."

How to Hunt for a Job

Employers visit college campuses to recruit MBAs. They don't travel to suburbia to recruit stay-at-home moms. You'll have to hunt for work when you're ready. Here's how to do it.

- **Leave no stone unturned.** I'm partial to the job search method popularized by Richard Nelson Bolles in his brilliant book *What Color Is Your Parachute?* Figure out what you'd like to do and who you'd like to do it for. Then call everyone you know personally and professionally to find out if they know of any suitable openings. Also, find out who hires people like you at companies you'd like to work for, as well as who does the kind of work you would like to do there. Send these people your résumé and ask to meet them, even if their company isn't hiring right now.

  Go ahead and post your résumé on job search Web sites, like Eileen Mulhern did. But don't expect a miracle. The same goes for visiting employment agencies or answering help wanted ads.

- **Organize the items on your résumé by function.** It doesn't make sense to list jobs in chronological order if you haven't had a full-time job in years. Eileen organized her résumé by the type of freelance work she had done. Her list included management, teaching, writing, and consulting. "When I put down all of the things I had done over the years, my résumé looked very full," she says.
- **Try hard to figure out how much you're worth.** This is a tough assignment. After all, how many of us knew if we

earned what we were worth when we worked full time? How do you find out the going rate for your job after you've been out of the work force for a while? It's hard, but you should at least attempt some research so you don't ask for a salary that's way too low. Chat up everyone you know who works for an employment agency or executive search firm. Also visit your local library and check out references like the *Occupational Outlook Handbook*. Peruse trade journals for salary surveys. Skim books like *The American Almanac of Jobs and Salaries*. Do what you can do and don't worry if you ask for too little. You can always ask for a raise once you prove yourself invaluable.

You may use the advice in this chapter next year, or you may not need it for fifteen or twenty years. The decision is yours. You now know that you can live on less than two incomes for as long as you want to. So, savor the extra time you have to spend with your children. Forgive me for ending on an old cliché, but I've got to say it because it's so true. Your children will be grown before you know it.

I Made My
Dreams Come True

What's life been like for my family since we began living on less than two incomes? I've never been happier, even though I'd planned to combine motherhood with a full-time career ever since I was a little girl.

Sure, I sometimes miss having more money to spend. Big-ticket expenditures, like replacing our fifteen-year-old Toyota Tercel or traveling to Europe, will just have to wait. On the other hand, scrimping has actually paid off in some ways. I've not only saved $4.00 a day by giving up the gourmet coffee and muffin I used to have at my desk every afternoon, I've also lost eleven pounds.

The most important thing I've gained is time—a precious eleven more hours each weekday to spend with my kids.

Do we spend all eleven of those hours on educationally enriching activities? Give me a break! Instead of having a nanny shop for groceries, I do the job with my daughters' "help." I now do laundry during the week instead of trying to squeeze it in on weekends between family outings. And I confess: I use videos (borrowed for free from the library, of course) as a baby-sitter while I cook dinner.

But extra chores don't chew up the fifty-five hours I gained each week. I now have time to savor lots of simple pleasures. I can take my children to the library myself, so I can steer them to books that I think they'd enjoy or that I loved when I was a girl. I can help my seven-year-old with her homework and still get her to bed on time. I can meet my kids' friends and rest assured that they're a good influence. I can eat dinner with my children (and sometimes my husband) on weeknights. I can volunteer to help more at my daughters' schools. I have more time to get to know our neighbors, so our family can really feel part of a community.

If I had to sum up what I've gained in one sentence, I'd put it this way: I now have the time to truly enjoy my children's childhood.

Index